HOW THE EU INSTITUTIONS WORK

Your handbook and guide to EU decision-making

Edited by Erik Akse

JOHN HARPER PUBLISHING

HOW THE EU INSTITUTIONS WORK
Your handbook and guide to EU decision-making

Published by John Harper Publishing
27 Palace Gates Road
London N22 7BW, United Kingdom
www.johnharperpublishing.co.uk
ISBN: 978-1-8380898-0-1

The publisher has no responsibility for the persistence or accuracy of the addresses of any external or
third party websites referenced in this book, and does not guarantee that the content on these websites
is, or will remain, accurate or appropriate.

Printed and Bound at the Short Run Press, Exeter.

Table of Contents

About the Authors

Erik Akse has a long track record in EU decision-making, policy development and Better Regulation. He has worked with the EU since 2002, including a nearly 5-year career stint at the European Commission.

He is co-founder of the Impact Assessment Institute and provides trainings and presentations on EU decision-making and policy development. He coaches public affairs professionals on their involvement in EU Impact Assessment and Evaluation. He enables organisations to align their advocacy activities with EU procedures for maximum effect.

Erik also advises administrations across the globe on implementing Better Regulation principles through systems for Impact Assessment, Policy/Legislative Evaluation, Public Consultation and administrative burden reduction.

Alan Hardacre is both a contributor to this book and the editor of the companion title *How to Work with the EU Institutions: A Practical Guide to Successful Public Affairs in the EU*. Alan created the predecessor single-volume book *How the EU Institutions Work and … How to Work with the EU Institutions* back in 2011 (with a second edition in 2015), and he retains his passion for both public affairs and trying to share and disseminate best practice. Alan has worked in varying capacities with the EU institutions and EU decision-making for over 15 years. He currently works in the private sector as a lobbyist having previously worked for the European Institute of Public Administration (EIPA) in Maastricht and as a lobbyist for the Confederation of British Industry in Brussels. Alan has also consulted for Brazilian, Thai and African business groups, and UN bodies, on advocacy and engagement strategies in the EU. Alan teaches and runs simulations on lobbying at the Institut des Hautes Études des Communications Sociales (IHECS) in Brussels and the University of Chulalongkorn in Bangkok. He also gives several speeches and presentations every year to different audiences on different aspects of lobbying.

Michael Kaeding is Professor for European Integration and European Union Politics at the Department of Political Science of the University of Duisburg-Essen, Germany. He graduated from the University of Konstanz and Leiden University, where he received his PhD and conducted postdoctoral studies on alternative forms of EU policy-making. Meanwhile, he has been a consultant for the EU institutions and various national ministries. Michael has written articles and edited books on the European elections, EU institutions, Comitology, EU Agencies, European social dialogue, and the implementation of EU legislation across Member States. He is a Visiting Fellow with the European Institute of Public Administration (EIPA) and Member of the Flying Faculty of the College of Europe (Bruges) and the Turkish-German University (Istanbul). Michael is a Fulbright alumnus and a former Carl Schurz Visiting Professor at the University of Wisconsin-Madison (USA).

Sabina Lange is Senior Lecturer in EU Governance at the European Institute of Public Administration, Maastricht (The Netherlands), and Associate Professor in International Relations at the University of Ljubljana (Slovenia). As an EIPA trainer she focuses on decision-making processes in the EU institutions and in particular on the work of the Council and the Commission's delegated powers. The world of 'Delegated and Implementing Acts' is also Sabina's recent research focus. She has published articles, think-tank pieces and book chapters on various inter-institutional topics, in particular on the role of the Presidency of the Council, the effect of the Trio Presidency, and the European Parliament and the Delegated acts.

Joost Mulder is a European affairs expert with more than 15 years of experience in EU legislation, and runs Better Europe Public Affairs (*www.bettereurope.eu*), advising a diverse set of clients including well-known NGOs defending environmental, human rights and shareholder interests. Joost previously worked as a political assistant to an MEP, a financial industry lobby consultant, and head of advocacy at the NGO Finance Watch. As an experienced Brussels insider, he has detailed knowledge of EU decision-making and first-hand lobby experience on trilogues, Council negotiations, secondary legislation and the implementation

of EU legislation. In addition to strategic and advocacy support for Better Europe's clients, Joost provides frequent open trainings and coaching on lobbying, and is a member of the European Commission's Financial Services User Group for Belgian NGO Fairfin.

The views expressed in this publication are those of the authors and are not in any way intended to reflect those of their respective employers, nor any of the institutions they describe, analyse and comment on.

Acknowledgements

Developing two new books by splitting up the previous single-volume *How the EU Institutions Work and… How to Work with the EU Institutions* has been a considerable endeavour. It could not have happened without the enthusiasm and energy of each of the contributing authors. I am very glad that the team that worked to produce the 'How the EU Institutions Work' part of the previous single volume was eager to step forward again to create this new book.

I was honoured that Alan Hardacre asked me to get involved in the development of the previous publication and then passed on to me the editing of the book that you are reading right now. Without his vision and drive to deliver, the cycle that started with the publication of the first edition of *How the EU Institutions Work and… How to Work with the EU Institutions* back in 2011 would never have got started. This time round, Alan has focused his efforts on the publication of what is in effect the companion volume to this book, looking at the same processes from a lobbyist viewpoint, *How to Work with the EU Institutions: A Practical Guide to Successful Public Affairs in the EU.*

I would also like to extend my appreciation to John Harper, the Publisher, for his continued support on this book and his endless patience. Always a source of ideas, contacts and suggestions it is a real pleasure to continue working with John.

I hope that this book answers your questions and helps you navigate through the maze of EU institutions and decision-making procedures.

Erik Akse

Synonymous EU

- multilat'l org
- supranat'l + intergvt'l syst of gvn
- pol + econ entity

↳ single mrkt
↳ customs union
↳ common currency
↳ dipl service

Introduction

By Erik Akse

The European Union (EU) is a multinational organisation of policy-making and law which encompasses 27 Member States now that the United Kingdom has left the club. Brexit had profound (geo-)political implications, but the decision-making system of the EU as such was not affected by it.

The European system of governance supersedes the national level, operates in 24 official languages and with institutions and bodies based in a number of European cities, but centred in Brussels. This supranational and intergovernmental system of governance is the largest political and economic entity in Europe, boasting a single market, a customs union, a common currency and a diplomatic service amongst other achievements.

The manner in which EU decision-making takes place is often referred to as a black box or a complex system that is difficult to understand. This image deserves correction. EU decision-making is certainly a comprehensive and elaborately-designed system that has been refined with substantial changes introduced in the past 20 years. But in many ways, it is more transparent and robust than decision-making in the individual EU Member States. It is geared more towards the involvement of stakeholders in decision-making, with the Commission taking tremendous steps in this respect in 2015.

This book focuses on how the EU institutions take decisions individually and collectively and how this leads to the adoption of legislation. In the end, the European Union is a cooperation between countries based on the implementation of common rules laid down in EU law. The EU budget and negoti-

From one book to two

How the EU Institutions Work and... How to Work with the EU Institutions was first published in 2011. An updated and revised edition then followed in 2015. This book combined a detailed description of how the EU institutions went about legislative decision-making with additional chapters on how to engage with that decision-making from a lobbying/stakeholder perspective.

This time round, we decided to make a clear split between the decision-making process on the one hand and the lobbying/advocacy engagement on the other. To do this we created two books, this one and its companion, edited by Alan Hardacre, called *How to Work with the EU Institutions: A Practical Guide to Successful Public Affairs in the EU.*

The two books are designed to work both as standalone titles or together, depending on the needs of the individual reader.

ations around it receive lots of media attention, but the fact remains that this budget is puny compared to the combined national budgets of the Member States. It is the policy development and law-making machine that is the core of the EU project. It shapes the life of every citizen in the European Union in some way or another.

Objectives and structure of the book

The chapters in this book aim to clarify the way in which EU law moves from the phase of ideas to binding legislation. It provides a practical overview of how the EU system works and, de facto, distills the core information from thousands of pages of law, procedural documents and official guidance – as well as showing where real-life practice diverges from the theory.

The five key objectives of the book are highlighted in the box on the next page.

To achieve its aim, the book has to cover a number of institutions, bodies and procedures in the EU policy cycle. The different key actors are highlighted below in Figure 0.1.

Figure 0.1 demonstrates the complexity of the EU decision-making process and the range of institutions and bodies that have a role. It gives an insight into why so many people regard the EU as an extremely complicated system. But as the rest of this book will show, EU decision-making is well organised and is based on clear rules and man-

Figure 0.1: Key actors in the EU

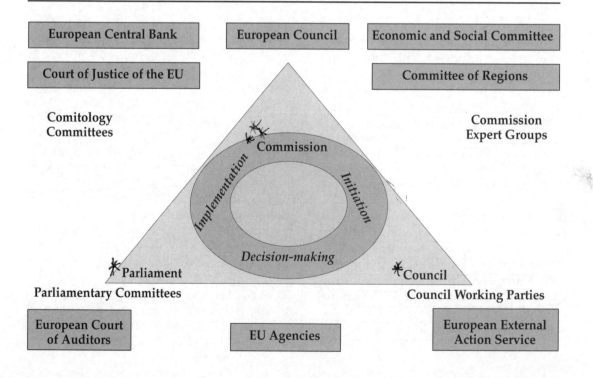

The five key objectives of the book

1. Understanding how the main EU institutions, bodies and Agencies work through a detailed analysis of their internal decision-making processes.
2. Identifying who the key actors within each institution are, at every stage of the internal decision-making process, and identifying what information they need.
3. Understanding where to find the right information in the myriad of sources that exist.
4. Presenting how the individual institutions come together to prepare and adopt EU rules.
5. Providing the foundation of EU knowledge for everyone who wants to understand EU decision-making better, be it for study or for work.

dates. It is distinctly different from decision-making in the Member States and the dynamics are truly unique. However, this does not necessarily mean that it is more complicated and more difficult to understand.

Figure 0.1 introduces the key institutions and key policy-making phases that this book deals with:

1. The three main phases of EU policy-making: initiation, decision-making and implementation.
2. The three main EU institutions: the European Commission, the Council of the EU and the European Parliament.
3. The four other EU institutions and EU Agencies and bodies.
4. Four of the most important Committees in the EU policy cycle: Expert Groups, Council Working Parties/Groups, Parliamentary Committees and Comitology Committees.

The lifecycle of a legislative proposal

The way in which EU legislation is developed is defined in in the EU Treaties, agreements between the Commission, Council and European Parliament, internal Rules of Procedure, guidelines and instructions. Together, they form a foundation upon which decision-making is built.

Figure 0.2 on the next page, showing the lifecycle of a legislative proposal, is based on the graphic presentation that the European Commission itself uses when presenting the way in which legislation is developed, amended, adopted, implemented and revisited.

While the separate elements presented in this lifecycle might appear to be of equal value, the figure should not be interpreted as such. That will become clear from reading this book. Nonetheless, as the graphic suggests and as this book will confirm, the Commission does play a crucial role in EU decision-making and is the only one of the institutions that is present in every phase of the lifecycle of a legislative proposal.

Moreover, the lifecycle highlights that policy development and law-making in the European Union is designed to be a circular process. In that sense it resembles a prod-

Figure 0.2: Lifecyle of a legislative proposal

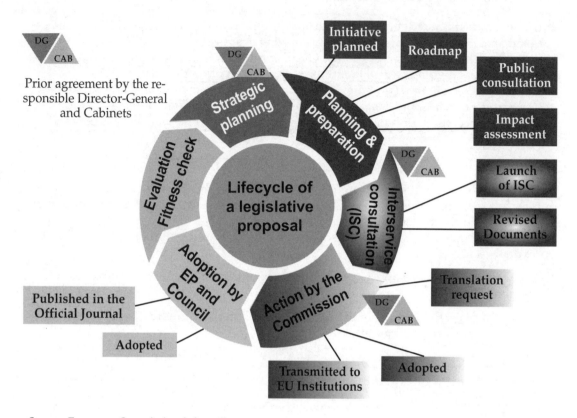

Source: European Commission (adapted)

uct cycle. Legislation is not simply kept in place forever after adoption. On the contrary, the effects that it brings about are monitored and evaluated. The findings that derive from those processes will determine whether an update of the rules is required. When this is the case, the process for developing a legislative proposal will start anew.

Book chapters

This book covers all decision-making phases in the European Union, its institutions, bodies, Committees and procedures.

1. **Part One** of the book deals with the institutions and their internal decision-making procedures. The three core EU institutions, the European Commission, the Council of the EU and the European Parliament, are addressed in detail in Chapters 1-3. These chapters have the explicit objective of detailing the internal decision-making

processes in a practical way. In addition to the three main EU institutions, the first part has a short chapter (Chapter 4) on the European Economic and Social Committee (EESC), the Committee of the Regions (CoR), the Court of Justice of the European Union and EU Agencies. These institutions and bodies can all play a role in the EU policy cycle and need to be discussed briefly to give the reader a full picture of the EU policy-making environment.

2. **Part Two** applies this individual institutional knowledge to how the institutions work together in the two main decision-making procedures in the EU – the Ordinary Legislative Procedure (OLP) and Delegated and Implemeting Acts. The section starts with OLP or Codecision (Chapter 5) because this is the principal legislative procedure used in the EU. Chapter 6 details the workings of the less well-known, but equally important, area of secondary legislation, Delegated and Implementing Acts. These two chapters explain in a clear step-by-step manner the workings of these main decision-making procedures, detailing formal and informal practices and the key inter-institutional dynamics.

2 Decmkg proceds

1) Ordinary Legisl Proced – OLP
– Codecision

2) Secondary legisl → Del + Imply Acts

PART I: THE DECISION-MAKING PROCEDURES OF THE INSTITUTIONS

1. The European Commission

By Erik Akse and Alan Hardacre

The European Commission (the 'Commission' or 'EC') is the largest institution of the EU, in terms of human resources, and equally the focal point of the EU system – the executive body of the European system of governance.

With the various formal and informal roles that it plays, the Commission is crucial to the pace of European integration, especially as it is the EU institution that is charged with thinking, acting and delivering European solutions to cross-national policy problems. But while the Commission is important for the big picture of European integration, it is equally, if not more, important for the minutiae and details of legislation. The Commission does not really allow for any form of national comparison given its idiosyncratic powers and nature – it really is a hybrid institution at the core of the EU project. This chapter will outline the roles, structure and functioning of the Commission whilst simultaneously identifying the key officials at each and every stage of the process. Key facts about the Commission can be found below in Table 1.1.

Table 1.1: European Commission – Key facts

Role:	EU Executive
Established:	1958
President:	Ursula von der Leyen
VP & High Representative:	Josep Borrell I Fontelles
Executive Vice-Presidents:	Frans Timmermans, Margarethe Vestager, Valdis Dombrovskis
Other Vice-Presidents:	Maroš Šefčovič, Věra Jourová, Dubravka Šuica, Margaritis Schinas
Term:	5 years (currently 2019-2024)
Decision-taking body:	College of 27 Commissioners (simple majority)
Internal structure:	33 Directorates-General and 15 Service Departments
Staff:	32,399 (2019 figure)
Procedural languages:	English, French, German
Location:	Brussels (Belgium) and Luxembourg

The Commission has been in place for over 60 years as the EU executive body. It has grown at both the political level, with subsequent enlargements bringing new Commissioners, and at the technical level as the EU project has widened and deepened, and its own powers have increased with treaty revisions. The Commission is headed by the 27-strong College of Commissioners as the ultimate decision-taking body, served by a staff of 32,399 officials (2019 figure) based mostly in Brussels (65%), but also with a presence in Luxembourg (11.6%), the EU Member States (10.9%, including Agencies and Commission representations), and in EU Delegations around the world (12.5%).

1.1   Roles of the European Commission

The Commission has four traditional roles that it derives directly from the Treaties (Article 17 TEU). These four roles are presented in Figure 1.1 below.

Figure 1.1:   The main roles of the European Commission

Guardian of the Treaty	– Ensures application of the Treaties & EU Law – Responsible for bringing infringement procedures
Right of initiative	– Proposes legislation except where the Treaty provides otherwise
Functions	– Coordinating & managing policies, projects, networks – Executive role – Managing EU Budget
External representation of the EU	– Represents the EU on the international stage in areas other than CFSP – Coordinated by the Vice-President of the Commission who is also High Representative for the Union for Foreign Affairs and Security – Observer, sole negotiator, mandated negotiator

common organ + seeks policy

1. Guarding the Treaty:

The first, and most important, Commission role is that of guardian of the Treaty because it covers all aspects of the Commission's activities, including the three others listed in Figure 1.1.

The main aspect of this guardianship comes through the Commission having the responsibility and authority to ensure that Treaty provisions

The European Commission promotes the European general interest. This role underpins all the tasks that the Commission undertakes: thinking European and delivering European solutions and value-added.

are applied correctly (with the Court of Justice of the EU as the final arbiter). Through these Treaty provisions the Commission is empowered to monitor the transposition, implementation and application of Union law by Member States.

If necessary the Commission is able to open **infringement proceedings**, of which there were 632 cases open by the end of 2018. These are 632 cases where the Commission investigates whether the Member States have breached EU law in respect to their obligations to implement and apply what they agreed at the European level. In recent years the number of infringement cases brought by the Commission, according to its own Annual Reports on Monitoring the application of European Union law, were: 932 in 2014, 721 in 2015, 967 in 2016, 814 in 2017, and 632 in 2018. Despite their steadily decreasing number (in 2009 there were 2,900 infringement cases), the still high volume of cases demonstrates the workload that guarding the Treaty requires of the Commission Services. Interestingly enough, a significant number of infringement cases stem from individual complaints which, as long as they are made in writing in an official EU language, can be submitted by anyone.

2. Initiating legislation:

As a link with the second role, that of the **right of initiative**, we should mention the right of the Commission to *promote legislation that is in the general interest of the Union.* This is a horizontal function that is derived from a number of Treaty-based provisions, notably those making the Commission the guardian of the Treaty and through the so-called Community method in

Technically the Commission now has the quasi-exclusive right of initiative – not the sole right as known before. The Treaty of Lisbon changed the provisions on Police and Judicial Cooperation in Criminal Matters, whereby in specific areas the Commission shares the right of initiative with the Council of the European Union.

which the Commission is the initiator of legislation. This second role, initiating legislation, is a sacrosanct right of the Commission, one that it generally guards jealously.

The von der Leyen Commission has taken the unprecedented step of providing the European Parliament with a political right to push the Commission to develop proposals. When the Parliament adopts an 'Own-Initiative Report' in which it calls upon the Commission to start an initiative, the Commission promises to do so (albeit in line with its own internal rules).

The right of initiative has some very important implications, not least that the Commission must prepare, draft and present every legislative proposal; a situation that gives the Commission a significant amount of influence over legislative outcomes. The ability to draft the initial text in the EU system of compromise and consensus means that a very high portion of what the Commission originally includes in a proposal remains at the end of the process.

This is even more significant when one considers that more than the vast majority of what the Commission proposes eventually becomes law, albeit after modifications by the co-legislators, the Council of the European Union (Council) and European Parliament (EP), the subjects of Chapters 2 and 3. This is, for example, almost the exact

Five exclusive competences of the EU

'When the Treaties confer on the Union exclusive competence in a specific area, only the Union may legislate and adopt legally binding acts, the Member States being able to do so themselves only if so empowered by the Union or for the implementation of Union acts.' (Article 2 TFEU).

The exclusive competences are (Article 3 TFEU):

1. Competition Rules for the Internal Market;
2. Customs Union;
3. Common Commercial Policy;
4. The Euro (Monetary Policy);
5. Conservation of Marine Biological Resources in the Common Fisheries Policy.

opposite of the United States legislative system where, in the 115th Congress (2017–2019), only 443, or 4%, of the 10,750 bills introduced became law. Having the sole right to draft the first text gives the Commission a considerable power in policy development and, in particular, in legislative and non-legislative procedures.

The right of initiative can lead stakeholders to the rather misleading conclusion that the Commission is only involved, and important, at the drafting stages of legislation. This could not be further from the truth because, as will be seen throughout this book, the Commission is omnipresent in the entire process of decision-making, operating influentially in both the European Parliament and the Council.

Some final points with regard to the right of initiative are important because there are limitations on the Commission's ability to propose legislation.

Firstly, the Commission needs always to have a **legal basis in the Treaty** for a proposal. Secondly, the proposal must respect the **principle of subsidiarity** under which in areas outside of its exclusive competence (see the box above) the EU can only take action in so far as the objectives of the proposed action cannot otherwise be sufficiently achieved by the Member States. Thirdly, the Commission must respect the **principle of proportionality**, whereby any action it proposes must be proportionate to the issues it is dealing with.

If these legal constraints are met then the Commission must also take account of political considerations, notably whether there is sufficient political will and appetite for the proposal in the Council and the Parliament as well as among civil society stakeholders. Assuming that all these conditions are fulfilled, the Commission will exercise its right of initiative and present the legislators with a text for them to base their negotiations on.

Having outlined that this right of initiative is so important for the Commission, it must be noted that it is something strongly coveted by the two legislators – the Parliament and the Council. The Commission's near-exclusive right of initiative does not mean, of course, that suggestions for action cannot come from other actors as well. Action can stem from Council Conclusions that request action from the Commission, or from international commitments, both of which are important influences on the Commission right of initiative. The Parliament also frequently requests action from the Commission in a variety of different ways, from Own-Initiative Reports to Oral and Written Questions.

The role of the European Parliament regarding the development of new proposals seems bound to become more important. The von der Leyen Commission has pledged a 'political' right of initiative for the European Parliament. This is a new way of working since, previously, the Commission did not regard Own-Initiative Reports as files it had to act upon. The new practice is that when the Parliament adopts resolutions requesting that the Commission develops legislative proposals, these requests will be heeded. These resolutions will from now on be the starting point for the Commission's work on developing proposals. Important to note is that such proposals will still have to follow the Commission's internal requirements, such as coordination between the DGs, Impact Assessment and public consultation. This means, that once these procedures are completed, the Commission can also decide not to present an actual proposal or – based on facts and evidence – choose to deviate from the original request from the EP.

> ## European Citizens' Initiative (Articles 11 TEU and 24 TFEU)
>
> The European Citizens' Initiative (ECI) enables more than one million EU citizens from at least seven Member States to directly request the Commission to bring forward a legislative initiative of interest to them in an area of EU competence.
> 'Right2Water' was the first ECI to have met the requirements set out in the Regulation on the Citizens' Initiative. On 20 December 2013 it was presented to the Commission to formally request a legislative proposal implementing the human right to water and sanitation, as recognised by the United Nations, and promoting the provision of water and sanitation as essential public services for all.

3. Managing and implementing EU policies and the budget:

This is a huge task that absorbs a significant proportion of the Commission's human resources. In addition to this, the Commission also has executive powers given to it by the Council or Parliament and Council in the form of Implementing and Delegated Acts, the subject of Chapter 6.

4. Representing the EU in external relations:

The final major treaty-based role of the Commission is that of representing the EU on the international stage. The Commission does this for all areas, except for the Common Foreign and Security Policy (CFSP) and in the international financial institutions and conferences, in a variety of different capacities. For example, it can act as a simple observer or member in international organisations, or it could be the sole negotiator for the EU. The most common form of representation, as understood by the outside world, is in the sense of trade negotiations in which the Commission negotiates on behalf of the Council with a strict mandate, as it does in trade negotiations such as the World Trade Organisation (WTO). The Commission also represents the EU through its staff posted in some 140 EU Delegations around the world as well as interacting on a daily basis with the approximately 163 non-Member State missions accredited to the EU and 39 international organisations and other representations to the Commission – all basd in Brussels (all figures from 2019). While much of this representation role has been incorporated into the European External Action Service (EEAS) since the Treaty of Lisbon, the Commission still has its staff on the ground across the world and has to deal with third country missions in Brussels.

In addition to these four Treaty-based formal roles, one needs to add a number of less formal, but by no means less important, roles. Firstly, the Commission plays a very important role as mediator and deal broker between the legislative institutions (loosely based on Article 294 TFEU). This role will be touched on later in this chapter, and again in a number of other chapters such is the im-

> **Official Journal of the EU (OJ)**
>
> The OJ is the official gazette of the EU and only legal acts published in the OJ are binding. It is available online at: https://eur-lex.europa.eu/homepage.html

portance of the Commission's role as 'honest broker'. A further informal role is that of information gatherer/disseminator and network organiser, because the Commission is at the centre of a huge network of experts, Member State officials and civil society representatives. Through these informal roles the Commission is usually extremely well-informed, connected and updated on all developments related to its dossiers.

1.2   *Internal structure of the European Commission: Outline*

To go about all of these important tasks, the Commission has structured its staff into some 48 **Directorates-General (DGs) and Services** and a number of **Executive Agencies**, reflecting the different roles and policy areas that it has to cover. Whilst the number of staff the Commission has might appear high to some eyes, it is in fact low relative to the tasks that the Commission has to carry out, which has important consequences. Compared to national administrations, in the EU Member States or internationally, the Commission has significantly less staff with 32,399 people. An example highlights the case in point: the US Food and Drug Administration (FDA) employs just over 17,000 people to focus on its specific areas of competence.

The main reason for this comparative under-resourcing, as decided by the Member States, is that the Commission does not implement EU legislation on the ground, hence does not need the same levels of human resources. The single biggest implication of this is that the Commission is constantly in need of information, notably about how things actually work on the ground as it does not necessarily have its own adequate sources of information and expertise (see Chapter 4.5 dealing with EU Agencies for more on this issue). It is for this reason that the Commission uses a variety of different means to get information, all of which will be considered in detail in this chapter.

The Commission was originally structured along the lines of the national administrations of its founding members, notably the French administration, but it rapidly evolved to meet the new challenges that Treaty revisions and enlargements have created. Whilst there are a sizeable number of DGs and Services, a corollary objective has been to increase internal coordination and cohesion, based notably on IT systems and internal procedures to avoid 'silo' effects (when DGs work alone and in isolation from their colleagues across the Commission).

The internal organisation of the Commission is underpinned by a series of internal rules, the most important of which are the **Commission's Rules of Procedure (RoP)**, which are published in the Official Journal of the EU (OJ), and hence publicly available. The Commission RoP have their own implementing rules to flesh out the details and give a precise guide as to how things happen in the Commission; this document is not officially made public but can be requested from the Commission. On an equal footing with the RoP, is the Communication from the President 'The Working Methods of the European Commission' (P(2019) 2 from 1.12.2019). Most of the details in this chapter have been taken from these documents and hence they will not be systematically referenced, other than in cases of importance where it is necessary to highlight the source of the information.

The internal structure of the Commission is presented in Figure 1.2.

Figure 1.2: *The internal structure of the European Commission*

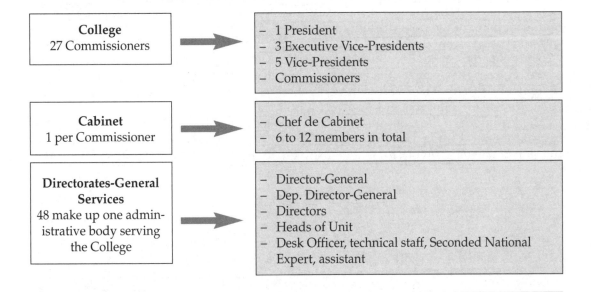

officially made public but can be requested from the Commission.

1.3 *Internal structure of the European Commission: The College of Commissioners*

At the top of the Commission's structure is the College of Commissioners, led by the President. The College represents the highest decision-making level of the Commission. The Commissioners together form the College and it is the College that formally takes decisions, gives political guidance to the Services and DGs and leads the Commission.

The Commissioners swear an oath to be completely independent when carrying out their functions which is as shown in the box on the next page. Despite swearing this oath, many Commissioners retain strong links to their home Member State, a fact that manifests itself in various ways, from their interventions in College meetings to the places in which they give speeches, as well as the emphasis individual Member States place on having 'their' Commissioner get a key portfolio that is most relevant to their national interests.

The College is made up of one Commissioner from each Member State. The Treaty

politics of EC !

of Lisbon foresaw a reduction in the number of Commissioners from 2014 onwards to two-thirds the number of Member States (Article 17 TEU). However the Member States had already agreed at the December 2008 European Council meeting to maintain the one Commissioner per Member State rule beyond 2014 (European Council Conclusions, 11-12 December 2008, point 2, page 2). The College is the focal point of the work of the Commission. All the DGs and Services of the Commission work to serve the College and assist the Commissioners in their decision-taking capacity.

It is worth briefly outlining how the Commissioners come into office and how they can be removed from office and hence the mechanisms that exist to scrutinise their activities and hold them to account.

The key political figure in the Commission is the **President** who has to find a balance between effective chairmanship of the Commission, maintenance of collegiate consensus and leadership of the policy orientation of the Commission. The President of the Commission has in recent decades usually been a pivotal and powerful voice in the EU and a consistent advocate of European solutions. President Ursula von der Leyen is affiliated to the centre-right Group of the European People's Party (EPP) in the EP and is a former federal minister from Germany where she had responsibility for several ministries. She occupies one of, if not the, most powerful political positions in Brussels.

The President of the Commission has a Service answerable directly to her, the **Secretariat-General (SG)**. This Service has about 600 staff who ensure that all the Commission departments work together effectively to meet the identified political priorities.

The Commissioner's oath

Having been appointed as a Member of the European Commission by the European Council, following the vote of consent by the European Parliament

I solemnly undertake:

- to respect the Treaties and the Charter of Fundamental Rights of the European Union in the fulfilment of all my duties;

- to be completely independent in carrying out my responsibilities, in the general interest of the Union;

- in the performance of my tasks, neither to seek nor to take instructions from any Government or from any other institution, body, office or entity;

- to refrain from any action incompatible with my duties or the performance of my tasks.

I formally note the undertaking of each Member State to respect this principle and not to seek to influence Members of the Commission in the performance of their tasks.

I further undertake to respect, both during and after my term of office, the obligation arising therefrom, and in particular the duty to behave with integrity and discretion as regards the acceptance, after I have ceased to hold office, of certain appointments or benefits.

Source: http://europa.eu/rapid/press-release_IP-10-487_en.htm

IN - Investiture (Article 17(7) TEU)

Step 1: The European Council proposes a candidate for President (taking into account the elections of the Parliament) to the Parliament, who must then vote to elect or reject the candidate by absolute majority of its members.
- President von der Leyen was approved by the Parliament in July 2019 by 383 votes in favour, 327 against and 22 abstentions.

Step 2: The General Affairs Council, along with the President-designate, adopts a list of intended Commissioners on the basis of suggestions by Member States. This happened in September 2019 for the von der Leyen Commission.

Step 3: Each individual Commissioner-designate is required by the Parliament to go for a hearing, where they will be questioned on issues of competence, and since the Treaty of Lisbon, on their 'European Commitment'.
- In 2004, 2010, 2014 and 2019 the EP requested that one or more Commissioner-designates be replaced - which was on each occasion respected.

Step 4: The Parliament votes its 'consent' to the full College in a single ballot.
- In 2019 the von der Leyen College was approved by 461 votes to 157 against, with 89 abstentions.

Step 5: The European Council appoints the Commission by qualified majority voting (QMV).

OUT – Censure of the College (Article 17(8) TEU)

- If the Parliament deems necessary it can bring a resolution for a motion of censure. This vote requires an absolute majority in which case the College must resign as a body.
- There have been nine motions of censure tabled in total, the last in November 2014 following the 'Luxleaks' plenary debate with Commission President Juncker.

- All motions have failed, but they have received varying levels of support.

In this vein, the job of the SG is to coordinate, advise and arbitrate to ensure that coherence, quality and delivery of policy, legislation and operations occurs smoothly and in accordance with the rules and the prescribed procedures.

Commission President von der Leyen in 2019 decided to reorganise the work of the Commissioners, taking further the approach of former President Jean-Claude Juncker of clustering Commissioners into groups that manage specific policy areas. Within her Commission, she appointed three **Executive Vice-Presidents (EVPs)** and five **Vice-Presidents (VPs)**. This implies that even though the College prefers to take decisions by consensus, there now is a more formalised distinction between Commissioners regarding their political relevance and importance and thus also their influence. There

Accountability of an Individual Commissioner

Step 1: Each Commissioner goes before the relevant Committee of the Parliament on a regular basis to give updates on their work and answer questions.

Step 2: In the Framework Agreement on Relations between the Parliament and Commission, voted by the Parliament in October of 2010, it states that the Parliament can request the resignation of an individual Commissioner - which the President of the Commission must either accept, or explain his reasoning to the next Parliament Plenary session.

Source: Article 17 TEU & Framework Agreement on Relations between the European Parliament and Commission

has, of course, always been an *informal* difference in influence between Commissioners based on their policy portfolios and political background. The important change is that President von der Leyen, in line with the process initiated by President Juncker, has established an official hierarchy within the College.

(Executive) Vice-Presidents have a lead role on specific topics and are in charge of coordinating and steering the delivery of projects that fall within their mandate. Individual Commissioners need to cooperate closely with their Vice-President as well as with the other Commissioners when developing new proposals.

Furthermore, President von der Leyen established six official Commissioners' Groups that embody the political priorities of her Commission. These groups are the following:

1. A European Green Deal
2. A Europe Fit for the Digital Age
3. An Economy that Works for People
4. A Stronger Europe in the World
5. A New Push for European Democracy
6. Promoting our European Way of Life

It can be expected that most proposals, in particular those that are politically important, will be prepared through one of these structures before they are presented to the College of Commissioners. This will also reflect the manner in which Commissioners' Cabinets (their private offices, see below), the Secretariat-General and DGs are involved in preparing files for decision-making by the College. The new structures will demand in-depth coordination since they put the emphasis on close cooperation during the decision-making process.

The Commission President

- is head of the European Commission;
- allocates portfolios;
- chairs the College meetings;
- establishes College meeting agendas;
- is a non-voting member of the European Council;
- is the representative of the Union on internal policies;
- is a crucial political actor in Brussels.

Some past Presidents:

2014-2019: Jean-Claude Juncker
2010-2014: Jose Manuel Barroso
2004-2009: Jose Manuel Barroso
1999-2004: Romano Prodi
1995-1999: Jacques Santer
1985-1995: Jacques Delors

Commissioners seeking to prepare, develop and table proposals to the College of Commissioners require prior approval by the responsible (Executive) Vice-President. This process, referred to as 'political validation', applies to each step in the decision-making process, such as the initial planning and approval for starting the initiative through the development of Impact Assessments etc. In addition, the President herself validates the initiation of the adoption procedure. This process implies a close follow-up and political scrutiny of the initiatives that the von der Leyen Commission is going to adopt during its mandate.

At the level of Commissioners, each is aided by their own private office (**Cabinet**) which is headed by the Chef de Cabinet. This post is a vital appointment and one that the Commissioner handpicks due to its importance:

Commission Executive Vice-Presidents and other Vice-Presidents

- Frans TIMMERMANS: Executive Vice-President for the European Green Deal and Commissioner for Climate Action Policy
- Margrethe VESTAGER: Executive Vice-President for a Europe fit for the Digital Age and Commissioner for Competition
- Valdis DOMBROVSKIS: Executive Vice-President for an Economy that Works for People and Commissioner for Financial Services
- Josep BORRELL FONTELLES: High Representative of the Union for Foreign Affairs and Security Policy and Vice-President for a Stronger Europe in the World
- Maroš ŠEFČOVIČ: Vice-President for Interinstitutional Relations and Foresight
- Věra JOUROVÁ: Vice-President for Values and Transparency
- Dubravka ŠUICA: Vice-President for Democracy and Demography
- Margaritis SCHINAS: Vice-President for Promoting our European Way of Life

Chef de Cabinet is one of the most influential positions in the Commission as he or she has access to significant information and has a high level of discretion to take decisions. Under the Chef de Cabinet there are usually between six and twelve people in the Cabinet, with at least three positions being reserved for Commission officials, meaning each Commissioner can bring in a number of advisors from outside the Commission. The Cabinet must also respect gender, nationality and geographical balance.

The main role of the Cabinet is to give political guidance and support to the Commissioner, which requires liaison and interaction with the Commissioner's DG(s). In this way the Cabinet filters the issues and the information for the Commissioner to ensure they are kept fully up-to-date, be it on political or technical issues. The Cabinets are rather unique in the technical and political overview that they have of dossiers and also in that they have a more holistic institutional picture within the Commission.

It is important to remember that all issues, files, questions and dossiers discussed later in this chapter cross the desks of the Cabinet and the Cabinet can have an important say in all of them. The Cabinet has to look over all texts to see what issues the DG has raised on a technical level. It then has to think about the Commissioner's political priorities, any promises they have made to either the Parliament or Member States, and any other issues the Commissioner might wish to see addressed. This is a very difficult balance to strike and leads to Cabinet members being heavily solicited internally and externally, resulting in a considerable workload. Most Cabinet members will get anything upwards of 50 e-mails per day from external stakeholders with information, reports, questions, meetings requests, etc. This is in addition to the internal Commission work that a Cabinet member will have to cover.

All Commissioners' Cabinets can be found on the Commission website, with very useful information on the composition of each Cabinet, their responsibilities and their contact details. Each Cabinet member has a portfolio that will include both sectorial and horizontal issues, and it is always important to identify the right person in the Cabinet. Whilst Commissioners' Cabinets work in different ways they all have an extremely good overview of the politics, detail and mechanics of a proposal – and crucially they have the influence to get involved in almost all procedures and proposals and can make changes.

> **A Commissioner's Cabinet**
>
> - composed of the personal team and advisers of the Commissioner;
> - provides a combination of private office secretariat, political advice and additional policy input;
> - acts as political antenna for Commissioners by keeping them aware of politically sensitive or difficult issues;
> - helps to coordinate policy and mediate among competing interests both within the Commission and from the outside;
> - reflects the personality and working style both of the Commissioner and the Chef de Cabinet.
>
> A Commissioner's reputation depends largely on their Cabinet's efficiency in providing sound advice and guidance.

1.4 Internal structure of the European Commission: Directorates-General and Services

Below the political level of Commissioner and Cabinet comes the administrative level. The basic operational building block in the Commission is the Unit, managed by a **Head of Unit (HoU)**, which varies in size and composition depending on its role. Within the Unit you will find a number of Desk Officers and administrative support staff, as well as Seconded National Experts.

Several Units form a **Directorate** which is overseen by a **Director**. These Directorates are sub-divisions of a **Directorate-General** which is managed by a **Director-General**, who is usually supported by a Deputy Director-General, special advisers and a dedicated administrative staff. A final important point about the internal staffing of the Commission is that there is an active mobility policy in place, which means that officials often move internally. For the sensitive positions this rotation can be every four years.

The Commission has two broad principles that guide its functioning and operations, principles that are rigorously pursued by the SG on a daily basis:

1. **Collegiality**: The College of Commissioners takes around 10,000 decisions a year, decisions that are taken collectively and are therefore the responsibility of all College members. This is a principle that is taken very seriously within the Commission and one that manifests itself in the working processes of the organisation. As every Commissioner is co-responsible for every decision in every policy area they

are all accorded the opportunity to participate in the formulation and approval of all decisions. However, this collegiality does not imply that each Commissioner is regarded the same, since (Executive) Vice-Presidents have an important role as gatekeepers in the process of the development of proposals.

2. **Administrative coherence**: All the Services and DGs of the Commission make up one administrative body to serve the College. This translates into a core area of work for the SG, ensuring coherence in Commission actions, especially when communicating with other institutions. So while it might sometimes appear that an individual DG operates as if it were a self-standing administration – the so-called 'silo' effect that used to dominate in the Commission – the DGs are clearly bound to the centre. The broad political objectives of the Commission filter down into the work of every DG, notably through the Strategic Planning and Programming cycle (SPP).

1.5 How the European Commission works: Strategic Planning and Programming

The internal decision-making procedures of the Commission can be split into a series of different phases. Before looking at these in more detail the broader context needs to be established.

The **Strategic Planning and Programming (SPP)** cycle is the macro-planning framework within which the Commission operates. What is shown in Figure 1.3 is an example for the year 2019.

The SPP system was born out of the desire of the Commission to define and deliver clear objectives and priorities and to allocate resources effectively in light of political priorities. The SPP system was a direct result of the 1999 Santer Commission crisis when all 20 members of the then College resigned. A resulting Committee of Independent Experts reported back to the new Prodi Commission with suggestions to avoid the errors of the past. A major part of the response by President Prodi was the SPP cycle, a cycle that has been evolving ever since at the heart of the Commission. Following this cycle is essential for solid upstream information and planning on behalf of an external stakeholder.

As Figure 1.3 on the next page shows, the SPP cycle is multi-annual, although there are three clear processes that we can identify and elaborate on:

1. **Discuss and establish priorities**:

In this phase the emphasis is on the Commission elaborating what it considers to be the policy and regulatory priorities, and discussing these with stakeholders before narrowing down to a more focused work programme detailing exactly what it intends to do. *The Political Guidelines for the Next Commission,* a 124-page document issued by President von der Leyen in July 2019, set out the broad strategic guidelines and objectives of the five-year Commission term.

2010 saw the first ever 'State of the Union' speech delivered by President Barroso to the EP Plenary in Strasbourg, a speech which is scheduled to take place every September as part of the process of discussing the major political priorities for the Union in

Figure 1.3: European Commission Strategic Planning and Programming (SPP) 2017-2019

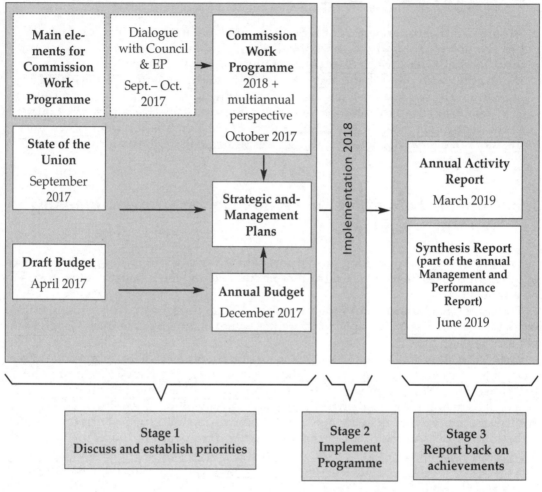

the coming year. This speech is therefore part of the broader discussions with stakeholders that the Commission then translates into concrete actions in the **Commission Work Programme (CWP)** by the end of October. The State of the Union speech quickly developed into a high-profile happening that seems bound to stay.

Since 2016, the Council, the Parliament and the Commission discuss the EU's legislative priorities and agree together on their top priorities for the upcoming year. These are set out in an annual Joint Declaration on the EU's legislative priorities. Of course, these priorities are integrated into the CWP.

The CWP gives a detailed list of forthcoming concrete actions that the Commission intends to undertake, generating transparency and predictability for stakeholders and facilitating cooperation with the legislators. The core of this document is a description of how the 'political guidelines' are being translated into concrete policy and legislative actions. Of more interest are its annexes which outline, in list format, the new initiatives that the Commission will take forward, the modifications or withdrawals of pending proposals, the simplification or evaluation initiatives foreseen and finally the adopted measures that will become applicable during the next year. This can be seen in the examples of new initiatives for 2020 in Table 1.2.

Table 1.2   ***Extract from Commission Work Programme, New Commission Initiatives for 2020***

No.	Policy objective	Initiatives
A European Green Deal		
1.	The European Green Deal	**Communication on the European Green Deal** (non-legislative, Q4 2019); **European Climate Law enshrining the 2050 climate neutrality objective** (legislative, Article 192(1) TFEU, Q1 2020); **The European Climate Pact** (non-legislative, Q3 2020)
2.	Financing the sustainable transition	**European Green Deal Investment Plan** (non-legislative, Q1 2020); **Just Transition Fund** (legislative, Article 175 TFEU, Q1 2020); **Renewed Sustainable Finance Strategy** (non-legislative, Q3 2020); **Review of the Non-Financial Reporting Directive** (legislative, incl. impact assessment, Article 114 TFEU, Q4 2020)
3.	Commission contribution to COP26 in Glasgow	**2030 Climate Target Plan** (non-legislative, incl. impact assessment, Q3 2020); **New EU Strategy on Adaptation to Climate Change** (non-legislative, Q4 2020); **New EU Forest Strategy** (non-legislative, Q4 2020)
4.	Sustainability of food systems	**'Farm to Fork' Strategy** (non-legislative, Q1 2020)
5.	Decarbonising energy	**Strategy for smart sector integration** (non-legislative, Q2 2020); **Renovation wave** (non-legislative, Q3 2020); **Offshore renewable energy** (non-legislative, Q4 2020)

Source: Annex 1 to Commission Work Programme 2020 - A Union that strives for more, COM(2020) 37 final, page 1

The CWP is a very important political, technical and practical document. Politically the Commission sets itself the target of delivering what it says it will do. Therefore it will be focused internally on delivering what it has stated in this document, and it will only delay, or not deliver, in light of strong mitigating circumstances such as an unexpectedly strong political opposition emerging. The actions that the Commission will

2020 CWP Annexes

Annex I: New policy and legislative initiatives.
Annex II: REFIT initiatives, to review existing legislation.
Annex III: The priority pending legislative files where the Commission wants the co-legislators to take swift action.
Annex IV: Intended withdrawals of pending proposals.
Annex V: Existing legislation which the Commission proposes to repeal.

focus on are the new initiatives, the major political priorities. From a technical and practical perspective the document, with its six annexes, gives a very transparent forward looking overview of the main actions to come from the Commission in the next few years – very useful for forward planning and anticipation.

With the new Commission taking office at the end of 2019, the process of developing and presenting the CWP after the elections was typical for an election year. Since the Commission President is appointed after European elections, the political priorities of the new Commission take over, in effect, the role of the State of the Union speech. The development of the CWP for 2020 is outlined in the list below.

The Commission updates the CWP on a monthly and annual basis. The Commission sends monthly updates on the CWP, with revisions, to the other EU institutions, simultaneously publishing these on the SG website. These updates give an extremely good picture of fluid and changing timelines to actions and priorities and allow stakeholders to keep up with progress and deadlines. The second way in which the CWP is updated

16 July 2019: The President-elect of the European Commission presents her Political Guidelines before the European Parliament.

18-19 October 2019: The President-elect exchanges views with European leaders at the European Council.

September – November 2019: During their hearings, Commissioners-designate discuss the priorities with the European Parliament Committees.

27 November 2019: The President-elect presents to the European Parliament her team of Commissioners and the distribution of responsibilities. The von der Leyen team is voted into office.

December 2019: The Commission participates in the exchange of views in the General Affairs Council.

December 2019: The Commission hears the views of the European Economic and Social Committee and the Committee of the Regions.

January 2020: The College of Commissioners meets with the Parliament's Conference of Presidents and Conference of Committee Chairs.

29 January 2020: The Commission adopts its Work Programme for 2020.

is through the annual update, whereby the Commission adopts a new multiannual CWP for the coming years.

Parallel documents of interest are the **Roadmaps and Inception Impact Assessments** which, for every single DG, offer a picture of the work that will be carried out by the DGs in preparation of the delivery in the 'Have your say' section of the website of the European Commission.

In parallel to this legislative planning through the CWP, the Commission also issues a **Draft Budget (DB)** in April of every year to launch the budgetary procedure. This 1000+ page document is drawn up on the basis of the activities that the Commission, and the other institutions, is undertaking and foresees, in the context of the CWP, and aims

> When an **Impact Assessment** is made, there will always be an Inception Impact Assessment. When a Roadmap is published, this means that there will be no IA.

to ensure that resources are allocated according to priorities. Although the **Annual Budget (AB)** operates in a multiannual framework – **the Multiannual Financial Framework (MFF)** which sets a 7-year spending framework– there is still room for manoeuvre on an annual basis, which is why there are such arduous negotiations taking place every October/November to finalise the budget before December of any given year. In this way, the Commission has set the priorities, outlined the concrete actions it will take forward and also received a budget to enact all of this.

The final documents are the **Strategic Plans (SPs)** and **Management Plans (MPs)**, documents with an internal focus, which are prepared by each DG to translate the Commission's priority objectives into general and specific objectives at the level of the DG. These plans are issued every year and they contain details of all initiatives in each DG and how they relate to the broad goals of the Commission. They present a multiannual approach that takes account of the multiannual nature of both the budget and the CWP.

The Strategic Plans are based on the Commission's political priorities. They are supported by impact indicators to help measure progress towards their achievement. Specific objectives for each DG are accompanied by result indicators, milestones and targets. This makes it possible to measure and report on the progress a department is making towards reaching its specific objectives.

Each Management Plan contains key outputs per year and targets for every single activity, as well as all the re-

Evaluation – The start, not the end

The 2015 **Better Regulation Guidelines** put ex-post evaluation as the key priority area for investment in the Commission. All policies are subject to an evaluation, which has extremely important consequences for any future action. This evaluation is the starting point for anything new.

For legislation specifically, the Commission's **Regulatory Fitness and Performance Programme (REFIT)** identifies opportunities for simplifying existing legislation and reducing administrative burdens.

sources that are being used on each activity. In this way the Commission, and also the legislators who receive this document, are able to monitor and evaluate its progress in an objective manner.

The SPs and MPs are published on the Commission website and are very useful documents to understand not only the initiatives within a DG, but the objectives and indicators of their work; this is helpful information if you are interacting with a DG.

With these three documents, the CWP, the DB (and ultimately the adopted budget) and the MP, the Commission has set its priorities, discussed them with stakeholders, crafted an Annual Budget to help it deliver its priorities (and other actions) and converted this into detailed internal documents stating the objectives and indicators that every DG has to strive towards in the coming year(s).

2. **Implement programme**:

The second stage is where the Commission endeavours to deliver everything it laid out in the CWP, to execute the budget and to achieve the indicators it set itself in the MPs. The Commission sends monthly reports to the other institutions on the execution of the CWP and an overview of planned Commission initiatives until the end of each year. The Commission will drive forward the strategic priorities politically, the SG acting as the President's lookout to make sure the DGs deliver on the Commission's most important promises. Every year there will be mitigating circumstances for a small number of initiatives, strategic and other items that were foreseen for the year in question – but for the vast majority the Commission will successfully deliver what it set out to deliver.

3. **Report back on achievements**:

The final stage of the SPP process concerns the **Annual Activity Report (AAR)** which is a report compiled for the Commissioners by each Director-General and Head of Service. These reports assess the results of their department against the objectives and indicators set in the MPs. These documents are also accompanied by a declaration of assurance on the proper use of resources and on the quality of financial management which is signed by the Director-General or Head of Service. These AARs are important evaluation documents that the Commission should then use in preparing future initiatives.

The outcome of the SPP cycle is the **Synthesis Report (SR)**. This report used to be published in June each year as a stand-alone document. Since 2016 it has been included

---

Effective work planning and execution

The work planning of the European Commission is highly effective. The European Parliament verified to what extent the Juncker Commission had completed its commitments by May 2019. The conclusion was that of the 547 proposals foreseen, the Commission had completed 512 (94 per cent). Of these, 361 had already been adopted and the others were either pending adoption or were still being negotiated. The remaining 6 percent of proposals that were not finished were held back for a variety of reasons, amongst them political issues, changing circumstances and other reasons that made the Commission change its mind regarding actually presenting a proposal.
See also:
http://www.europarl.europa.eu/RegData/etudes/IDAN/2019/637943/EPRS_IDA(20 19)637943_EN.pdf

in the annual management and performance report for the EU budget. The SR reports on achievements by the Commission as a whole, but is more important as the moment when the College of Commissioners takes political responsibility for the management and work of its Directors-General and Heads of Service.

This brings to a close the SPP cycle, although at any given point in time the Commission Services will be dealing with implementing their actions for the given year, preparing actions and priorities for the next year and simultaneously reporting back on (and learning from) what they did in the previous year. The SPP cycle places a heavy workload on those involved within the Commission, but from an external perspective it allows for a transparent and accessible process in which all stakeholders are able to identify their issues at an early stage. It is from this broad framework of prioritisation and resource allocation that individual files are taken forward within the Commission, as the next section describes in detail.

1.6 How the European Commission works: Preparation of a dossier

If a legislative dossier is under preparation in the Commission it will have already been flagged in the CWP. If it is a legislative proposal, it would also have been flagged in the Roadmap or Inception Impact Assessment. This section will follow the process from the macro-level of Commission planning into the detail of the preparation of an individual dossier by the Commission Services. Here the emphasis will shift away from the President of the Commission and high-level political discussions to the basic organisational building block of the Commission: the Unit.

A proposal will be taken forward within the most relevant Unit of the most relevant DG, the so-called lead Unit in the lead DG. This Unit will take responsibility for a dossier and thus coordinate the preparation of the proposal and all supporting documentation. The Unit will draft the documents, proposals and Impact Assessment (when required), and consult other relevant DGs

EU legal acts

When the Commission is preparing its legal acts for adoption by the College it can use one of the following:

Regulation – shall have general application and be binding in its entirety and directly applicable in all Member States.

Directive – binding as to the result to be achieved but leaves to the national authorities the choice of form and method.

Decision – binding in its entirety. A decision which specifies those to whom it is addressed and shall be binding only on them.

Recommendation & Opinion – encourages those to whom addressed to act in a particular way, without being binding on them. This allows the Commission to issue non-binding rules.

The choice of legal act is very important and has significant consequences for Member States.

and external stakeholders, before tabling the resulting documents for final adoption by the College. It is these stages that will be addressed in the next sections. The initiation of work in the Commission is presented in Figure 1.4.

Figure 1.4: **Proposal – From European Commission Work Programme (CWP)**
to Regulatory Scrutiny Board (RSB)

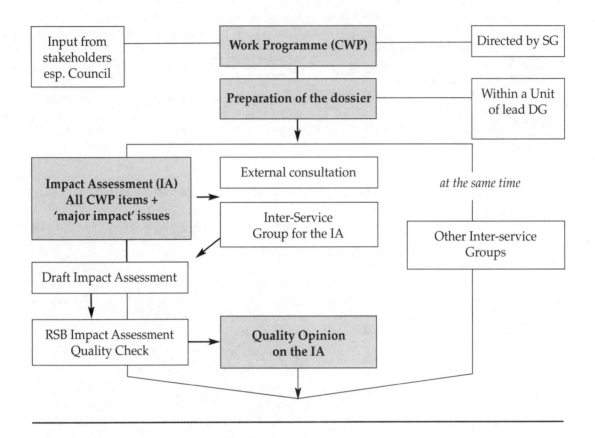

The flowchart in Figure 1.4 shows the start of an individual dossier's journey. The dossier will be included in the CWP once it is advanced enough that the Commission can confidently announce to the outside world that it will be delivered within the period of the CWP. Otherwise the earliest the outside world will officially know about the dossier is through it being flagged in the Roadmaps and Inception Impact Assessments.

Within the Unit that has been designated as the lead on a specific issue, one or two Desk Officers will take a lead on the specific file. At this stage the first major undertaking, for a legislative proposal, often is the development of an Impact Assessment which we will come to shortly. There are two major aspects of the Unit's work that need to be addressed in relation to its drafting of a proposal and all supporting documents. This is the dual obligation for the Unit to consult internally and externally.

Internal consultation: At the very earliest stage the Unit has to associate other DGs to its preparatory work through **Inter-Service Groups (ISGs)**, which bring together representatives from different DGs and Services of the Commission.

The first set of ISGs are groups with a mandate to discuss a series of issues such as general policy coordination. They have the objective of increasing cooperation and coherence between DGs in the medium- to long-term. Through such groups the responsible Unit will hope to generate internal agreement on its proposals and work, and associated DGs will hope to influence the proposal to take into account their specific points and interests.

The second internal mechanism is setting up a task-specific ISG, which is focused on assisting the Unit with the development of proposals and, when an IA is made, the IA process.

The Unit before starting the work on a proposal, must circulate details of the proposed plan and activities to all other DGs who can then respond by taking a place in the ISG for an IA if they feel their DG's interests are touched on in some way. This is of particular relevance when an Impact Assessment is made since such proposals are the most substantial in nature and are often also politically the more relevant ones.

The Unit will keep close contact with the ISG for the IA throughout the development process for a proposal, again with the objectives of internal cohesion and consistency. We see therefore that while it is the Unit that drafts everything, there are a significant number of other associated officials closely involved in the process.

Generally, the Unit can be expected to chair the Inter-Service Group for an Impact Assessment directly. However, when a proposal is deemed of particular political relevance or when it is a highly sensitive file or for a major initiative, the Secretariat-General will chair the ISG for the Impact Assessment.

External consultation: The other side of the coin is external consultation, where the Commission has a variety of tools at its disposal, any of which can be used, in varying combinations, from the very inception of the drafting process in the Commission. The main forms that are used by the Commission for engaging with external stakeholders are as follows.

1. Commission Work Programme (CWP)

https://ec.europa.eu/info/publications/european-commission-work-programme_en

As described above, this is a rolling multi-annual programme that outlines the main Commission proposals to be adopted in the future, with the most detail being concentrated on the next 12 months. The CWP is constantly open to consultation, internally and externally as new priorities and issues arise.

2. Impact Assessment (IA)

https://ec.europa.eu/info/law/law-making-process/planning-and-proposing-law/impact-assessments_en

A major component of an IA is consultation of the stakeholders in the area being investigated. In this sense stakeholders will likely be formally consulted, via the Feedback option after publication of the Roadmaps, Inception Impact Assessments, hearings or questionnaires etc. If an IA is ongoing, interested stakeholders should make their opinions known to the lead Unit running the IA, as well as any other impacted/interested DGs likely to support their position. This topic will be taken up in more detail in the section on IAs.

3. **Open hearings** (check individual DG websites to keep informed)

The Commission organises a number of open hearings to gather together interested stakeholders and exchange views and collect information. As a forum for consultation they are limited because they will usually bring together 50-250 people listening to presentations by the Commission and/or key interested stakeholders. Whilst limited in the sense of information exchange they are extremely useful events for visibility with the Commission and other stakeholders. These events are very good networking opportunities.

4. **Green Papers**

https://ec.europa.eu/info/consultations_en

A Green Paper is one of the old-school formal consultation techniques used by the Commission, whereby it presents a paper (not actually green) outlining the options that it is considering on a certain question. This document must be no longer than 30 pages and is translated into all official languages. There are minimum standards of consultation that apply, meaning that everything, including responses and the Commission's summary, has to be published on the website of the DG concerned and that stakeholders get a minimum of twelve weeks to reply. A response to a Green Paper is an excellent opportunity to bring concerns to the attention of the Unit and Desk Officer that will eventually draft the proposal because at this stage the ideas are still general.

5. **White Paper**

https://ec.europa.eu/info/consultations_en

A White Paper is, like the Green Paper, one of the formal consultation techniques used by the Commission. It is a document in which the Commission outlines which (legislative) option(s) it favours, seeking any additional comments and ideas. This document must be no longer than 15 pages and it is translated into all official languages. The same minimum standards of consultation as explained above apply. A White Paper is an excellent opportunity to bring concerns to the attention of the Unit and Desk Officer that will eventually draft the proposal – but, compared to the Green Paper, at this stage the ideas are more concrete and established.

6. **Small and Medium-sized Enterprises Test (SME Test)**

https://ec.europa.eu/growth/smes/business-friendly-environment/small-business-act/sme-test_en

The SME Test is the application of the 'Think Small First' principle and is an integral part of the Commission's regulatory Impact Assessment. The aim is to take into account the impact of regulation on SMEs as soon as possible during the policy-making process. The SME Test is aimed at avoiding legislation which could put a disproportionate burden on small and medium-sized enterprises. It entails a separate analysis that comes under four main steps:

- Consultation with SME representatives (via focus groups, business test panel, questionnaires and interviews among others).

- Preliminary assessment of businesses likely to be affected (based on the previous consultation step to determine whether SMEs are affected and the extent of impact).
- Measurement of impacts on SMEs (quantitative analysis of cost and benefits of the policy options to SME operations, performance and administrative compliance).
- Assessment of alternative options and mitigating measures (full/partial exemption, transition period, financial aid and general simplification initiatives benefiting SMEs). The Commission obliges itself to focus on the findings of the SME test in one part of the Impact Assessment report and provide as much detail as possible for each of the different steps.

> **'Have your say'** is the single portal on which the Commission posts all consultations. It is also used for stakeholder feedback on documents that are published.
>
> It is here that you can find the Commission summary and all responses to closed consultations and feedback rounds. This is an invaluable source of information for mapping the position of stakeholders and getting a good overview of the issues at stake. Moreover, it shows the files that are being prepared and will be published within a reasonable timeframe. It also shows the files that are soon expected to be adopted by the College. https://ec.europa.eu/info/law/better-regulation/have-your-say_en

7. Feedback

https://ec.europa.eu/info/law/better-regulation/have-your-say_en#give-feedback-on-commission-initiatives

The Commission publishes documents at two key stages of the development of proposals. At the start, these are Roadmaps and Inception Impact Assessments that indicate that a proposal is being prepared. At the end, it is the final proposal (where required with an accompanying Impact Assessment) that is published after adoption by the Commission.

Publication of these documents is the start of the so-called 'feedback period' of at least four (and a maximum of eight) weeks. Those interested in the topics addressed in the files can use this time to analyse the materials and get in touch with the Commission to discuss the subject matter.

8. Public consultation through online questionnaires

https://ec.europa.eu/info/law/better-regulation/have-your-say_en#gathering-evidence-public-consultations

The Commission systematically consults via the internet these days with different types of questionnaires. This is mostly done via the 'Have your say' consultation website. See the box above for all the details. Before these public consultations can be launched, they must be politically validated.

9. Expert Groups (see below)

https://ec.europa.eu/transparency/regexpert/

10. Informal meetings, events, gatherings, etc. (see below)

The Commission will use differing combinations of the consultation tools identified above according to its needs. It is often obliged to use several during the preparation of an initiative as it seeks to find all the relevant stakeholders and information.

There are a series of minimum requirements that surround these consultation tools. For example, when undertaking a public consultation there should be adequate time to respond, usually taken to be 12 weeks. If the Commission is organising a meeting or a hearing it should allow at least 20 working days' notice; consult representatively; make sure stakeholders know exactly what they are being consulted on; report back on the consultation, and report back, with justifications, on what it intends to do based on the suggestions it received. A key aspect of all of these forms of consultation is the requirement that the Commission posts a summary on the internet so that external parties can see how the Commission has analysed and evaluated the information that was submitted. Moreover, the Commission also publishes all contributions that stakeholders submitted.

The two most important sources of information for the Commission, above and beyond open consultations, are without doubt **Expert Groups** and informal meetings and gatherings. Expert Groups are possibly the single largest source of information for the Commission, because they give the organisation access to information that it would otherwise have difficulty attaining. The Commission, in late 2019, had around 730 Expert Groups registered on its Register of Expert Groups (https://ec.europa.eu/transparency/regexpert/).

As and when a Unit in the Commission considers that it needs expert input the most convenient and substance-rich way of doing this is to create an Expert Group. This used to be done by the Commission most frequently to assist it with legislative proposals, but Expert Groups are now regularly used to assist the Commission with different types of non-legislative work as well.

The Unit in question is free to invite who it wants to participate in its Expert Group, depending on its needs. The Commission calls the meetings, sets the agenda and the objectives (discussion, draft a report, etc.), chairs the meetings and drives discussions according to its needs. Members of these groups are entitled to claim travel and accommodation costs if needed. Expert Groups are extremely important sources of information for the Commission, notably on how things work in Member States, and through this importance they represent a direct channel of influence on the development of proposals by the Commission.

Expert Groups

• approx. 730;

• 80% created informally by the Commission;

• 20% created formally by legislators or political decision of College;

• Chaired by Commission;

• Objectives set by Commission;

• Meet (usually) in Brussels as and when needed;

• Most members of Expert Groups are national Member State officials.

A vital source of information for the Commission

For this reason there has been persistent pressure on the Commission to be more transparent about what the Expert Groups do and who sits on them, resulting in a more accessible and detailed Register of Expert Groups (Commission Decision on establishing horizontal rules on the creation and operation of Commission expert groups (C(2016)3301)). On this register you can find information on all the existing Expert Groups and their composition, with names for those sitting in an individual capacity and affiliations for those representing an association or Member State. In addition to all of this the register also identifies the Unit responsible in the Commission, and is thus overall a useful source of information.

Expert Groups will be constantly feeding into the drafting process within the Commission, alongside the internal support from Inter-Service Groups. This creates an early crucial network of about 40-50 people with strategic input on a Commission draft text. The crux of this process is without doubt the Impact Assessment, the process of which is outlined in Figure 1.5.

Impact Assessment is a process that prepares evidence for the College, as political decision-makers, on the advantages and disadvantages of possible policy options by assessing their potential impacts. It ensures that when the Commission brings forward a proposal it does so in a transparent, comprehensive and balanced way based on a solid bank of evidence. In this way an IA is a tool for the College and not a formal Treaty-based legal obligation. That said, the Commission has committed to undertake IAs as stated in the Inter-institutional Agreement on Better Lawmaking of 2003 that was updated in 2016.

Figure 1.5: 'Average' Impact Assessment process and timeline

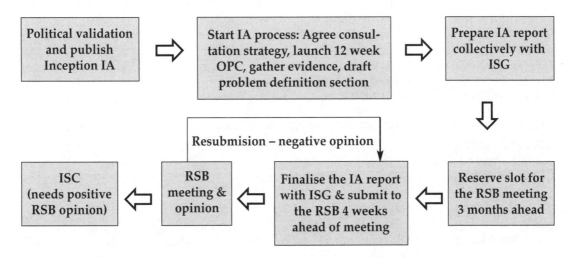

The time needed will depend on the evidence which is already available, the need to rely on the results of the study contracts etc. Typically up to 18 months although can be significantly shorter.

Figure 1.5 highlights all the important stages in the drafting of an IA and the average time attributed to each stage of the process. Seeing all of these stages and the time involved allows an appreciation of the investment and workload made by the Commission in this stage of policy development – the single biggest investment of the Commission in its Better Regulation package.

An IA is required for all major policy initiatives and legislative proposals in the CWP and other proposals with potential significant impacts. The first category is quite clear-cut and can be seen transparently in the CWP and the Inception Impact Assessments, but the second category is one of increasing importance, including Implementing and Delegated Acts. The Commission has now put a screening mechanism in place so that a Unit in a DG or the SG can request, or suggest, an IA on a non-CWP measure that is on the Commission's agenda.

Impact Assessment: Key facts

- All major policy initiatives, legislative proposals + proposals with significant impacts.
- Three pillar approach: economic, social and environmental.
- Better Regulation Guidelines to guide desk officer.
- Assisted by Inter-service Group.
- Is an analytical and consultation-driven aid to the political decision of the College.

Final documents:

IA report RSB
Opinion
Executive summary of IA (24 languages)

Once it has been established that the proposal requires an IA the Unit sets up the Inter-Service Group in order to involve other DGs directly and officially in the analytical process. This group is often chaired by the Unit. However, when the file is of particular political importance, the SG will chair the group.

The first port of call of the Desk Officer(s) responsible for drafting the IA will be the Better Regulation Guidelines prepared by the SG. The Unit responsible will in most cases do the research and consultation itself, with some Units choosing to outsource data collection to external consulting companies. This is the most important and time-consuming part of the IA process, which along with the initial drafting of the IA can take around one year. To give a clearer picture of what an IA seeks to address a list of fundamental IA questions are in the box below.

Once the Unit has drafted the IA report and the Inter-Service Group is satisfied (this

1. What is the nature and scale of the problem, how is it evolving, and who is most affected by it?
2. What are the views of the stakeholders concerned?
3. Should the Union be involved?
4. If so, what objectives should it set to address the problem?
5. What are the main policy options for reaching these objectives?
6. What are the likely economic, social and environmental impacts of those options?
7. How do the main options compare in terms of effectiveness, efficiency and coherence in solving the problems?
8. How could future monitoring and evaluation be organised?

is not a procedural obligation, but an internal political constraint), the Unit will submit the draft IA report to the **Regulatory Scrutiny Board (RSB)**. The RSB succeeded the Impact Assessment Board in 2015 as the central quality control and support body for the quality of Impact Assessments.

The role of the RSB is to scrutinise the quality of all Commission IAs and important evaluations. In essence the RSB is the internal quality control mechanism to guarantee horizontal standards and provide solutions to common issues and problems. The RSB issues an opinion on each and every IA and is a formal procedural requirement in the Commission decision-making procedure. Without an RSB opinion, a proposal should not be submitted to the College.

The RSB issues a maximum of two opinions for the same Impact Assessment, thus allowing DGs to improve their IA if they fail to meet the applicable standards the first time they present the document to the Board. In cases where the RSB issues a second negative opinion, the launch of the Inter-Service Consultation must be specifically approved by the Vice-President for Inter-institutional Relations and Foresight. There can thus still be political reasons to go ahead with a proposal in cases where the Impact Assessment is not considered to be of sufficient quality.

Once the author DG has submitted its IA to the RSB, the RSB sends back detailed comments. The author DG then responds to these comments, either in writing or orally during an RSB meeting. From this the RSB will proceed to issue an opinion. These opinions are also made public and are posted, along with the IA, in the Register of Commission Documents: https://ec.europa.eu/transparency/regdoc/?fuseaction=ia.

Once the RSB has delivered its opinion and the modifications have been made by the lead DG, the IA is ready to accompany the proposal into the formal internal procedures that follow, on its way to adoption by the College. After the IA has been finalised, the Unit will also have to draft its legislative (or non-legislative, such as a Delegated Act) proposal, based on the IA findings. The proposal and the IA are intimately connected and should be complementary.

It is important to stress the significance of the IA for all EU-related actors. The Commission IA is the basis for discussions and negotiations within the Commission as to

Reform of the Impact Assessment Board

The Impact Assessment Board was established in November 2006 by a note of the then Commission President Barroso. Its role was to oversee Impact Assessment quality within the Commission. The Board operated under the direct authority of the President and consisted of high-level Commission officials.

The Juncker Commission decided in December 2014 to strengthen the Commission's approach to Better Regulation and to further increase the quality of its Impact Assessment system. The IAB would be remodeled as the Regulatory Scrutiny Board. The RSB consists of four Commission officials and three external members that work full-time. This is in contrast to the part-time nature of the position of the members of the IAB.

The members of the RSB are presented online: https://ec.europa.eu/info/law/law-making-process/regulatory-scrutiny-board/members-regulatory-scrutiny-board-0_en

The 'evaluate first' principle

In 2015 the European Commission published updated guidelines on the implementation of the so-called Better Regulation principles. The Commission declared that its most favoured approach to developing new legislative and policy proposals was to first evaluate the actual effects that the existing EU acquis had brought about. Such evaluations are meant to provide insight into the costs and benefits of EU legislation. They also should provide evidence if there are (regulatory) shortcomings and thus be the basis of an Impact Assessment for a new proposal.

The von der Leyen Commission works along the same lines with exceptions to this rule needing approval by the Vice-President for Inter-institutional Relations and Foresight.

what options it should present to the legislators. The Council and the Parliament increasingly use the IA in their discussions and internal negotiations, before coming together for their inter-institutional negotiations on a Commission proposal. The importance of following and engaging in the IA process for all involved actors is now taken for granted.

For more information on how to work with the Impact Assessment process, see also: E. Akse, *Influencing the Preparation of EU Legislation: A Practical Guide to Working with Impact Assessments*, John Harper Publishing, London, 2013.

1.7   How the European Commission works: Administrative decision-preparation

Once the IA has been completed it is possible to proceed internally with a dossier. This phase is represented in Figure 1.6.

In Figure 1.6 we see the progress of a dossier from its draft form into the final decision-making procedures. At this stage the draft proposal will have been crafted by the Unit responsible with internal and external input through the various groups and tools we have identified thus far. The launch of the Impact Assessment process and the initiation of the online public consultation were both politically validated, which shows close political involvement in what is actually published.

Once the Unit has obtained a satisfactory RSB opinion (or political green light to proceed without such a positive opinion), and has prepared its draft proposal and all supporting documents, it will check with the DG hierarchy and the Commissioner's Cabinet to seek political approval (validation) to launch the procedure in the **Inter-Service Consultation, the ISC**. This is the formalised procedure to seek input from all other Commission DGs and Services and is done via a dedicated IT tool called 'Decide'. The ISC has been compulsory in the Commission since 2001 and about 40-60 ISCs are

Figure 1.6: Proposal: From Regulatory Scrutiny Body (RSB) to College adoption

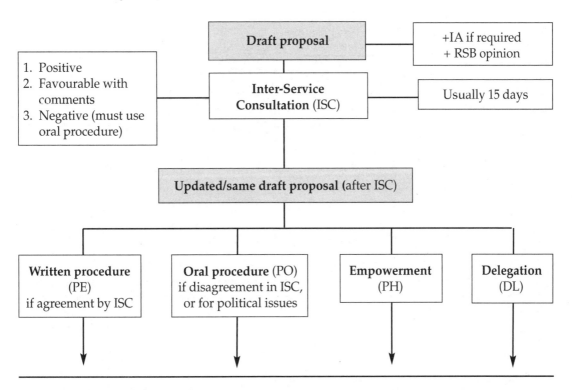

launched in the Commission every day. When the ISC is validated, it is launched since the file is considered to be sufficiently advanced and can move forward to formal adoption by the College.

From CIS-Net to Decide

Inter-Service consultations used to be managed through a system called CIS-Net. In 2015, the Secretariat-General started a fundamental redesign of the software underpinning the Commission's internal decision-making.

Decide will be the single platform though which decision-making is managed, from the planning stage to adoption by the College by incorporating of E-Greffe into the system (see also further below). Furthermore, the Decide system is expected to support legislative drafting as well and will replace the LegisWrite system.

Decide will provide for a more streamlined decision-making process since documents do not have to be transferred from one system to the other. It also facilitates the process of political validation, which happens several times during the time a proposal is developed.

The DGs and Services consulted via the ISC will often be similar to those which have already worked with the Unit via ISGs, although there will now be additional compulsory consultation of DGs and Services depending on the issues raised. For example, the SG will be consulted on any CWP item as it will be interested in the political ramifications and any institutional matters (such as Subsidiarity, Implementing and Delegated Acts, etc.); the Legal Service will be consulted on any draft legal acts (including Implementing and Delegated Acts) as well as any document with legal implications; DG Human Resources will be consulted on any proposal with personnel implications; DG Budget on any proposal with financial implications; OLAF on any proposal with the possibility for fraud; Communication on any proposal with a possible impact on Commission communication policy; and the EEAS on any document with relevance for EU's External Action.

Through the Decide platform, all consulted parties receive the documentation and

Commission decision-making procedures

Oral Procedure (PO) (approx. 200 a year)
What: The College decides during its weekly meeting on issues that are sensitive, political or otherwise in need of the attention of the College. The President decides the agenda.
Documents: Major political or financial implications, CWP strategic priorities, no agreement among DGs and Services at ISC, need for discussion of College.

Written Procedure (PE) (approx. 3,000 a year)
What: The proposed decision is submitted to all members of the Commission (at Cabinet level) and is deemed adopted if there are no reservations stated within the deadline (five days for a normal PE). Urgent PEs are possible and have a shortened deadline (usually three days).
Documents: Issues where all DGs and Services agree that a discussion by the full College is not needed, no negative opinions in ISC.

Empowerment (PH) (approx. 2,500 a year)
What: A mandate is given by the College in its meeting, or there is a standing mandate, to one or more College members to take measures in its name, under its responsibility within strict limits and conditions. Empowerment does not have to be exercised, but if it is the Commissioner, he/she must notify the next College meeting.
Documents: Management or administrative measures.

Delegation (DL) (approx. 4,000 a year)
What: The principle is exactly the same as the Empowerment Procedure but a Delegation can be given to a Director-General or Head of Service, unless the empowerment explicitly prohibits it.
Documents: Management or administrative decisions with a more limited margin for discretion and manoeuvre.

the deadline for responses. The minimum deadlines for answering are either 10 or 15 working days, depending on the size of the documents submitted to ISC.

Submission of texts to the ISC is the point at which there is the most document leakage in the Commission. It is here that many stakeholders get hold of Commission proposals and are able to exert some influence over the ISC process. At this time consulted DGs and Services are expected to deliver one of three possible answers:

1. **Agreement**: The consulted DG, or Service, is in agreement with the documents circulated and has no comments to make.

2. **Favourable opinion subject to taking comments into account**: The consulted DG is in general agreement with the documents circulated, but has one, or a series, of comments that it would like the lead DG to take into account.

3. **Negative opinion**: The consulted DG has one, or several, fundamental objections to the content of the consulted documents.

There is one further possibility in the ISC, and that is that a consulted DG does not actually respond within the deadline. In this case automatic agreement is assumed in the form of a tacit accord after the deadline passes. In almost all cases consulted DGs will be prepared for the ISC because they have already worked with the lead DG in the ISG and they have already formed their positions.

We need to say more about two of the possible outcomes above. Firstly, if a DG gives a 'favourable subject to comments' opinion the lead DG is not obliged to take these comments into account, but it must justify to the DG concerned why it did not do so. Secondly, if the lead DG receives a negative opinion it is also not obliged to take it into account, so from a technical perspective it could continue with its proposal. From an internal political perspective, however, this is unlikely to happen because a DG, and ultimately the Commissioner, will not want to leave the issues unresolved. The lead DG and the DG(s) and/or Service(s) that gave the negative opinion(s) may have a bilateral meeting to try and iron out their differences and agree on a final ISC text.

The resulting ISC text will likely be a modified version of the original document submitted for consultation, the first of a series of modifications that are likely to take place to the text before final adoption by the College. The philosophy behind the ISC boils down to the fact that one DG cannot go ahead on its own because it has to respect the principle of collegiality. Final Commission texts are therefore always the result of compromises between different internal perspectives and represent the Commission position.

Once the ISC is closed, the Unit, with the authorisation of the Director-General and the Commissioner's Cabinet, requests validation in order to start the procedure that is expected to result in approval by the College. As Figure 1.6, and the box on the page opposite, highlight there are four formal decision-making procedures in the Commission, and the lead DG has to follow one of these to get its file adopted. The initial indication regarding the procedure that will be followed is entered already in the IT system.

The box opposite highlights the low number of Oral procedures (known internally by its French acronym, PO – Procédure Orale) that are used each year, but this is a reflection of the fact that only the most important files are left for discussion and adoption by the

Table 1.3 Documents in the dossier submitted to E-Greffe

Obligatory documents submitted for approval by College
Act (in up to 24 languages) + Annexes. This is the only document to be 'adopted'.
Fiche de Renseignements – identity card of the file. Drafted by official in charge.
+ Supporting documents when necessary
Impact Assessment – the full version as drafted by the Unit.
Executive Summary of Impact Assessment – (in 24 languages) a short description of the main elements of the IA.
RSB opinion on the Impact Assessment
Financial information – if there is going to be financial incidence.
Results of Inter-Service Consultation
Committee voting results – If the act is an Implementing Act that required a Committee vote.
Technical support documents, memos and info notes, Staff Working Papers, etc.

College. The most common approach to bring proposals before the College for adoption is through the Written Procedure. It is also important to stress that all the decision-making procedures detailed in the box are the ultimate responsibility of the College.

Once the lead DG has chosen which procedure to submit their dossier under, their Unit will have to submit the full dossier into E-Greffe, the IT tool that manages this stage of the internal decision-making procedure. The dossier is not simply a single draft proposal, but an important collection of documents. E-Greffe is expected to be replaced soon by the Decide system. However, the documents that will have to be provided will surely remain the same.

The course of the dossier depends, therefore, on the decision-making procedure chosen, or imposed, within the Commission. It is important to consider the Written and Oral procedures in more detail because this is where the politically and financially important decisions are made.

1.8 How the European Commission works: Political decision-taking

The flowchart in Figure 1.7 details the processes of the **Written and Oral procedures**. The most widely used of the two is the **Written procedure** (known internally by its French acronym PE, Procédure Écrite). In this case the dossier that has been through ISC and needs College approval will be submitted electronically to every Cabinet. The

Figure 1.7: Preparation of a dossier: Written and Oral adoption procedures

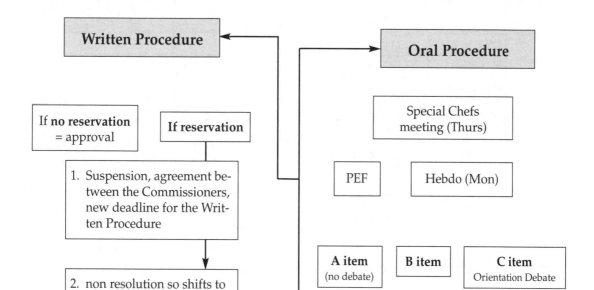

Cabinets, acting on behalf of their Commissioner, have five working days to respond. Most cases will lead to no reservations being made, and the decision is therefore deemed to be adopted. This decision is taken on behalf of the College. When the deadline passes, the SG will ensure that all of the post decision-making formalities are respected, something we will come to a little later.

If reservations are placed by one or more Cabinets then the Cabinet of the lead DG and the Cabinet(s) with reservations will have bilateral discussions to try and find common ground with a view to jointly opening a new Written procedure with a new deadline. If such an agreement proves impossible the dossier that was foreseen as a Written procedure is switched to an Oral procedure item and it drops into the weekly Oral procedure cycle.

The **Oral procedure** effectively operates over a two-week cycle, as outlined in Table 1.4. The objective of this system is the efficient preparation of the College meetings that take place, in general, every Wednesday morning on the thirteenth floor of the Berlaymont, or on Tuesday afternoons in Strasbourg when the Parliament has its Plenary weeks. The cycle starts on Thursday of week W-1, when the dossiers that are being placed in Oral procedure for College discussion and decision are uploaded into E-Greffe for transmission to all Cabinets. From this point we can address each stage in the process individually.

Table 1.4: The Oral procedure weekly cycle

Week	Day	Events
W-1	Monday	
	Tuesday	**Delivery of files 48 hours before Special Chefs**
	Wednesday	
	Thursday	**Special Chefs**
	Friday	
W	Monday	**HEBDO (pm)**
	Tuesday	
	Wednesday	**College Meeting**
	Thursday	Special Chefs
	Friday	
W+1	Monday	HEBDO (pm)
	Tuesday	
	Wednesday	College Meeting (am)

1. The Special Chefs meetings (Thursdays)

The initial discussions are those that take place in the Special Chefs configuration. These meetings are chaired by a member of the President's Cabinet and are composed of a member from each Commissioner's Cabinet, a Legal Service representative and the SG as the organiser of the meeting. The official acronym is RSCC, after the French name 'réunions spéciales des chefs de cabinet'.

In addition, the Cabinet member from the lead DG of a proposal under discussion can invite officials from their DG to accompany them on their specific files. In this sense this is the last involvement of the technical officials from DGs before the political decision-making takes over. The agenda for the meeting is done by drawing the dossiers that are ready for, or need, a decision or discussion from the Commission internal rolling four- to six-weekly agenda of all items on the Commission's immediate radar (known by its French acronym of LPP for Liste des Points Prévus).

The objective of these meetings is to start preparing the next meeting of the College by holding in-depth discussions on the dossiers on the initial draft Ordre du Jour (OJ), the meeting agenda for the College. The outcome of the discussions in the Special Chefs meeting is a more concrete OJ that is then sent to the Hebdo meeting of the Chefs de Cabinet, the next step in the process for approval and completion. The

'Special' Special Chefs

If an issue needs in-depth discussion, a special meeting of the Special Chefs will be convened i.e. outside of the standing Thursday meeting.

Special Chefs meeting seeks to find agreement where possible and highlight sensitivities for the Chefs de Cabinet, and if needed the College, to deal with. The Special Chefs meetings work from the text that came out of ISC, likely to be version II of a proposal. The Special Chefs can also make modifications during their meetings which can lead to them sending a version III to the next step in the process.

2. The Hebdo meetings

The Hebdo meeting is the weekly meeting of the Chefs de Cabinet that takes place in the Berlaymont every Monday. The Hebdo meeting is chaired by the Secretary-General and is composed of the Heads of all the Commissioners' Cabinets, the Director-General of the Legal Service and the Director-General of the Spokesperson's Service. This Monday meeting has the objective of finalising the agenda for the College meeting by splitting the decisions that need to be taken into the following categories:

- A items: Hebdo has found agreement, therefore to be adopted without discussion.

- B items: Hebdo has not reached agreement, therefore College discussion is needed before decision. There are also a number of so-called 'false B' items, where there is agreement but also a need for visibility, thus College discussion.

Figure 1.8: Commission meetings cycles

	Thursday	Friday	Sat/Sun	Monday	Tuesday	Wednesday
When the College meets in Brussels	RSCC(s)	GRI				College (am) in Brussels
	RSCC(s)			HEBDO (pm)		EXCO
When the College meets in Strasbourg (12 x/yr)	RSCC(s)	GRI		HEBDO (am)		
	RSCC(s)				College (pm) in Strasbourg	EXCO

RSCC(s)	Special meeting(s) of Cabinets (1 file/meeting). Usually on Thursday, but possible on other days (the more files, the more meetings)
EXCO	External Coordination Group
GRI	Inter-institutional Relations Group = Deputy Heads of Cabinet. They prepare inter-institutional files for the next HEBDO meeting.
HEBDO	Weekly meetings of Heads of Cabinet to prepare all files for the next College meeting

Hebdo has, next to the 'Special Chefs', two other preparatory forums: the Group for Interinstitutional Relations (Groupe des Relations Inter-institutionnelles, GRI) and the Group for External Coordination (EXCO).

GRI serves as a forum to exchange information and to prepare positions on all aspects of the Commission's interinstitutional work that require coordination between Cabinets and/or services. It monitors the legislative process until adoption of legislative proposal that are debated by the co-legislators.

EXCO has been newly established to ensure more strategic and coherent external action by the European Union, i.e. a stronger foreign policy in line with the aim to have a more geopolitical Commission.

- C Items: These are orientation debates, where the College needs to hold a broader discussion around an issue or current event.

At the end of the Hebdo meeting, an agenda will be in place for the next College meeting, which usually has four to ten 'B' items and a series of 'A' items for adoption.

It is also at the Hebdo that a fifth decision-making procedure is possible, the **Finalisation Written procedure** (see box). The minutes of the Hebdo meeting are called the Compte Rendu (CR) and they are sent to the College meeting with the agenda and documents (they are not made public).

3. The College meetings

As mentioned earlier, the College meets once a week in Brussels or Strasbourg. The President can also call special meetings on

> ### Finalisation Written Procedure
>
> A dossier is submitted as an Oral Procedure and hence goes into the weekly cycle, ending with the Chefs de Cabinet. At this meeting they can decide to switch the dossier to a Written Procedure and simultaneously decide when the Written Procedure will expire. The switch has a double objective:
>
> - Better timing of press conferences because there is more control of when to announce news – not everything 'big' is decided on a Wednesday.
> - College will discuss only the key issues.

her own initiative or at the request of one or more Commissioners. The President chairs the meeting and presents the agenda items in order. 'A' items will therefore be adopted at the meeting without any discussion, and 'B' items will be subject to discussion and adoption or deferral. If a 'B' item is deferred it will fall back into the weekly cycle for further discussion, or be sent back to the DG responsible for further work and modifications. Formally, the Commission Rules of Procedure provide for the College to vote by simple majority but in practice the College tends to decide by consensus, despite some very difficult and controversial dossiers passing through the College.

The College meeting minutes, called the Procès-Verbal (PV), are drawn up by the SG after the meeting. These minutes are in two parts. The first part is general information on the matters discussed and the decisions that will be made public. These minutes are duly posted on the website of the SG.

Figure 1.9: Preparation of a dossier - Transmission

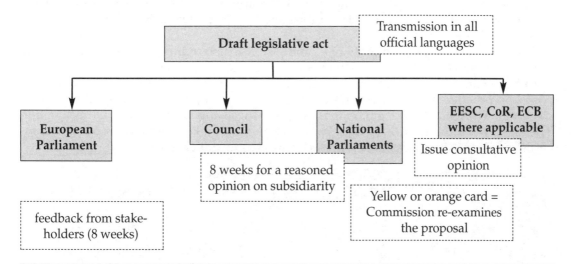

The second part of the minutes is the restricted section which contains other decisions, any votes held and any declarations specific Commissioners wanted entered in the minutes. (You can find the agendas and PVs at https://ec.europa.eu/transparency/regdoc/index.cfm?fuseaction=gridyear).

In general, however, the best source of information on what happened in a College meeting is the specialist press, which is usually a better source than the press conference that takes place in the Berlaymont after the College meeting. The press will report, on Thursdays, in some detail the discussions of the previous day's meeting.

The College meeting represents the culmination of the work of the Commission whereby the final political choices are made on the basis of all the technical and supporting material that has been provided by the DGs and Services. The final aspect of the Commission internal procedure, concerns the transmission of the draft proposal, outlined in Figure 1.9 above.

The Commission SG is responsible for the transmission of draft legislative acts to the other institutions, for the notification to external addressees (certified documents) and also for the publication in the Official Journal of decisions taken by the Commission.

Of most interest in the context of this book is the transmission of documents to the other institutions, as illustrated by Figure 1.9. The SG is responsible for making sure that the Commission proposal is correctly transmitted along with the key accompanying documents (such as the IA). Only the most important legislative proposals are adopted by the College on a Wednesday and here the Registry is tasked with sending all the relevant documents, in all the relevant languages, within 48 hours to the institutions that require these documents. The majority of legislative proposals are adopted by Written procedure and are thus not necessarily finalised on a Wednesday, in which case their transmission can take place on any day of the week.

First and foremost the documents need to be sent to the co-legislators, the Parliament and the Council, for the formal start of their decision-making procedure. The legislators will not formally start their clock until they receive all language versions. In addition, the Commission is also legally obliged, in a series of determined cases, to send the proposal to the European Economic and Social Committee (EESC) and the Committee of the Regions (CoR). All of these institutions and bodies will be dealt with in later chapters of this book.

The final obligatory recipients of Commission legislative proposals, following the entry into force of the Treaty of Lisbon, are the national parliaments, which are required to have the documents to carry out their eight-week subsidiarity check. It is also now common practice for the Commission to send national parliaments all other official documents (outside their legal obligations) that they send to the European Parliament. The eight-week timeframe for national parliament to make known their possible concerns overlaps with the feedback period provided to stakeholders.

The role of National Parliaments (Article 12 TEU and Protocol 1)

- Each Member State accorded 2 votes (may be one per chamber if applicable).
- Eight weeks for a reasoned opinion on subsidiarity and proportionality.
- If 1/3 oppose a draft (1/4 for Police Cooperation / Judicial Cooperation in Criminal Matters), draft must be reviewed (so-called 'yellow card').
- If simple majority opposes draft, it must be reviewed (so-called 'orange card').
- If Commission maintains the proposal, Council and Parliament may take account of the position of national parliaments and either may halt procedure (55% of Council or majority of votes in EP).

1.9   The European Commission: media channels

The European Commission has its own extensive web domain 'europa.eu'. All structures that are part of the Commission will have a website under that domain. Keep in mind that all official documents of the Commission are published under 'europa.eu'. Therefore, it is important to make sure to use this domain when looking for official documents.

You can follow the Commission on: Facebook, Google +, Instagram, LinkedIn, Pinterest, Storify, Twitter, Vine, YouTube, etc.

Individual members of the Commission, such as the Commission President, Commissioners, Spokespersons and even Commission Representations are present on Twitter, Facebook or both.

The link to the overview of the social media presence of the European Commission: https://europa.eu/european-union/contact/social-networks_en

1.10   Key stages and key actors – European Commission

This chapter has detailed the internal procedures of the Commission by following the process of an individual proposal through the pipeline to the point where it enters the decision-making processes of the Parliament and Council. The chapter has identified all the stages of internal decision-making and the key groups and individual actors that are involved but it is now worth underlining some of the key aspects of how the Commission operates.

A very important distinction in the work of the Commission that needs to be stressed is that between the technical and political. The work of the Commission is all under the collegiate responsibility of the College at the very highest political level. It is the weekly meeting of the College that takes the decisions and then assumes the political responsibility for them. Below the College, yet still political, is the level of the Commissioner's Cabinet where the objective is to ensure that the interests of the Commissioner and DG are adequately represented and defended across the Commission. It is at this level that conflict is resolved and outstanding technical details are finalised for College approval.

The Chefs de Cabinet provide the essential link between ultimate political decision-making and the technical details of all proposals and dossiers. It is the Chefs de Cabinet who agree on the College agenda, with the ability to designate 'A' items and switch Oral procedures to Finalisation Written procedures. The interface between technical and political is the Special Chefs meetings, where members of the Cabinet discuss detailed proposals with lead DG technical officials for the last time.

At the technical level, the lead DG is obviously the most important actor driving a proposal through all the various stages of Commission decision-making. The principal powers of the Unit in the lead DG are the fact that it has done all the research and consultation and it has all the facts and information at its disposal, and also the fact that it drafts the original proposal. But while these powers are important, they need to be put into context because the lead DG must, at all times, collaborate closely with other interested DGs through the ISG and then finally through the formal and obligatory ISC and final decision-making procedures for the College. Through these interactions, draft proposals presented by the lead DG are often altered in small, but important, ways for the sake of collegiality.

From this analysis the main actors (in chronological order) in the elaboration of a Commission proposal are listed in Table 1.5

Every proposal that needs to be adopted by the College will go through the stages outlined in Table 1.5, and all of the people identified will play a role (which will be different on a case by case basis). The exact role will, of course, depend on the issue at stake and also to an extent on how external stakeholders engage in the processes detailed here. The volume of procedures, documents and decisions also highlights that the officials identified here are involved in a significant number of dossiers at any given time.

Table 1.5: Key stages and key actors: The European Commission

Key stage	Comment	Key actors
Political Guidelines State of the Union	The overarching political guidelines have, over time, become increasingly Presidential documents. Key for political direction and major political issues.	The President Secretariat-General President's Cabinet
Commission Work Programme	The CWP is the technical translation of the political priorities. The annex is an outline of what to expect in the next 12-24 months – a key planning document. Key for individual issues and 12-24 month planning.	(Executive) Vice-Presidents Secretariat-General DGs
Impact Assessment	The IA is the most important part of the drafting process as it will have a direct bearing on the text of the proposal The lead DG must form an Inter-Service Group to assist its work. Key for detail of a proposal – will underpin legislative proposal.	Unit within lead DG Secretariat-General Inter-Service Group members RSB
External consultation	The lead DG can choose to use an Expert Group, open consultations, hold hearings as well as have informal contacts. Interested Units in other DGs will also use their informal contacts for their specific interests. Key for the detail of a proposal – the Unit will need to find (and justify) a compromise position.	Unit within lead DG Units within associated DGs Expert Groups
Inter-Service Consultation	Once the IA is sufficiently advanced, the Unit in the lead DG will turn to drafting a legislative proposal and this it will do accompanied by an ISG. Once the lead DG Unit is ready to submit the file for formal ISC it will seek Cabinet approval. Key internal process for finding Inter-service positions. Important, and detailed, changes can be made.	Inter-Service Group (ISG) Decide Inter-Service Consultation Units in other DGs Lead DG Cabinet Cabinet of responsible Vice-President Other DG Cabinets in case of problems

Key stage	Comment	Key actors
Special Chefs	The Special Chefs meeting is an important interaction with technical Services as they try to put together a draft College meeting agenda. Key meeting to finalise agreement, iron out technical differences and highlight potential political problems.	President's Cabinet Members of Cabinets Lead DG Unit officials Legal Service
Hebdo	The weekly Chefs de Cabinet meeting is tasked with finalising the College agenda. It also has a considerable discretionary power to take decisions. Key meeting that can take important decisions and make important changes.	Chefs de Cabinets Secretary-General
College meeting	The decision-taking body of the Commission meets once a week to take final decisions, give political impetus and take responsibility for the actions of the Commission as a whole. Key political decision-taking body.	President Commissioners Members of Cabinets

Council of Min

- → Council of EU
- → EU Council
- → Council

- x # configs of EU mins
- * legisl body
- * poly making body
- * exec body
- * complex vtg proced

Europ Council

- → hds of St/Govts
- → Pres + EC Pres
- → 1974 + insti alt
- → Lisbon Traty 2009
- → top decis maker
- → defender of inter-gov'su + nat'l int.
- → strategic decis
- → unanimity
- → regular summits
- → pol natl ints
- → highest pol body
- → EU key priorities
- → mts quarterly

2. The Council of the EU and the European Council

By Sabina Lange[1]

The Council of the European Union (most commonly referred to as the Council of Ministers or the EU Council and in short form simply as the Council) lies at the heart of EU decision-making. It brings together the EU Member States at the level of Ministers. It is first and foremost an EU legislative body, sharing its legislative powers in the vast majority of policy areas with the Parliament. But the Council is also a policy-making and an executive body. Although there is only one Council, it takes decisions in various configurations, depending on the policy field, with foreign policy-making forming a world of its own. Its work is prepared in numerous preparatory bodies of a diverse nature, meeting in the Council's Justus Lipsius and Europa buildings in Brussels, under the watchful eyes of the rotating Presidency (see below) and with the support of the General Secretariat of the Council (GSC), while the work in the capitals of the Member States also feeds into the work of the Council.

The **European Council** brings together Heads of State or Government of the Member States, together with its President and the President of the Commission. Its role is to provide momentum and direction in the development of the EU. The European Council was established as a body in 1974, after a series of 'Summit meetings' at the highest political level in the Member States in the 1960s. It was finally turned into a fully-fledged institution of the EU with the Lisbon Treaty. In the first decade following the entry into force of the Lisbon Treaty the Euro-

Which Council?

The **Council**, also referred to as the Council of Ministers or the Council of the European Union or EU Council, is one of the three key EU institutions, together with the Parliament and the Commission. Member States' Ministers take policy-making and law-making decisions.

The **European Council** became an EU institution with the entry into force of the Treaty of Lisbon. The Heads of State or Government, together with the European Council President and the President of the Commission meet as a rule four times a year to provide the Union with the necessary impetus for its development and define the general political directions and priorities.

The **Council of Europe** is not part of the EU but a separate pan-European organisation based in Strasbourg, whose primary aim is to promote human rights.

1 The author would like to express special thanks to Daniela Cuciureanu for background research and her valuable comments on the chapter in the first edition of this book.

pean Council played a decisive role in managing one crisis after another. It thus asserted its role as the top decision-maker. The Council tagged along, proving wrong those who initially saw it as a loser from the Lisbon Treaty.

Sometimes confused with the Council and the European Council is the Council of Europe, whose seat is in Strasbourg. This is NOT an institution of the European Union. The Council of Europe was established by the 1949 Treaty of London and therefore pre-dates the creation of what is now the EU by the Rome Treaties of 1957. It is an intergovernmental organisation comprising both EU and non-EU European states which operates primarily through the adoption of conventions, the first and most important of which is the 1950 European Convention for the Protection of Human Rights and Fundamental Freedoms. The European Court of Human Rights, sitting in Strasbourg, exists to hear cases involving the Convention. It is unrelated to the Court of Justice of the European Union, which sits in Luxembourg.

This chapter will focus mainly on the Council of Ministers, in view of its legislative role, but we will first outline the main characteristics and roles of the European Council.

2.1 The European Council

There are a number of characteristics which make the Council and European Council easy to differentiate. Firstly, their composition: while the Council of Ministers (as the name suggests) is composed of Ministers from Member State governments, the European Council is composed of Heads of State or Government (thus Presidents or Prime Ministers, depending on the constitutional order of the Member State), together with the President of the European Commission. The Lisbon Treaty created a new position of full-time **President of the European Council**. This post was first held by former Belgian Prime Minister Herman van Rompuy, who was succeeded in December 2014 by Donald Tusk, who stepped down as Polish Prime Minister. Tusk was himself succeeded in 2019 by Charles Michel, who was also elected like van Rompuy from the position of Prime Minister of Belgium. The **High Representative** of the Union for Foreign Affairs and Security Policy (the 'High Representative') also takes part in its work. In contrast, the Presidency of the Council of Ministers rotates on a six-monthly basis among the Member States.

A second distinguishing characteristic is the nature of the decisions taken: the Council is mainly a legislative and executive body (it also has other functions which will be explained in detail later). The European Council does not have legislative functions, but it is the highest body for setting the strategic goals and direction for the Union, as well as being the last instance in striking compromises in negotiations.

A third important difference derives directly from the previous one – the way in which decisions are taken. While the Council is characterised by complex decision-making rules and a voting system based on a double majority of Member States and of population, the European Council largely operates by unanimity.

Although European Council meetings originated in summits held since the late 1960s, and were brought within the realm of the European Communities' Treaties with the Single European Act in 1986, it was given the formal status of an EU institution only with the Lisbon Treaty in December 2009. The European Council is often por-

Table 2.1: European Council – Key facts

Roles:	General political direction Priorities of the Union High-level political discussions
Established:	1974 (as a political body), 2009 (as an EU institution)
Members:	Heads of State or Government, President, President of the Commission (High Representative of the Union for Foreign Affairs and Security Policy takes part)
President:	Charles Michel (took office on 1 December 2019)
Term:	2.5 years, renewable once
Location:	Brussels

trayed as a defender of intergovernmentalism and national interests in the EU, but its composition, which includes the President of the Commission and now also a full-time President who does not hold a national mandate, as well as the participation of the High Representative in its work, makes such claims more relative. The European Council is the highest level political body in the Union, charged with giving political guidance and defining the Union's priorities. It also nominates the President of the Commission and the High Representative, appoints the Commission as a whole (after approval by the European Parliament), and chooses its own President.

The European Council meets at least four times a year. Traditionally the custom has been for the European Council to concentrate on the economic situation in the Union at its spring meeting and to look at monetary policy and enlargement at its autumn meeting. The other two meetings have traditionally taken place before the end of the six-month term in office of the rotating Presidency of the Council of Ministers (such terms running from January–June and from July–December).

Additional meetings can be convened by the President if the situation so requires, and in recent periods of crisis meetings have been more frequent. Such additional meetings were a feature of the Presidency of Herman van Rompuy as European leaders sought to tackle the financial crisis and its consequences. Meetings tackling the migration wave of 2015-2016 featured prominently during the presidency of Donald Tusk and subsequently in handling crisis points in the Brexit negotiations. Regular meetings are occasionally preceded (or succeeded) by a meeting of the Euro Summit (only Heads of State or Government of Member States which have adopted the euro, and the institutional members). Occasional thematic one day meetings have also become customary.

Since the second half of 2003, European Council meetings have taken place in Brussels and no longer in the country of the Council Presidency. Meetings of the European Council are often accompanied by demonstrations, protests and road blocks in Brussels making travel around Rond-Point Schuman very difficult on these days (important to be aware of if one is planning a meeting in the area).

A meeting of the European Council can last one day or be spread over two days, starting on the afternoon of the first day and finishing at lunch time of the following day, not rarely with negotiations stretching long into the evening hours and compromise papers appearing in the early morning hours. Delegations, whose size is limited to 20 official staff (excluding technical staff), usually arrive on the previous afternoon to participate in numerous bilateral and multilateral meetings.

It is customary for the leadership of the Political Groups from the Parliament to meet on the evening before the European Council with the Heads of State or Government belonging to their Political Group. Several bilateral meetings also take place over breakfast on the morning of the day of the meeting itself, with the President of the European Council also meeting Heads of Delegations bilaterally or in smaller groups to facilitate later negotiations. The President of the European Parliament addresses the European Council (but does not participate in its meetings).

> It is always important to keep an eye on European Council Conclusions as they indicate priorities for the Commission and the legislators and set a particular direction for the Commission's policy choices. They can request the European Commission to prepare legislative proposals, reports or other forms of action.

Prior to the Lisbon Treaty's entry into force, European Council meetings were the highlight of the rotating Council Presidency's activity. With the creation of the post of full-time President of the European Council, the Treaties charge the President with chairing European Council meetings. The President proposes the agenda of the meetings and drafts the conclusions, in cooperation with the Commission President, building on the work of the General Affairs Council (GAC, see section 2.5) and, after the preparation in Coreper and consultations with the so-called 'sherpas', the Heads of State or Government cabinet members in the capitals. The President also ensures the follow-up to the meeting.

At the end of the six-month Council Presidency term the Head of State or Government of the country holding the rotating Presidency reports to the European Council, in consultation with the President of the European Council, on progress achieved in the Council.

The President of the European Council is no longer 'first among equals', but is instead entirely dedicated to serving the European Council, although without a vote. There have been many characterisations of this new role, but Van Rompuy as the first holder of the office defined it as that of 'facilitator', preparing the ground and brokering compromises among Member States. Even though the personal styles of the office holders thus far have differed, the characterisation of the position as that of a facilitator still best explains the role.

With 27 Member States, European Council meetings are a far cry from the original intention of small intimate gatherings of national government leaders. With successive rounds of enlargement those participating in meetings became so numerous that the Lisbon Treaty made a significant change – since December 2009 Foreign Ministers no longer have an automatic seat at the table. The Heads of State or Government may be joined by a Minister with responsibility for the subject under discussion, but this is very seldom. A representative of the General Secretariat of the Council (GSC) orally briefs the group of senior officials from all the Member States seated in a neighbouring room (the Antici, see below) who then inform their respective Delegations.

The outcome of European Council meetings is **European Council Conclusions** which can touch on a variety of subjects (with annexed strategic documents and declarations) which provide guidance for the future work of the Council of Ministers. A press conference is held after the meeting, jointly by the Presidents of the European Council and of the Commission. Press briefings during and after the European Council are also given by staff members from all Delegations. Shortly afterwards the President of the European Council presents the achievements of the meeting to the Plenary session of the Parliament.

The European Council is the apex of the pyramid of EU politics. The President of the European Council and his Cabinet, and the support provided by the GSC, give the European Council a solid presence in Brussels and ensure that it is well-integrated into the EU structures. The Presidents of the European Council and of the Commission meet weekly. The Cabinet of the President of the European Council works closely with the rotating Council Presidency to ensure continuity in the work of the Council and the European Council.

2.2 The Council

Table 2.2: Council – Key facts

Names:	The Council of the EU, the Council of Ministers, the Council
Role:	EU (co-)legislative and (co-)executive body
Established:	1952, 1958 (separate for the three Communities), 1967 (a single Council)
Presidency:	rotating, among Member States (six months term)
Decision-taking body:	Council (10 configurations)
Internal structure:	Working Parties/Groups (approx. 150) Committees Coreper, parts I and II Council of Ministers General Secretariat of the Council
Working languages:	24 official and working languages
Location:	Brussels, Luxembourg

As the key facts in Table 2.2 show, the Council is not only complex with regard to its roles and structures, but also because of its rotating Presidency, with a different Member State taking the steering wheel of the Council's machinery every six months (with the exception of the Foreign Affairs Council). In this sense the Council is the most intangible of the EU institutions due to its nature of being a body of national decision-makers, which stretches it (and its legitimacy base) right back to the Member State capitals.

In addition, the Council also uses all EU official languages. Although in practice only a handful of meetings take place in full interpretation regime (all 24 official languages), and more and more meetings are taking place in a lesser number of languages or without interpretation altogether (with only English spoken), the fact that all documentation for Council meetings needs to be translated into all the official languages is an onerous burden on the work of the Council Secretariat.

The Council's headquarters are in the heart of the EU quarter of Brussels, spread across the Europa and Justus Lipsius buildings opposite the Commission's Berlaymont building on the Rue de la Loi. The Ministers meet there, all the preparatory meetings take place there and the GSC is based there as well. While each Member State has its delegation room on the Council premises, Member State representatives coming to the preparatory (and Council) meetings are either based at the Permanent Representations scattered around the EU quarter in Brussels or in the Member State capitals. In the months of April, June and October the Council, as a decision-taking body (i.e. the Ministers), meets in Luxembourg. In comparison to the monthly move of the Parliament to Strasbourg, the Council's move is on a much lower scale, meaning that not all the GSC's services are present in Luxembourg.

The **rotating system of the Presidency** had in the past long been a source of confusion and even frustration to those trying to deal with the EU; every six months a new Head of State or Government would lead the European Council, a new country represented the EU externally and a new set of priorities seemed to have been developed for the work of the Council. However, the system remained virtually unchanged until it was reformed by the Lisbon Treaty in 2009, with the aim of achieving more continuity and a stable leadership in the EU.

By introducing the post of the full-time President of the European Council, and with the Foreign Affairs Council Presidency being taken over by the new High Representative, the rotating Presidency has been curtailed and the role of President of the European Council decoupled from it. Nevertheless, the rotating Presidency still remains in place and still holds the Presidency of nine (out of ten) Council formations. The GSC serves both institutions and thus provides a link at the service level, supporting coherence and continuity in the work of both institutions.

2.3   The roles of the Council

The Council brings together representatives of the Member States who are able to make decisions on behalf of their respective governments. First and foremost the Council's role is to safeguard national interests while acting on the basis of the Treaties. The Treaties not only define the scope of the action, but also the competences of the Union, which affect the powers of the Council as well as the way in which it takes decisions.

The Treaty (Article 16.1 TEU) clearly defines the legislative and budgetary powers of the Council (both exercised jointly with the Parliament) and extends its powers to carrying out policy-making and coordinating functions. The more the legislative and budgetary powers came to be shared with the Parliament, the more the policy-making and coordinating powers grew in scope and importance. Although the Commission is the primary executive body in the EU, the Council exercises executive powers in some specific cases as well.

The primary role, and the primary activity, of the Council is the exercise of its legislative powers. No legislative decision in the EU is taken without the Council's involvement and approval. The way in which it decides, the procedure (and with it the involvement of other actors) and the nature of the act adopted, despite it having been simplified to an extent, still varies.

The first key element of how the Council works relates to the way it votes.

Figure 2.1: Voting in the Council

	Weighting (%)	Weighting (%)
Germany	16.13	18.54
France	13.08	14.98
UK	12.96	0
Italy	11.88	13.65
Spain	9.13	10.49
Poland	7.39	8.49
Romania	3.77	4.34
Netherlands	3.39	3.89
Belgium	2.23	2.56
Greece	2.09	2.40
Czech Republic	2.05	2.35
Portugal	2.00	2.30
Sweden	1.99	2.29
Hungary	1.90	2.18
Austria	1.72	1.98
Bulgaria	1.36	1.56
Denmark	1.13	1.30
Finland	1.07	1.23
Slovakia	1.06	1.22
Ireland	0.95	1.10
Croatia	0.79	0.91
Lithuania	0.54	0.62
Slovenia	0.40	0.47
Latvia	0.37	0.43
Estonia	0.26	0.30
Cyprus	0.17	0.20
Luxembourg	0.12	0.14
Malta	0.09	0.11

figures to 31/1/2020 from 31/1/20

Qualified-Majority Voting
(for 2020 until 31/01/2020 and from 01/02/2020 to 31/12/2020)

A qualified majority needs
– 55%* of Member States (i.e. at least 15/27) AND
– 65% of population

A blocking minority needs
– 45% of Member States OR
– 35% of population (representing ≥ 4 Member States)

Council Decision 2009/857 of 13/12/07 deliberations to continue if (since 01/04/17) 55% of the blocking minority indicate opposition

* 72% if not on proposal by Commission or High Representative (at least 20 MS)

The Lisbon Treaty broke with the weighted voting system which had been in place since the European Coal and Steel Community was established, though the new, much-simplified system of a dual majority of Member States and population only came into effect in November 2014. In order for a decision to be adopted a **qualified majority** of at least 55% of Member States, which must comprise at least 65% of the Union's population, need to vote in favour of the decision.

As Figure 2.1 shows, the weighting of the votes by Member States had to be significantly adjusted in 2020 to take account of Brexit, with a redistribution of the UK's weighting.

An additional rule states that at least four countries are needed to block a decision. Without this extra rule there could be as few as three countries representing more than 35% of the EU's population, thus forming a so-called 'blocking minority' – the minority which prevents the Council from reaching a qualified majority to adopt a decision.

Passerelle Clauses

These are clauses within the Treaty of Lisbon that allow the European Council to unanimously decide on:
- changes in voting in the Council;
- change from SLP to OLP;
- specific policy areas or issues to be subject to QMV or OLP.

Qualified majority is the general rule unless the Treaties provide otherwise. The first alternative is **simple majority** which is mainly used for procedural issues, but also in cases where Council requests the Commission to undertake any study it considers desirable for the attainment of the common objectives and to submit to it any appropriate proposals (Article 241 TFEU).

The second alternative is **unanimity** which is needed mostly for (non-implementing) decisions in the areas of Common Foreign and Security Policy (CFSP) and Common Security and Defence Policy (CSDP) (which are non-legislative in nature), in some policies in the area of freedom, justice and security, as well as in Passerelle Clauses (entrusted to the European Council, see box above) and for establishing Enhanced Cooperation. These also characterise most decisions taken by Special Legislative Procedures (SLP) requiring the consent or consultation of the Parliament. Unanimity is also needed in the Ordinary Legislative Procedure (OLP) in cases where the Council wants to adopt changes to the Commission's proposal without the Commission's agreement to these changes (see Chapter 5).

Although qualified majority voting is the general rule, it is important to understand that a highly consensual tradition and practice have become cemented into the functioning of the Council. Being aware of the long-term nature of EU integration, the Council strives to accommodate as many national interests as possible and, at the same time and with increasing difficulty reach an agreement with the European Parliament under the OLP.

An estimated 70% of all decisions which could have been taken by a qualified majority are in fact taken by consensus. This proportion is still relatively high, but it needs to be noted that the number of decisions in which at least one Member State voted against has risen in the last decade and the number of Member States which contest an individual decision has also risen on average.

Both the inclination to seek consensus and the difficulty of achieving it have implications for the nature of negotiations. Negotiations involve long-term relationships which do not end after the adoption of one act, and decisions often come in packages. There are also implications for the character of the measures adopted, reflected in compromises allowing for transition periods, exemptions, differentiations, etc.

Given the importance of the population factor and the vast differences in size of population among the Member States, it might easily be assumed that the big Member States are more influential and dominate proceedings in Council. While this partly holds true, one should not underestimate the influence and expertise of smaller Member States, especially on specific issues and dossiers. It is often the case that certain smaller Member States can steer the direction of the debate with convincing arguments – and they are often the source of compromises. Therefore due attention should always be given to all Member States in the Council.

Since the Lisbon Treaty came into force the **Ordinary Legislative Procedure** has been, as the name suggests, the ordinary way of taking legislative decisions. The procedure is described in detail in Chapter 5. Worth pointing out here are the agenda-setting practices in the Council with regard to the files in OLP. While the deadlines are fixed once the Council has adopted its position in the first reading (if it is not in total agreement with the Parliament's position), the Treaty sets no time limit for the first reading.

However, since almost 90% of legislative files under OLP are now concluded with first reading agreements, the negotiations with the EP take place at this stage. The Presidency will be in close touch with the rapporteur in the Parliament in order to find possible compromises between the two institutions. The Presidency thus has a key role in finding and steering compromises through the Council. One should always keep track of the discussions taking place between the two legislative institutions and the compromise proposals coming from the Presidency. The role of the Presidency at this stage can prove to be quite instrumental.

This does not mean that the Presidency is completely unconstrained when setting its six-monthly agenda and the files it will put on the agenda. The **Trio 18-month Presidency programme** which outlines the activities of the three successive Presidencies in the period provides guidance. The 18-month programme was introduced in 2007 in order to tackle the problems of discontinuity and having varying priorities every six months. The trio for 2019 and the first half of 2020 was formed by Romania (holding the Presidency January–June 2019), Finland (July–December 2019) and Croatia (January–June 2020). The subsequent trio was formed by Germany, assuming the Presidency of the Council in the second half of 2020, Portugal and Slovenia and these three began well in advance to seek to coordinate their approaches.

The programme itself is prepared by the three Presidencies (heavily assisted by the GSC) in close cooperation with the Commission, and since the entry into force of the Lisbon Treaty, also the President of the European Council and the High Representative for the Foreign Affairs Council (FAC). This means that decisions on what to put on the agenda are already, to a certain extent, taken when setting up the 18-month programme, thus giving a rough sense of orientation on what the Council intends to deal with in the coming 18 months.

Furthermore, the annual Joint Declaration on the EU's Legislative Priorities (introduced by a 2016 Interinstitutional Agreement on Better Law-Making agreed among the three institutions) guides the Presidency in structuring the agenda. The actual operational programme under the term of each Presidency is fine-tuned in the last month before the beginning of each Presidency. When finalising the programme the Presidency takes into consideration progress under the previous Presidency, the Commission's Work Programme, the above-mentioned Joint Declaration and also the arrangements it sets with the Parliament on cooperation in terms of agenda-setting for files in OLP. It is thus only in this period that it becomes a lot clearer which files are going to be prioritised and put on the agenda of the Council – and for the OLP files, by definition also of the Parliament – in the coming six-month period.

Although the OLP is the most common procedure, the **Special Legislative Proce-**

dures (SLP) are characterised by the greater role of the Council. There is more than one type of SLP and they vary in terms of the majority needed in the Council (usually unanimity, but qualified majority in the case of specific R&D programmes) and by the nature of the involvement of the Parliament. In some cases the latter is only consulted (among them, tax harmonisation, approximation of laws, measures in energy policy with a fiscal character, sensitive areas of social policy, family law with cross-border implications, operational police cooperation and system of own resources); in other cases the consent of the Parliament is required (e.g. in actions to combat discrimination, strengthening citizens' rights, the establishment of a European Public Prosecutor's Office, implementing measures for a system of own resources). The consent of the EP is also required in many cases to conclude international agreements, including bilateral agreements with third countries.

Furthermore, there are still areas of decision-making with no involvement of the Parliament (such as measures on fixing prices, levies, aid and quantitative limitations on the fixing and allocation of fishing opportunities, approving state aid in exceptional circumstances, implementing measures to freeze assets). The procedure for the adoption of the Annual Budget is also a Special Legislative Procedure. Before approaching any institution it is important to clarify under which procedure, with what majorities, and with what involvement of the Parliament and the Commission the issue in question is to be adopted.

The Council's role as **budgetary authority** is of course extremely important and hardly a year passes without intense and difficult negotiations with the EP in an effort to settle the budget appropriations for the coming year. After a series of budgetary crises in the 1980s a multiannual financial perspective, known as the **Multiannual Financial Framework (MFF)**, was introduced in order to set the broader lines for the period across several years (the most recent perspectives have covered seven years), which would make the Annual Budgets less vulnerable to the negotiating powers of the institutions. With the Lisbon Treaty the budgetary procedure was simplified, reducing the number of readings to one, after which there is a Conciliation meeting should there be no agreement in the first reading. Between 2010 and 2019 all Annual Budgets for the Union were adopted in time. The Conciliation meeting was convened each year and the Commission submitted new budget proposals for 2011, 2013, 2015 and 2019 after the failure of the two budgetary authorities to agree in Conciliation.

It is important to understand that since the Lisbon Treaty (and for the first time in 2010) the Parliament and the Council have an equal say over the entire budget. The MFF, however, is according to the Treaty to be adopted by the Council unanimously, after obtaining the consent of the Parliament. Given that the MFF needs to be observed in adopting the Annual Budget, it could, on a strict reading of the Treaty, be claimed that by setting the contours via the MFF, the Council limits the action of the Parliament. This is legally speaking true, and, the Parliament is aware of that, which is why it also strives to assert its role in the process of the adoption of the MFF.

The **policy-making function of the Council** is widely understood to be prevalent in the areas which do not fall under the exclusive or shared competences of the Union, but are subject to coordinating and supporting or supplementing competences of the Union. The Council adopts non-binding measures primarily in order to coordinate economic and employment policy. Other areas in which the Council coordinates are industrial policy, research and technological development, space and most aspects of public health policy. In exercising its coordinating function the Council usually adopts guidelines in the form of **Council Conclusions** or Council recommendations.

Perhaps the most widely known policy-making in the Council, with the aim of co-ordinating Member State policies, is in the area of foreign policy, more specifically CFSP, including the CSDP. However, Member States of course exercise their individual rights to make their own foreign policy, as indeed across all areas where the Council acts as a legislator.

In the initiation phase of the EU policy cycle, the representatives of the Member States take part in the expert and consultative bodies. In the decision-making phase, Member States (as the Council) scrutinise and amend the Commission's proposal. In the implementation phase, Member States provide an opinion on the Commission's draft Implementing Acts and in the Council they can object to Delegated Acts (see Chapter 6). This means that the Member States, both individually and acting collectively in Council, are a crucial actor all through the EU policy-making process even if the interventions of the Member States, and their room for manoeuvre, can change from file to file and during the policy cycle stages.

A distinction can be made between representatives of the Member States who take part in the decision-making processes of the Council because they represent the position of their Member State, usually via an explicit mandate, and those officials from Member States who sit in Committees scrutinizing proposed Implementing Acts and/or Expert Groups. These national officials are only very rarely based in Brussels and come from the Member State capitals only for the purposes of the meetings. In these cases the officials often have a greater margin of influence over their positions, notably because they are usually the technical experts in the domain. This distinction is important if you are trying to approach a national official because knowing their room for manoeuvre and possibilities will condition how you can work with them. It is therefore important to clearly establish in what capacity and in what relationship to the decision-making authorities, representatives from the Member States take part in these meetings.

Lastly, there are some **executive powers** that the Council shares with the Commission. There are three aspects to this.

One is the implementation of EU legislation and (coordinated) policies at the national level, which gives Member States (and not the Council) the executive powers.

The second is the involvement of the Council in the implementing stage of EU policies via Implementing and Delegated Acts (dealt with in detail in Chapter 6).

And, thirdly, there are a limited number of areas in which the Council acts as the body in charge of exercising implementing powers itself. The area of CFSP is partially subject to this (e.g. the missions in the framework of the CSDP) as well as monitoring economic developments in the Member States and the EU.

Having reviewed the functions of the Council, we will now turn to the internal structures which enable it to carry out these roles.

2.4 Internal structure of the Council

This section explains the main elements of the Council architecture with the objective of detailing the key actors and structures. Figure 2.2 outlines the broad picture of the internal structure of the Council. We will address each hierarchical level in turn, high-lighting the basic organisational features of the Council: **Coreper**, **Special Committees** and **Working Parties** (also referred to as **Working Groups** – the two terms are used synonymously in this book as they are by the Council itself). At the end the GSC is presented in detail. The next section thus starts to explain how these levels all work together in order to produce the legislative and policy-making activities of the Council, starting at the top with the Council of Ministers.

Figure 2.2: The internal structure of the Council

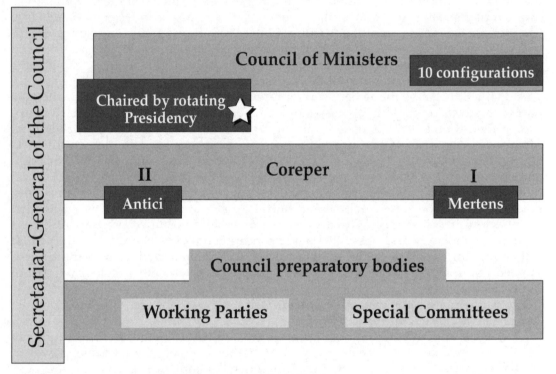

 With the exception of the Foreign Affairs Council and some of its preparatory bodies. Some specialised committees also have elected chairs.

2.5   Internal structure of the Council: The Council as a meeting of Ministers

The Council as a meeting of Ministers constitutes the final stage of the work of the entire Council machinery composed of the preparatory bodies and the GSC. The Treaty states that the Council consists of a representative of each Member State at

Ministerial level, who may commit the government of the Member State in question and cast its vote.

The attendance lists of the various Council meetings point to differing practices of the Member States with regard to the seniority of their representatives. Although Ministers' attendance is a rule, junior Ministers, State Secretaries, even Directors-General or Permanent Representatives and Deputy Permanent Representatives to the EU might represent their Member States at a particular meeting. The decision on attendance can be based on competences, domestic priorities, or other reasons for unavailability of the Minister.

With regard to the membership it also needs to be mentioned that in some instances involving federal or largely decentralised Member States, representatives of a sub-federal level might take part, either in a capacity to take decisions (Belgium, Germany) or to coordinate sub-state units (Spain) in Council formations (or policy fields) for which in that particular Member State a sub-federal level has a legislative competence. Some Council meetings also cover areas which are the responsibility of more than one national Ministry and are therefore attended by several representatives. It is always necessary to establish at what level and under which competence of which Minister, and in what capacity, a Member State will take part in a Council meeting.

Although there is only one Council, it meets in several **configurations** to discuss different policy areas. It is worth noting, however, that any Council configuration can adopt (legislative) acts in any policy field. Following the changes introduced by the Lisbon Treaty there are now ten Council configurations, as indicated in Figure 2.3.

Figure 2.3: Council configurations

- General Affairs
- Foreign Affairs (including European Security and
  Defence Policy, Trade and Development Cooperation)   } **Coreper II**
- Economic and Financial Affairs (including Budget)
- Justice and Home Affairs (including Civil Protection)

- -

- Employment, Social Policy, Health and Consumer Affairs
- Competitiveness (Internal Market, Industry, Research and Space)
- Transport, Telecommunications and Energy   } **Coreper I**
- Agriculture and Fisheries ★
- Environment
- Education, Youth, Culture and Sport (including Audiovisual)

★ Dossiers based on Common Agriculture Policy are studied by the Special Committee on Agriculture, instead of Coreper I, before going to Ministerial level

There used to be many more configurations, but with the reforms undertaken in the late 1990s and early 2000s (the Conclusions of the 1999 Helsinki European Council and 2002 Seville European Council), their number had fallen even pre-Lisbon Treaty from over 20, first to 16 and finally to 9, resulting in many Council meetings being so-called composite Councils, covering issues which spread across several Ministries in Member States. The Lisbon Treaty finished the process, started already at Seville, of enhancing the role of the GAC, by splitting the General Affairs and External Relations Council (GAERC) into the General Affairs Council (GAC) and Foreign Affairs Council (FAC). These two Council formations are the only ones with a Treaty base; the rest of the Council configurations are determined by the European Council.

The **General Affairs Council** is charged with ensuring the consistency of the work of the Council (in all its configurations), preparing the work of the European Council and ensuring the follow-up of its meetings. The GAC is thus placed in a somewhat awkward position between a primus inter pares and a coordinator.

In the Council's Rules of Procedure (RoP) this role is further elaborated, charging the GAC with responsibilities for overall coordination of policies, institutional and administrative questions, and horizontal dossiers which affect several of the EU's policies, such as the MFF in regard to operating rules for the Economic and Monetary Union (EMU). The awkwardness of the GAC's position is more understandable once you see this detailed list. By dealing with enlargement it crosses the thin line between enlargement and foreign policy, which is the subject of the FAC. On the other hand, its coordinating function, and especially the part to do with EMU, places it in competition with the Economic and Financial Council (ECOFIN).

One question that arises from these vast areas of policies is: who is the most appropriate Minister to take part in the GAC meetings? By looking at the attendance at GAC meetings in the years following its separation from the Foreign Affairs Council, we can observe four broad categories of representatives of the Member States in the GAC: Foreign Affairs Ministers, European Affairs Ministers, State Secretaries from the Foreign Affairs Ministries and State Secretaries from the Prime Minister's cabinet. It needs to be added that, more often than in case of other configurations, it is the Permanent Representatives to the EU who represent Member States at GAC meetings. The choice depends largely on the tradition and current system of coordination of EU affairs in each Member State.

Delegation sizes to the Council meetings vary by Member State. In the Council meeting room itself the Minister is accompanied by the Permanent Representative (or the Deputy Permanent Representative) seated next to the Minister (except in the case of the ECOFIN Council where Ministers sit alone at the inner table) and a small number of advisors are seated behind in the second row. The Presidency is given more seats and it usually uses its Member State seat for the highest-ranking civil servant in the administration covering the given policy area.

The Commission is present with a Delegation composed of a Commissioner, Director-General and a small number of staff, including staff from the Secretariat-General of the Commission (SG). The representatives of the GSC are also in the room. The relevant Director-General is seated on the left of the Presidency to assist it and further officials as well as a representative from the Legal Service are seated behind. For the meetings of the FAC the European External Action Service (EEAS) is also present. With around 100 people in the room, the Council meetings are far from intimate, though the

Council formations meeting on a regular basis tend to have a more intimate atmosphere. Legislative parts of Council deliberations can be accessed via the internet (see box on the right).

There are around 70 to 80 formal Council meetings a year. The average number of meetings per year has grown by about 20% in recent years (2016–2019) compared to the pre-Lisbon period. Some configurations meet monthly (GAC, FAC, ECOFIN, Agriculture and Fisheries) and others once or twice per Presidency term. Usually a Council meeting lasts one working

> ### *Council live on the Internet*
>
> You can follow the Council on the Internet for:
> 1. Council deliberations under the OLP.
> 2. The Council's first deliberations on legislative acts other than those adopted under the OLP.
> 3. The Council regularly holds public debates on important issues.
> 4. The Council regularly holds policy debates on Council programmes.

day, but some are scheduled over two days, starting after lunch on the first day and finishing with lunch on the second day. Besides the official agenda, the draft version of which is distributed by the GSC two weeks prior to the Council meeting, the attending Delegations and Ministers can engage in a number of other meetings. Bilateral meetings in the morning or on the margins of the Council are a routine part of the co-operation among Ministers.

Sometimes there is also an informal dinner among the Ministers on a preceding evening. We can also find Ministers holding meetings in different groupings, usually in the evening before the meeting. The custom of Prime Ministers meeting the leadership of a particular European Political Group in the Parliament before European Council meetings has been replicated in some cases before Council meetings. However, more often the so-called 'like-minded' countries meet to discuss and possibly align their views before important decisions are to be taken. Such groupings have included the Visegrad four (Poland, Czech Republic, Slovakia and Hungary), the Hanseatic League (Sweden, Finland, the Baltic States, the Netherlands and Ireland), the Franco-German couple or the Baltic and Nordic states.

Ministers also meet in **informal Council meetings** hosted by, and held in, the country of the Presidency. Although the 1999 Helsinki European Council agreed to limit the number of informal Council Meetings to five per Presidency, in practice almost every Council formation holds an informal meeting during each Presidency.

These meetings are informal in the sense that they do not adopt any decisions and they do not follow the Rules of Procedure of the Council. They are intended to advance the work of the Council on specific issues, to promote a certain issue of the Presidency or to discuss long-term policy developments. Discussions at informal Councils, which are usually only followed by a statement of the Presidency, may be formalised at a subsequent formal Council meeting.

Informal Council meetings are attended by the Minister and usually up to two assistants. The Commission as well as the GSC are also present. It has become customary to invite a prominent expert to speak on the subject matter under discussion. Often a Presidency underpins discussions on its prioritised subjects by background studies it orders or requests (e.g. from the Commission), and by its own so-called 'non-papers' as well as those contributed by other delegations. (A non-paper is a position paper that is supposed to trigger a discussion but does not bind the organisation that issues it. They do not have an official status.) It is important to watch out for the informal Council's agenda and discussions as major breakthroughs might happen on legislative or non-legislative files and issues. It holds true for the informal Council meetings just as for the formal meetings, however, that they are not an occasion at which Ministers are available for a meeting or susceptible to persuasive arguments. These need to be channelled through the Council hierarchy.

2.6   Internal structure of the Council: The Presidency

The top of the Council hierarchy, as first among equals and changing every six months, is the Presidency of the Council. Already in setting up the European Coal and Steel Community, the founding governments opted for a rotating Presidency to manage the Council's work and represent it internally as well as externally. The tasks of the Presidency came to extend far beyond management (which also became an extraneous task itself with the widening and deepening of the Union) to include tasks such as political initiator and broker. This relatively stable system of a single Council Presidency resisted any major change until its reform with the Lisbon Treaty in 2009.

Following the entry into force of the Lisbon Treaty, the rotating Presidency has been somewhat curtailed, with the view of ensuring more continuity, especially with regard to the European Council, and coherence with regard to external action and external representation of the Union. The European Council, as explained in detail above, is thus no longer chaired by the rotating Presidency, but by its full-time President. Likewise, the Foreign Affairs Council is chaired by the High Representative (except when trade is on the agenda, in which case the rotating Presidency remains in the chair). Some of the Working Parties which feed into the FAC (including the Political and Security Committee, PSC), but not all, are chaired by permanent chairs from the European External Action Service (EEAS). With the European Council and the FAC being chaired by the European Council President

> ### Forthcoming Presidencies
>
> The current order in which the office of President of the Council shall be held was decided through a Council decision in 2016 and covers the period up to and including 2030. The six-monthly Presidencies for the period 2020-2024 are:
>
> 2020:   Croatia, Germany
> 2021:   Portugal, Slovenia
> 2022:   France, Czech Republic
> 2023:   Sweden, Spain
> 2024:   Belgium, Hungary

and the High Representative respectively, the most visible role of the rotating Presidency – that of external representative of the Union – has been reduced.

There are two possible exceptions to this. Firstly, a Foreign Minister of a country of the Trio-Presidency can be asked to act as a deputy to the High Representative in matters of CFSP; and, secondly, in a sitation where the EU lacks representation in a third country or within an international forum, a rotating Presidency, if present, represents the Union in that country or in that forum. The rotating Presidency may also be asked to represent the Member States internationally in cases where the Union lacks competence but Member States wish to act together. But aside from this representational role for the rotating Presidency in the area of CFSP, representation of the EU in external affairs is no longer in the hands of the Presidency.

For all the other nine Council configurations, however, the tasks of the Presidency have not changed. The issues of continuity and coherence have been addressed with regard to regular Council work (in addition to the above-mentioned strengthened coordinating roles for the GAC) via the establishment of the system of pre-established Trio-Presidencies. As noted above, in a Trio a group of three consecutive Member States holding the Presidency work towards the execution of the joint programme. Each Presidency still draws up its own individual programme, prioritising issues it feels strongly about. It also presents the list of all forthcoming Council agendas, indicating the dossiers that will be discussed as well as the objectives of the deliberations.

This list is prepared at the latest one week prior to taking up the Presidency. The calendar and the agenda of the Council's work for the Presidency's term, subject to modifications as required, are thus available within the last weeks of the previous Presidency's term. It is worth keeping this in mind for planning purposes, especially longer-term planning. With these agendas you have a good idea when a particular issue is going to reach Coreper or Council levels.

These calendars and agendas are also important if you are trying to set up meetings with the representatives of the Presidency, because the days around any meeting of the Council are extremely busy for the Presidency. In addition, in order to plan its Presidency, the Member State will know in advance when a certain new legislative proposal will be issued by the Commission. Even though this information will not be included in the calendars and agendas made available, the Presidency is an additional source of information when trying to establish more precisely when the Commission will issue a specific proposal.

The Presidency convenes the meetings, drafts the agendas and chairs the meetings at all levels of the Council machinery (with the aforementioned exceptions in the foreign affairs area and with exceptions to some Committees and Working Parties, outlined below). It aims at driving the Council's work forward by trying to bring the discussions to the adoption of decisions.

The norm of having an 'impartial Presidency' has become deeply rooted in the Council's culture, though each Presidency can exercise its tasks with different objectives in mind. These may be promoted consciously by the government or adopted individually by its Presidency teams, especially the chairs of Working Parties, Committees and Coreper, and eventually by the Ministers. An outline of 'ideal' styles by the Presidency as identified often in the literature is presented in Table 2.3 on the next page.

Table 2.3: Different styles of the Presidency

Organiser (task-oriented)	Broker (group-oriented)	Political leader (transformational)
• Plans meetings (with GSC) • Drafts agendas (with GSC) • Makes sure that the machinery is running smoothly (with GSC)	• Listens to the Member States positions • Creates a good atmosphere • Identifies the midway position, bargains and trade-offs • Formulates compromises • Serves the group process	• Puts current discussions in a long-term perspective of EU challenges • Steers the debate in specific directions • Convinces delegations to abandon short-term interests
Focus on **effectiveness**	Focus on **fairness**	Focus on **long-term objectives**

Source: adapted from Schout, J.A. and Vanhoonacker, S. (2005) 'Nice and the French Presidency'. In Laursen, F. (ed.) The Treaty of Nice: Actor Preferences, Bargaining and Institutional Choice (Dordrecht: Martinus Nijhoff)

The Presidency has three advantages which allow it to exercise its brokerage role: procedural control, access to information and support from the GSC.

First, in respect of **control over procedures**, the Presidency arranges the meetings and sets the agendas; not in a vacuum, but it does have a certain margin of manoeuvre for prioritisation on all levels, from Working Party to the Council of Ministers, bringing attention to new issues, reviving issues, speeding up (or slowing down) dossiers. It does so by deciding on the frequency of the meetings, shaping of their agendas, proposing the introduction of a new (ad hoc) Working Party and deciding its composition, forming a Friends of Presidency group, etc. The Council RoP set the framework for the business-like conduct of Council meetings, aimed at efficiency (Article 20 and Annex IV).

Second, the Presidency also enjoys an advantage in **access to information**. Presidencies start preparing for their term of office a couple of years in advance; they pay attention to the process and the dossiers they will tackle; they consult their counterparts in other Member State capitals; and during the Presidency they enjoy privileged access to information. This is why it is important to take into consideration the Member States that will hold the rotating Presidency in the future and engage with them in good time. In the run-up to taking over the Presidency, the Member State and its Permanent Representation are very busy with planning the next six months and it is very challenging to be able to secure a meeting with the relevant persons at that time.

Third, **the GSC gives full support to the Presidency** in its tasks by providing advice on procedures, positions, strategies and tactics, as well as suggestions on compromise proposals. In order to promote issues and policies the Presidency wants to prioritise, it organises numerous events, in Brussels and in its own capital; in addition, its embassies organise events in other Member State capitals.

These are also occasions to establish contact with the most relevant attachés, advisors to the (Deputy) Permanent Representatives, or the person in charge of your particular issue, if you have not done so previously. All these actors can be instrumental when trying to find out the progress reached on a certain dossier during Council workings. During the Presidency all its representatives in Brussels are under enormous time pressure, filling in the time between meetings with bilateral talks and testing the water for compromise proposals in order to achieve the objectives the Presidency set itself and those it announced in the draft agendas of the Council submitted prior to its Presidency. Therefore, approaching the Presidency is much easier in the period before, when it is still reshuffling its priorities and when it is becoming clearer what issues it will have to deal with and is seeking information on.

2.7   *Internal structure of the Council: Coreper I & II*

The **Committee of Permanent Representatives** (**Coreper**, after the French acronym) of the governments of the Member States is charged with the preparation of the work of the Council and with carrying out the tasks assigned to it by the Council. Hiding behind this very modest, and rather general, job description is a body with the highest level of political awareness and insight. It is also the only horizontal body in the Council architecture. With two exceptions explained below, every single dossier passes through the discussions of the Coreper meetings prior to being placed on the agenda of the Ministers' meeting.

As the name suggests, Coreper (pronounced 'co-repair') is a body composed of Permanent Representatives of the Member States in Brussels. They head Permanent Representations of the Member States to the EU. Already in 1962 Coreper split into two, with **Coreper II composed of the Permanent Representatives (PR)** ('ambassadors') and **Coreper I composed of Deputy Permanent Representatives (DPR).**

Coreper II ambassadors are usually very senior diplomats from the national Foreign Ministries. Coreper I representatives may be slightly junior to their Coreper II colleagues, and they may also come from outside the Foreign Ministries (e.g. from bodies coordinating EU policies in the Member States). Both carry out tasks which are very time-consuming and also very different from the work done by their diplomatic colleagues in embassies around the world. As Figure 2.3 showed, the split refers to the Council meetings they prepare. In Coreper II the more senior 'ambassadors' deal with horizontal, institutional, financial, justice and home affairs and foreign affairs. Coreper I is seen as more technical as it prepares for the other six internal market orientated Council configurations.

It is worth briefly outlining the main roles and functions of a Permanent Representation in Brussels because they are such important actors in the Council architecture. Table 2.4 highlights the main elements of the role of a Permanent Representation.

Figure 2.4: Composition of Coreper

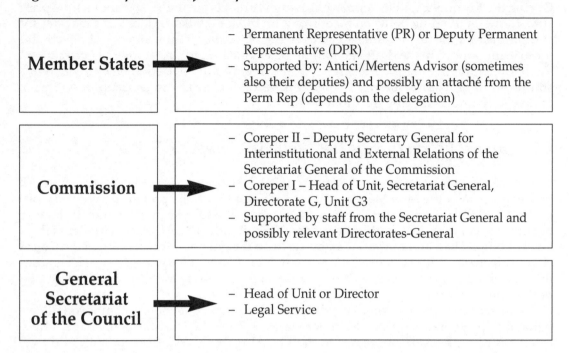

Member States ➤	– Permanent Representative (PR) or Deputy Permanent Representative (DPR) – Supported by: Antici/Mertens Advisor (sometimes also their deputies) and possibly an attaché from the Perm Rep (depends on the delegation)
Commission ➤	– Coreper II – Deputy Secretary General for Interinstitutional and External Relations of the Secretariat General of the Commission – Coreper I – Head of Unit, Secretariat General, Directorate G, Unit G3 – Supported by staff from the Secretariat General and possibly relevant Directorates-General
General Secretariat of the Council ➤	– Head of Unit or Director – Legal Service

Coreper II and Coreper I representatives are highly knowledgeable and experienced. They are unique in public administrations in the sense that they are diplomats with an in-depth knowledge about the policies they negotiate on in the Council and, in case of the Presidency, with the European Parliament for the files under OLP (see Chapter 5 for details on Codecision). They prepare the meetings of the Council with the objective of facilitating progress in negotiations, while at the same time they have their own national mandates and need to observe national interests.

Due to the frequency and intensity of the meetings, Coreper representatives are very familiar with each other and can be very informal in their dealings, resulting in meetings being open and efficiency-oriented. The representatives are usually rotated after four or five years, in line with national diplomatic practices. Some countries, though, prolong their term of office, usually in order not to change them in a period before assuming the Presidency.

Coreper meets weekly (both I and II), usually on Wednesdays, although it can also meet on Thursdays (Coreper II). Coreper I often continues working on the weekly agenda on Friday. Meetings usually begin at 10:00h and occasionally last long into the evening hours. The precise arrangements vary from one Presidency to the other. Meetings are trilingual (English, French and German, with interpretation). They are extremely dynamic meetings, with people rushing in and out as the dossiers under discussion follow each other. As Figure 2.4 shows, in addition to the PRs or DPRs, there are also senior officials (Antici and Mertens, see below) assisting them and the relevant attachés on the dossiers under discussion on the Council side.

Similarly, the Commission is present with senior officials from its SG and a shifting

Table 2.4: Roles and functioning of a Permanent Representation

Information gatherer	Monitor the proposals being generated by the Commission and, where appropriate, work for changes.
Information conductor	Link EU institutions and national governments. Assist national organisations to contact the Commission, Parliament or other EU institutions for lobbying purposes.
Information provider	Brief ministers who attend meetings of the Council, with particular attention to negotiating tactics and the politics of the files.
Policy formulation	Assist in putting together national policy on EU issues and proposals (takes place in national capitals, although to differing degrees depending on the Member State).
Negotiator	The staff negotiates at official level in line with instructions given by national governments. This can be done either through informal contacts or the formal process.

representation of experts from the relevant DGs. A small delegation from the GSC assists the Presidency, takes notes and advises on separate files. Officials from its Legal Service may also be asked to clarify any legal questions.

The senior officials assisting the representatives form special groups which normally meet on Tuesday to go through the agenda, clarify positions and signal points of contention that could arise during negotiations. In the case of Coreper II this preparatory group is called the **Antici group** and in each Permanent Representation there is an Antici attaché. Similarly the **Mertens group** meets to go through the agenda of Coreper I and Mertens attachés assist the DPRs.

The Antici attachés are usually more senior, often coming from the Foreign Ministries. Their discussions can also go beyond technical and procedural issues and they can indeed undertake limited political negotiations themselves. The Antici attachés also have a special role with regard to the meetings of the European Council. There they act as information carriers for their delegations on the proceedings in the European Council meeting. Mertens attachés also act as a point of contact for a number of attachés and experts and have a coordinating role in the Permanent Representation, as well as a reporting role to the national capital (though this may vary between Permanent Representations). The Presidency's Antici and Mertens attachés are also important actors with regard to negotiations with the Parliament. They are another channel for the Presidency to brief other Member States and also to check on their positions with regard to the continuation of the process.

Considering all of the above it is necessary to stress the importance of Mertens and Antici attachés as they can be crucial contacts to have in the Permanent Representations. They have a bird's eye view on all the dossiers, access to in-depth and updated information on of the dossiers leading to Coreper I or II respectively, and they are also updated regularly on other Member State positions and compromise solutions once negotiations are at Coreper level.

2.8   Internal structure of the Council: Committees and Working Parties

The work of Coreper and the Council is assisted and prepared by a number of Committees and Working Parties (WPs).

Committees have a higher standing in the Council hierarchy and can be of a very diverse nature with regard to their status (Treaty-based or based on Council decision), tasks (delivering opinions, giving recommendations, contributing to policy developments), composition (especially with regard to chairmanship), relations to the Council (direct or via Coreper) and frequency of the meetings (from several meetings in a single week in the case of the Political and Security Committee to only twice yearly in some other cases).

The **Special Committee on Agriculture** (SCA) is a unique case in the sense that it is an equal counterpart to Coreper I in preparing the work of the Agriculture and Fisheries Council. It covers issues of a technical nature in the agricultural markets and rural development, while Coreper I deals with fisheries, food safety and budgetary issues.

The **Political and Security Committee** (PSC, also known by the French acronym COPS) is a Treaty-based Committee (Article 38 TFEU) charged with monitoring the international situation in the area of CFSP, contributing to the definition of policies by issuing opinions, and also monitoring the implementation of the agreed policies. Its members usually also hold the rank of ambassador and might be referred to as PSC (or COPS) ambassadors or even CFSP ambassadors. Like the Coreper they have a senior-level official group called the Nicolaidis group, which prepares their work. They usually meet on Tuesdays and Thursdays, but can also be convened when an international situation so requires. Though, unlike the SCA, the PSC does not enjoy the position of being a parallel counterpart to Coreper, and there are occasional tensions between the two, issues considered by the PSC are rarely re-opened by Coreper II. Following the implementation of the Lisbon Treaty, the PSC is no longer chaired by the ambassador from the Presidency, but by a representative of the High Representative.

The **Economic Policy Committee** (EPC) provides analyses, opinions and draft recommendations on structural policies and its chair (together with the chair of the **Economic and Financial Committee** – EFC) assists the meeting of the ECOFIN Council.

Other Committees are tasked with reporting and giving opinions. They are usually composed of high-level experts coming from the capitals, joined by the attachés from the Permanent Representations.

The PSC is not the only Committee not to be chaired by the Presidency. The EFC has an elected chair for two and a half years (and as an exception a Secretariat provided for it by the Commission and not the GSC). The Employment Committee, the Social Protection Committee and the Economic Policy Committee have an elected chair for two years. The EU Military Committee has an appointed chair for three years and the Security Committee (dealing with security issues related to Council proceedings) is chaired by the representative of the GSC.

Other important Committees with a specific position in their respective policies include the Trade Policy Committee (TPC), Committee on Internal Security (COSI), Article 36 Committee (CATS) and Strategic Committee for Immigration, Frontiers and Asylum (all chaired by the Presidency) and Committee for Civilian Aspects of Crisis

Management (chaired by the representative from EEAS). Committees' websites (others than those pertaining to the CFSP) are available on the Europa portal under respective policies.

About 140 **Working Parties (WPs)** (also called **Working Groups**, **WGs**) prepare the work in the Council. There are 15 to 20 meetings every day. WPs are tasked with examining all the relevant files and dossiers in their area. This reduces the number of open issues to be dealt with by Coreper and eventually by the Ministers. WPs tackle general questions as well as technical issues related to any file.

Different WPs meet with a varying frequency. Some meet several times a week, others fortnightly and others again on a much less frequent basis. Also, some have a fairly stable and well-established schedule of meetings, while others might be more irregular. This all depends on the different traditions that the WPs have developed over time. They also vary with respect to the breadth of issues they might cover, with some being highly specialised (e.g. WPs under the Agriculture and Fisheries Council) and others covering policy more broadly (e.g. Environment Council is mainly, but not exclusively, served by one Environment WP, with an International Environment WP addressing specifically the international dimension of environment policy).

It is important to know that unless urgency requires differently, a WP will not discuss the same issue with less than two weeks passing from one meeting to another due to logistical constraints related to translation and document production (i.e. if they do meet more often, they will discuss other items from the agenda). WPs are composed of national representatives, based at the Permanent Representations in Brussels and/or flying in from the national capitals, along with a representative from the Commission. Similarly to higher up in the Council's hierarchy, representatives from the GSC are charged with providing assistance to the Presidency and drawing up notes. Figure 2.5 on the next page depicts the delegations in the WP meetings.

Member States may be represented in a WP by up to four people, coming from the Permanent Representations or from the national capitals. They may be counsellors, attachés or experts in the area and they work based on instructions given to them by the national capital. The breadth of their mandates, as well as their involvement in coming up with the mandate and their level of autonomous action, vary enormously not only between Member States and among issue-areas, but also depending on their personalities, expertise and experience. It is vital to understand that Council WPs work on the basis of consensus and according to some estimates they resolve around 70%–75% of all issues, with the rest being left for Coreper and the Ministers.

Figure 2.5: Working Party composition

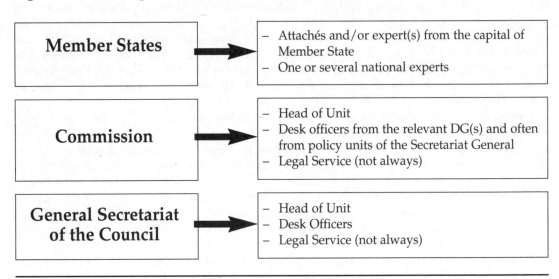

WPs, especially those which meet regularly and are frequented by staff from the Permanent Representations, can develop a very informal atmosphere. The members may have friendly relations and their contact goes beyond just WP meetings.

The line between what is political and what is technical is hard to draw. WPs aim at agreeing on as many issues as possible and only pass them on for consideration by Coreper where further instructions are needed, or for placement on the Ministers' agenda when the Presidency believes that all possibilities for finding a compromise have been exhausted.

Although it is left to Member States as to how they organise their representation at the WP meetings, efficiency and economic considerations determine whether the representatives are permanently based in Brussels or travel to the meetings from the capital. Usually, for those WPs which meet more regularly the representatives come from the Permanent Representations, while the not so regular groups are attended by both an attaché from the Permanent Representation and an expert from the capital. It is first and foremost the attachés, due to their permanent status in Brussels, deep knowledge of procedures and understanding of broader processes beyond the file under consideration, who can give you the information you need regarding a certain dossier and who have a better overview of the negotiations.

Before we go on to look at how this machinery works, in the opposite hierarchical order, we need to look at the mostly invisible helping hand provided by the relatively small number of officials in the GSC.

2.9 Internal structure of the Council: General Secretariat of the Council

As already indicated several times, the GSC is the backbone of the Council's work. It provides logistical services, gives advice and guidance and delivers legal opinions. The key functions of the GSC are highlighted below in Figure 2.6.

Figure 2.6: Functions of the General Secretariat of the Council

1. Logistics

Prepares meetings, drafts reports, briefings, minutes, prepares and records draft agendas. Hugely important function, especially for the Presidency.

2. Advice and Guidance

Provides intellectual infrastructure, assists the Presidency in finding compromises, coordinating work, summing up situations. Provides reports and data on an ad hoc basis. Gives advice also on the process – timeframes, language issues.

3. Legal Opinion on form, substance, procedure

The Legal Service gives opinions to the Council. Its opinion is very important – it is difficult for Member States to go against it. It is a politically aware body that can provide strategic advice.

It is a relatively small secretariat, headed by a Secretary-General (who by tradition enjoys a long term of office), with roughly 850 administrators. It is divided into the private office of the Secretary-General, policy DGs, a Legal Service and a Press Office. In the period following the entry into force of the Amsterdam Treaty in 1999, and until the entry into force of the Lisbon Treaty, the Secretary-General of the GSC was also the High Representative. Since the introduction of the post of full-time President of the European Council, the GSC also supports him and his Cabinet.

Over the years the GSC has earned itself the reputation of being not only an impartial, but also highly competent and highly dedicated, service. Its officials are almost invisible and its services, such as document production (and ensuring the quality of drafting of Council's documents), interpretation and translation, are taken for granted by the delegations. For the Presidency, however, the GSC provides crucial support. Not all Presidencies make use of it to the same extent. Bigger Member States, which can rely on their large domestic administrations, are less likely to use the GSC's full potential, while smaller Member States tend to rely heavily on it. Officials of the GSC also help the Presidency in its preparation stage, by providing it with information from the screening of files and helping it in setting up the 18-month agenda.

During the Presidency, the GSC officials help by arranging the meetings and structuring the agendas, briefing it before and supporting it with any advice needed during the meetings. Representatives of the GSC also sit next to the chair during all meetings, at all levels. They advise the Presidency on how to achieve its objectives and they help draft compromise proposals.

Approaching the GSC staff can be very useful when engaging with the Council, especially when it comes to Treaty provisions, trilogue discussions or general decision-making procedures. They know the issues in detail as they need to be able to offer advice and expertise to the chair at any time during the negotiations. Also, due to their extensive experience, the GSC is often aware of the direction that a dossier is likely to take inside the Council. At the same time, it must be stressed that the GSC's officials work under a strong code of conduct, with the principles of professionalism and confidentiality observed in any contacts with the delegations and other actors.

2.10 How the Council works: Setting the agenda

The internal decision-making procedures of the Council can be split into a series of different phases, which will be elaborated on one by one in the following pages. At the outset it needs to be said that, in comparison with decision-making in the Parliament and in the Commission, decision-making in the Council can be considered much more straightforward and simpler to understand. On the other hand, however, when it comes to the level of an individual file it is much more elusive and less transparent, making it more difficult to work with. Furthermore, with the Presidency changing every six months, practices can change as well, to better suit the goals and the style of the Presidency.

Given the variety of the Council's roles, the output of the Council is highly diverse. The box on the right presents a variety of types of decisions the Council can adopt.

As explained above, the bulk of decisions that the Council takes are of a legislative and policy-making nature. In principle, the Council works in the same way irrespective of the nature of the decision to be adopted. Differences in proceedings, however, arise among some policy areas due to the difficulty of the issues being decided, the urgency of a matter, and the varying styles of the Presidency (see Table 2.3). The procedures of the Council are laid out in its RoP.

Before we look at how the Council works, we first need to establish how the Council plans its work. It has already been mentioned that the Trio-Presidencies prepare and present their 18-month pro-

A variety of activities undertaken by the Council:

1. adoption of legislative acts;
2. signing international agreements;
3. signing accession treaties;
4. adopting Council conclusions;
5. adopting decisions on the seat of the EU agencies;
6. concluding inter-institutional agreements;
7. adoption of decisions in foreign policy area;
8. monitoring military and civilian operations.

gramme. The programme is prepared in close cooperation with the Commission and the President of the European Council, and the High Representative contributes for the activities of the FAC.

Since the establishment of the Trio programmes in 2007, the practice of cooperation in preparation of the programme has varied among them and across the sectors. Member States may attribute different levels of importance to the Trio programme and have a different view of the approach to preparing it (top-down or bottom-up and with a different role given to the GSC). The first Trio programmes were composed of two parts: a strategic framework and an operational programme, these were tedious and fragmented. From the Trio that started in 2016 onwards, the programmes are structured in line with the Strategic Agenda adopted by the European Council in 2014. They are shorter and more focused, but remain similarly general in their aims. A new Strategic Agenda was agreed in Spring 2019 and it will guide the programme of the Trio starting in mid-2020.

Preparatory practice differs, but the necessary components are:

1. Screening of the dossiers to understand the state of play and legal and procedural issues to be tackled (i.e. ongoing negotiations, mid-term reviews, reports, health checks and observing deadlines in the Codecision procedure).

2. Double-checking with the Commission's Work Programme.

3. Alignment with the Strategic Agenda and other obligations stemming from European Council's conclusions.

From this point onwards, the three countries can add or prioritise issues they feel strongly about. Negotiations follow in order to finalise and produce a coherent text. The final programme is presented at the GAC at least a month before the first of the Trio members takes office. In some sectors, the three countries may prepare separate programmes. Each Presidency is then obliged, on the basis of this programme and after consultation, to prepare draft agendas for Council meetings for the entire time of its Presidency, showing the legislative work and operational decisions envisaged. The box to the right lists the types of work the Council does and the decisions that it takes.

Though not required, Presidencies usually prepare and publish their own programme and their own priorities, which can be found, alongside many other useful documents, on the Presidency's website.

Based on this programming, and taking into consideration the cooperation with the Parliament, the Presidency arranges the work of the Council. A simplified version of the work of the Council follows the pattern presented below. This process is elaborated in more detail in the subsequent sections.

1. The Commission submits the proposal.

2. The proposal is assigned to a specific WP.

Operational objectives

for the Council agenda items:

1. information and presentation;
2. policy debate and exchange of views;
3. orientation debate;
4. progress report;
5. general approach;
7. political agreement;
8. position;
9. adoption;
10. adoption of Council conclusions.

3. The WP discusses it and when it reaches an agreement, or exhausts its discussions, it passes it on to Coreper.

4. If discussions are still needed, it is first screened by the Antici or Mertens group.

5. Coreper then, if needed, further negotiates the proposal and decides whether it is ripe for discussion by the Ministers or sends it back to the WP for further discussions there.

6. The Ministers adopt a decision on the file or instruct Coreper on further proceedings.

2.11 How the Council works: The Working Party

The process in the Council starts at the WP level, as represented in Figure 2.7.

Figure 2.7: Working Party level

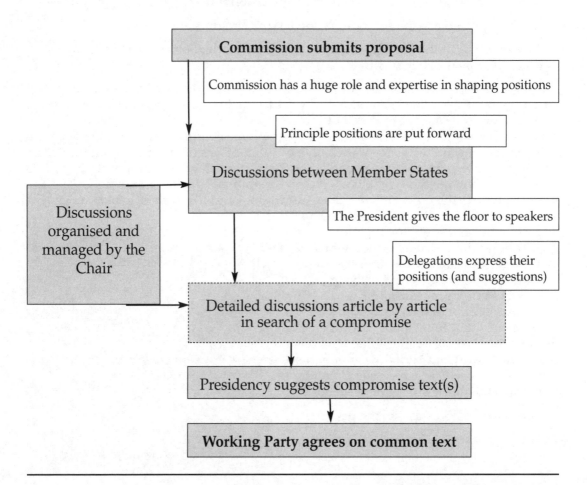

The Presidency announces the assignment of a file to a WP. At the last session of the WP under an out-going Presidency (also at any other hierarchical level in the Council) or at the first session under the incoming Presidency, the chairperson briefly outlines the Presidency programme and objectives for the coming six months. The WP schedule is also drafted in advance for the entire Presidency term of office, although it is obviously subject to changes and only indicative. Often a Presidency will only plan the exact WP meetings a month ahead.

In cooperation with the chairperson, the GSC sends out the invitations, the agendas and relevant documentation to the delegates coming to the WP (the same holds true for other levels in the Council hierarchy as well). A Presidency generally aims at discussing a dossier at no more than three WP meetings, this obviously being subject to the complexity and length of the dossier, with the first meeting dedicated to the more general debate on a dossier and the consecutive meetings to a more detailed examination. As a dossier can go quickly through the WP, it is important to know in advance when the meetings will be held and to get in touch in due time with the attachés concerned. It is important to keep in mind that 70%–75% of all dossiers are agreed at this level; therefore from an advocacy point of view, the window of opportunity should not be missed.

The WP meeting is chaired by the Presidency, which is assisted by the GSC (whose Legal Service is also present), with the Commission seated opposite to it. The national delegations are seated around, with the previous Presidencies to the left and national delegates of the Presidency and future Presidencies to the right of the chair. Prior to the meeting, usually an hour before, the Presidency, the Commission and the GSC hold a meeting to go over the issues and exchange views on potential problems, to agree on the way to proceed and on the tactics to use. The Presidency opens the meeting of the Working Party and announces how it wants to proceed on any item of the agenda.

It is customary for the Commission to be given the floor first to present the proposal. The strength of the Commission is its knowledge of the content of the proposal, its expertise in the subject area and, since it went through the various consultation phases (see Chapter 1.6 and 1.7), also its understanding of Member State positions and the interests behind them. The Commission representative is tasked with defending the proposal but at the same time working, in cooperation with the Presidency, towards the adoption of a compromise proposal. The Commission presents the objectives, the measures and the impact of the proposed document or the relevant part of it to be discussed according to the agenda.

After the Commission, the national delegates are invited to take the floor. The Presidency determines the order and manner in which these exchanges unfold. It can hold a general debate on the proposal, or a debate on the recitals first; it can cluster articles,

> ## Council Rules of Procedure (RoP)
>
> The Council outlines, in detail, all its offices, powers, procedures and much more in its Rules of Procedure.
>
> Pay attention because the Rules of Procedure can change.
>
> It is extremely useful, even necessary, to know these rules if you interact with the Council.
>
> The current Rules of Procedure were adopted on 1 December 2009 (2009/937/EU). An amendment to incorporate the changes in the qualified majority was adopted on 29 September 2014 (2014/692/EU).

or go article by article, and so on. The choice of the manner also depends on how advanced the discussions are, whether it is the first time the dossier is under discussion or whether it has reached the point where there are only a few contentious issues remaining that need to be resolved.

Full round tables are not very welcome and are not encouraged by the Council's RoP. Therefore more often than not the Presidency invites the Delegations to speak directly. The representative of the GSC keeps the speakers' list. Delegates express their countries' position with regard to the issue under discussion, according to the mandate they have been given. They enter reservations, on different grounds, to parts of the text (or a general reservation on a text as a whole).

The more technical reservations can and should be eliminated before the proposal is passed on to Coreper. However, WPs vary with regard to how political they are. As a rule, they are technical bodies, but the line between one and the other is blurred, and WPs often discuss and negotiate elements of the proposals which would qualify as political. The Commission is regularly invited to explain and clarify questions from the Delegations and to express itself on the changes proposed by the Delegations or the Presidency. The chair is in charge of steering the debate towards an agreement, by consensus, on as many issues as possible. The chair summarises the debate, draws conclusions and presents possibilities for further proceedings and, eventually, compromise proposals.

A lot of work is done between meetings. The Presidency might ask a specific question and request answers to be sent in writing; it might invite Delegations to submit proposals in writing; it might arrange bilateral meetings with Delegations; and it spends a lot of time on the phone negotiating as well as keeping in contact with Delegations and with its own superiors when it needs a renewed mandate or seeks help. It should be pointed out that the autonomy given to the WP chairs by different Member States holding the Presidency varies – and it also varies with respect to the position of the issue on the Presidency's list of priorities, as well as its relationship to other issues (and therefore the possibility of a 'package deal'). The WP chair also discusses with his or her Mertens or Antici attaché and the Permanent or Deputy Permanent Representative how to advance the file and when the file is ready to be moved to Coreper. The same item is usually discussed with at least a two week break in between, to allow for the translations and document production and also to allow the Presidency to make progress between meetings.

If the urgency of a matter requires more meetings, the Presidency has a few alternative ways to advance. It can organise an attaché-only meeting which does not require the same interpretation regime as a regular WP. **Attaché-only meetings** also have different negotiating dynamics: experts' meetings may dwell on technical elements too long, whereas attachés may find solutions by employing their negotiating skills and building on their closer relations. It is not unusual for WPs to enjoy an informal so-

Reservations the delegates enter on a proposed text can be on linguistic grounds, or because they need to check with their superiors or because they want to verify the effects or because the involvement of a legislator in their country requires that body's primary agreement. Reservations can also be due to a profound disagreement with a part of a proposal, be it in a recital or in the body of the proposal.

cial occasion during the term of each Presidency in the country holding the Presidency or at a destination nearby Brussels.

On very particular subjects the Presidency may also organise a **Friends of the Presidency** group. These groups are usually set up to discuss big policy-making decisions or especially difficult files. They are equally composed of representatives of all Member States and the Commission, but do not strictly follow the RoP of the Council. They are nevertheless assisted by the GSC.

Ad hoc working parties are set up to deal with specific cross-cutting dossiers which do not fit simply in one existing Working Party. Recent examples include the Ad hoc working party on Article 50 TEU, which dealt with Brexit negotiations, and the Ad hoc working party on the Multiannual Financial Framework 2021–2027 which was also set up in 2018. The previous MFF (2014–2020) was discussed in the framework of the Friends of the Presidency group.

It needs to be stressed that a WP never votes. They agree by consensus on the common text. If there are still reservations by some Delegations, they are added in square brackets or in footnotes. The chair reports to their Permanent/Deputy Permanent Representative on the support the proposal has among the delegations based on the discussions in the WP. An exception to this is an indicative vote sought on Commission's Delegated Acts.

2.12 *How the Council works: From Working Party to Coreper*

Once a WP chair concludes that a common text is ready to be included on the agenda of Coreper, they forward it, together with a written report, to Coreper for examination. The Council RoP require the WPs to terminate discussions on a dossier within five working days prior to the Coreper meeting (unless urgency requires otherwise). If the dossier does not need any further discussion by Coreper (and is deemed ready for adoption by the Ministers) it enters the Coreper agenda as a I item (the 'I' being Roman number one). If however, Coreper is expected to discuss the item it is placed on the agenda as a II item (Roman number two).

In preparation of a Coreper meeting, the Antici and the Mertens group meet on the day before to go through the agenda and clarify positions and also to see if there have been any developments in the meantime (since the dossier was put on the agenda). Coreper meetings are guided by the same rules as the WP meetings (and so are the Council meetings) and follow the same procedural pattern. Due to the number of issues covered by a single Coreper meeting (be it Coreper I or II) it can resemble organised chaos, with experts from all three institutions exchanging chairs during the meeting depending on the issues under discussion. Ahead of a regular Wednesday Coreper meeting the Presidency, the GSC and the Commission hold preparatory meetings earlier in the week, separately for Coreper II and Coreper I.

Figure 2.8: From Working Party to Coreper

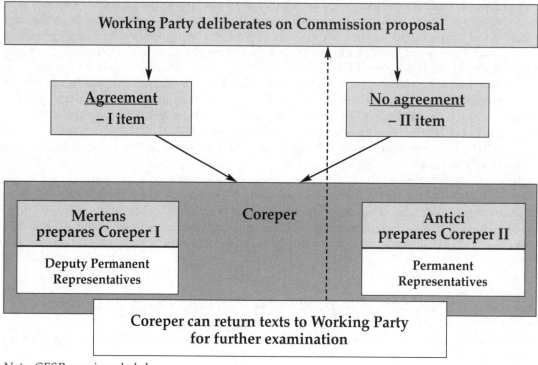

Note: CFSP area is excluded

2.13 *How the Council works: From Coreper to Council*

Discussions in Coreper are much more political and many of the dossiers under II items are resolved at the level of Coreper and do not require further discussion by the Ministers at the Council meetings. Some items will of course be left for the Ministers to discuss and reach a decision. The statistics suggest that in addition to about 70%–75% of all issues being resolved at the level of WPs, a further 15%–20% are resolved by Coreper.

Items that do not require discussion by Ministers at a Council meeting will be placed as A items on the Council agenda, to which I items from Coreper's agenda are (almost) automatically included, and those requiring discussion are placed as B items. However, Coreper can also return dossiers back to the WP for further discussions.

Coreper is a horizontal body and dossiers which are going onto the agendas of different Council configurations are discussed at a Coreper I or Coreper II meeting, depending on the Council formation. Provisional agendas of the Council meetings need to be sent to the members of the Council and to the Commission at the latest 14 days before the meeting. This implies that about three weeks before a given Council meeting

Figure 2.9: From Coreper to Council

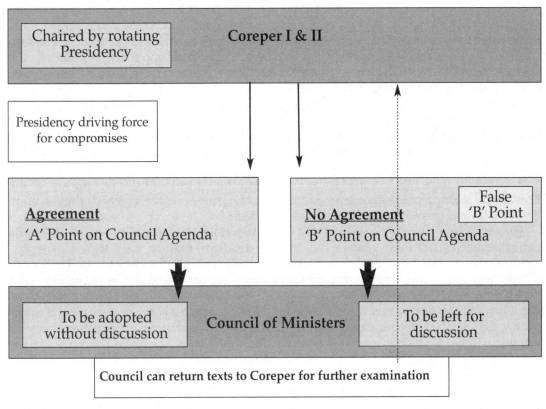

Note: CFSP area is excluded

Coreper adopts a provisional agenda for that meeting. Requests for inclusion of an item on a provisional agenda of a Council meeting, by the Commission or any Delegation, must therefore reach the GSC at the latest 16 days prior to the Council meeting in question. Coreper can still discuss an item already placed on the Council's agenda.

The decisions prepared by Coreper all have to be formalised by a Council meeting. However, in the case of files in OLP, Coreper can agree, without the need for formal verification by the Council, on the mandate for the Presidency to enter into trilogue discussion with the Parliament. It should be said, however, that the Council increasingly decides to agree on a so-called 'general approach'. This is a political agreement ahead of Parliament's first reading position of the Parliament, and it can help to expedite agreement between the two institutions, as Parliament has an idea of the Council's position prior to taking its own position in first reading. The Council's final position, however, cannot be adopted until the Parliament has delivered its own first reading opinion.

Provisional dates for Council meetings are communicated by the Presidency about seven months in advance and the draft agendas, as we have seen earlier, are established at the latest one week prior to each Presidency's term in office. Provisional Council meeting agendas are distributed no later than 14 days prior to the Council meeting, with requests for inclusion of an item on the agenda to be received no later than 16 days prior to the meeting. It is generally acknowledged that in the area of foreign affairs these rules cannot always be respected due to external events and the urgency of a response. The Presidency is expected to observe a 21-day deadline for disseminating the agenda, with the entire documentation for the Council meeting, in the case of the Area of Freedom, Security and Justice (AFSJ).

On the other hand, it is possible to suggest inclusion of any item on the agenda of any Council meeting after the expiry of the time limit of 16 days – but the suggestion has to be accepted by consensus in the Council. It is easier to place items under the 'any other business' section of the agenda, which does not need to be voted upon; however, a request needs to be accompanied by a written explanation.

A couple of days prior to the Council meeting the Permanent Representative of the Presidency holds a press conference in the Council press centre in which they outline the agenda and answer questions from journalists.

The definitive agenda is adopted by a simple majority in the Council. By a simple majority, items included within the 16-day deadline can be withdrawn from the agenda. The agenda, and the Council meeting itself, are split into two parts. The Council meeting is split into '**legislative deliberations**' and '**non-legislative activities**'. The first are open to the public (web-streamed on the Council's website) as are the documents on which the deliberations are based. Non-legislative activities are closed to the public. Council or Coreper can decide to hold a public debate on an important issue of interest to the EU and its citizens. Such an item is marked as 'public debate' on the Council's meeting agenda, whereas the legislative deliberation is marked as 'public deliberation'.

Part A of the agenda includes items which can be adopted without discussion. These are items on which agreement has already been achieved – either at the WP level, at the level of Coreper (or SCA in case of Agriculture and Fisheries Council), or at a previous Council meeting where only an administrative or legal clarification was left over to be made afterwards. They can be adopted item by item or 'en masse', while verifying that the sufficient majority has been achieved (the proof that a necessary majority has been achieved is displayed on the screen in the meeting room). B items are subject to a discussion in which the Ministers proceed in a way similar to the proceedings explained above in the case of the WP. A so-called '**false B**' item is an item on which an agreement has already been achieved, but on which one, or more, Ministers want to express themselves, mostly for domestic political purposes.

The process in Council is illustrated in Figure 2.10.

Adoption of items normally proceeds without a vote, but a vote can be requested by any Member State or the Commission.

We explained above (Section 2.3) how the qualified majority is formed. Here we focus on the effect the voting regime has on **negotiations in the Council**. The possibility of a qualified majority vote, meaning that one country (or more) could be outvoted, changes the dynamics of negotiations. Member States who might be outvoted try to modify a proposal closer to their interests, prolong the decision-making procedure or form a **blocking minority** (see Figure 2.10). In the course of the negotiation of a dossier the Member States, and especially the Presidency, pay attention to the blocking minori-

Figure 2.10:   The Workings in the Council

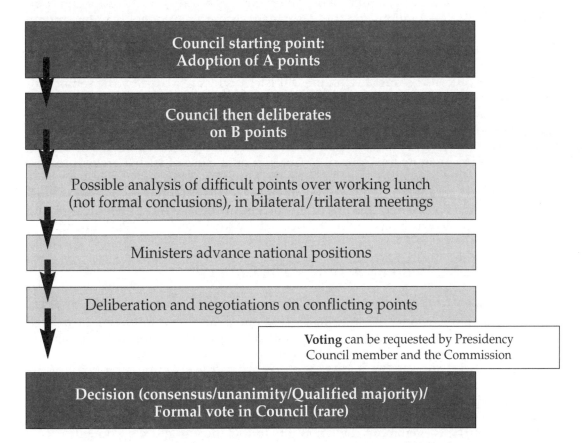

ties being formed; the major negotiation activity on highly contentious files centres on those Member States who are not (yet) with the blocking minority, but whose position seems to be close to it.

Though only about 10%–15% of all decisions taken by the Council are discussed by the Council, this is still enough for vigorous discussions at every Council meeting, for decisions to be taken, or to enable progress on key files. While WP chairs, and also Coreper chairs, are permanently based in Brussels and can therefore stretch their bilateral meetings and plan their work between meetings, Ministers do not have this luxury. They meet over one or maybe two days.

If discussions in a Council meeting are not showing any progress, the Presidency has a few options. It can adjourn the meeting in order to meet bilaterally or with a small number of Member States; it can instruct the PRs to leave the meeting room and try to find a solution among them; and it can also decide to discuss the subject over lunch or dinner. While the rest of the Council meeting takes place in a room with about 100 people, in most cases the Ministers' lunch is restricted to Ministers only and the responsible Commissioner. Normally only the Presidency may be accompanied by its PR or another senior official and by the GSC. Many dossiers are advanced or agreed upon during lunch. The lunch discussion items are usually decided a few days in advance and communicated to the Delegations via the Permanent Representations. It can be an item from the agenda of the meeting, with the aim of discussing it freely over lunch, but it can also be something completely unrelated, like a discussion on the seat of a new Agency or how to tackle a certain imminent issue. A separate lunch is also organised for the senior officials accompanying the Ministers, who are joined by the senior officials (Director-General) from the Commission and the GSC.

In addition to decision-making by the Council at the meeting, the Council can also adopt decisions via an **Ordinary Written Procedure** or a **Silence Procedure**. The Ordinary Written procedure can be used in cases of extreme urgency provided there is unanimous agreement by the Council or Coreper on the use of such a procedure. The simplified Silence Procedure can be used on the initiative of the Presidency, where the issue is deemed adopted if no objections have been raised within the period of time laid down by the Presidency. The use of this procedure is seen most often in adopting the text of replies to questions put to the Council by Members of the Parliament.

2.14 Key stages and key actors – The Council

This chapter has detailed the decision-making process in the Council by first explaining how a file gets on the agenda of the Council and then following it through the Council machinery. The chapter has identified all the stages of the decision-making process and the key groups and individual actors that are involved.

The first observation to be made is with regard to the seeming simplicity of the Council workings. Though the process is linear, the content can be subject to many different influences which impact the dynamics of the policy-making process. Given that there is significantly less transparency in the Council (in comparison to the Commission and Parliament) it is even more challenging to follow the work of the Council.

While the 18-month Trio programme gives only a rough idea as to what the priorities of the Council workings might be during the coming three Presidencies, the operational programmes of each Presidency present a clearer picture as to which files will be worked upon in the Council in the following six months. Even these, however, need to be checked against the actual agenda (for things such as leftovers from the previous Presidency), the Commission's execution of its planning, international events or domestic developments which demand sudden attention. In addition, the progress of files depends on factors such as the general mood surrounding the file and the dynamics over the file in the Parliament (in the case of a Codecision file). This does not mean that the programme the Presidency set for itself will not be pursued, but it does mean that due to various factors this or that file may be set aside and another one occupy its place on the agendas.

Council Working Party, Committee, Coreper and Council meetings are scheduled well in advance due to logistical constraints with regard to the availability of rooms and interpreters, the translation of documents and also the availability of officials and Ministers – as well as a desire to avoid surprises as much as possible. With all of this in mind, the margin for setting up extra meetings to overcome difficulties or to examine new issues is limited but not entirely impossible. Management of the Council workings lies in the hands of the rotating Presidency; therefore it is important to watch closely how the Presidency ranks a certain file on its list of priorities and how much of an extra mile it is willing to go to achieve its objectives on the file.

The Presidency can advance work during the meetings by inviting the Delegations to submit proposals in writing and by careful preparation of compromise proposals. Although all the Presidency actors are extremely busy and under time pressure, they will have an ear for constructive proposals. This is probably mostly the case at the level of the WP. In principle, political issues with regard to the proposals under examination are not discussed at this level, but the Presidency of course aims at getting a very good sense of everyone's position on the proposal and a possible solution in order to be able to prepare the compromise at this or at any later stage. A WP chair who is well-informed and strong on the substance of a file can be crucial in developing compromise proposals at the later stages.

The linear progress in the Council (passing from the WP/Committee stage to Coreper and finally to the Council) can sometimes be disrupted and reversed in the case of extremely difficult files. Examples of these would be files on which there are divergent positions either due to new developments in positions, or due to the fact that the file is simply not yet ripe for decisions to be taken and more work needs to be done at the technical level. It is up to the Presidency to manage such situations. Its options include referring the file back to Coreper (from a Council meeting), to the Mertens or Antici groups or to the WP itself. It can also propose to set up an ad hoc WP or a meeting of a WP in the composition of attachés only, or even invite officials from the national capitals to its own capital for a high-level discussion to find a compromise. Such options are used by the Presidency very carefully, in order not to create a sense of chaos and haste, but it is precisely with these developments that one can lose track of the progress on a file.

Once again, closely watching the steps of the Presidency is important for understanding the dynamics and progress on a file. It is also important to develop a sense of the majorities the Presidency is pursuing for the adoption of a file. Naturally, legal conditions for unanimity are strictly observed, but as explained above, in the vast majority of cases where a decision could be taken by qualified majority, the Council adopts a decision by consensus. This tendency affects the dynamics of negotiation, the framing of the compromise and eventually the timing of the adoption of the file. However, if consensus does not seem probable and (or) there is time (or peer) pressure, the Presidency can decide to conclude the file with the majority it has obtained. Therefore the voting system outlined earlier in this chapter (see section 2.3 and Figure 2.1) is highly relevant and careful monitoring of majorities throughout the process is still essential.

Following this analysis, the main stages and key actors in the decision-making process in the Council are outlined in Table 2.5.

The Council and the European Council on Social Media

You can follow the Council and the European Council on: Facebook, Flickr, Google +, Instagram, Storify, Twitter, YouTube. The link to the overview of the Social Media presence of the Council and the European Council:
http://www.consilium.europa.eu/en/contact/social-media/

Table 2.5: Key stages and key actors – The Council

Key stage	Comment	Key Actors
Setting the 18-month Trio-programme	Provides a rough sense of orientation as to what will be tackled in the programmed period.	Permanent Representations and Heads of State or Government + Cabinets of the three countries holding the Presidency
		General Secretariat of the Council and Commission
Setting the operational agendas of the Presidency	Gives a clearer indication as to what will be worked on and with what operational objectives.	Key focus on personnel of the Permanent Representation holding the Presidency
		General Secretariat of the Council
Discussion of a file in a Working Party/ Committee	Rarely only a technical discussion thus this is the stage (and the level) to closely watch for direction in a discussion and for compromise proposals coming from the Presidency.	Attachés/Member State delegates in the Working Party
Discussion of a file in COREPER	Several open issues might be addressed and successfully closed at this stage, or grounds tested for the Ministers' deliberations.	Attachés/Advisors/(Deputy) Permanent Representative
		Antici/Mertens group
Council meeting	Final decisions taken, also in package deals; Presidency to advance compromise; intense negotiations immediately prior and during the meeting.	Ministers, Cabinets
		(Deputy) Permanent Representative

The Council of the European Union Register

The register lists references to documents produced in the General Secretariat of the Council of the EU since 1/1/1999 in the official languages. The database includes agendas of meetings, draft conclusions of Council meetings and a wide range of other documents. Though a large proportion of the documents in the register are not available in full text due to classification rules, the register is the first step in your search, providing you with, at the very least, information on the existence of the document. In addition, the register also contains documents from other institutions, relevant for decision-making in the Council.

3. The European Parliament

By Joost Mulder and Alan Hardacre

The Parliament is the only directly elected institution in the EU, and as such is the source of direct democratic legitimacy in the Union. Direct elections first took place in 1979, and are held every five years, meaning that in 2019 we started the ninth legislature. While few would have heard of, or worked with, the Parliament back in 1979 it is now a formidable political institution increasingly comparable to influential national parliaments, if not even more powerful. The Treaty of Lisbon, which entered into force in December 2009, ushered in a new era for the Parliament, the repercussions of which have been seen over the subsequent decade and all of which will be outlined in this chapter.

Table 3.1: European Parliament – Key facts

Role:	EU legislative body
Established:	1979 (as elected body); 1952 as Common Assembly
Voting system:	Party list and proportional representation
President:	David Sassoli (Socialists and Democrats) 2019-2022
Vice-Presidents:	14
No. of MEPs:	705
Term:	5 years (currently 2019-2024 session, 9th legislative term)
Decision-making body:	Plenary
Political Groups (Figures as of 23 March 2020):	187 European People's Party (EPP) 147 Socialists and Democrats (S&D) 98 Renew Europe (RE) 76 Identity and Democracy Group (ID) 67 Greens/European Free Alliance 61 European Conservatives and Reformists (ECR) 39 Confederal Group United European Left/Nordic Green Left (GUE-NGL) 29 Non-Attached Members (NI)
Internal structure:	20 Standing Committees and 43 Delegations approx. 6,000 officials under Secretary-General
Working languages:	24
Location:	Strasbourg (France), Brussels (Belgium) and Luxembourg

There are 705 **Members of the European Parliament (MEPs)** who sit in, currently, seven different **Political Groups**, as well as a number of non-attached MEPs (known by their French acronym NI - for *non-inscrit*). It is within, and between, these Political Groups that the Parliament has to find its position(s) in its decision-taking body, the Plenary session.

This chapter will present the Parliament's decision-making process in detail, although trying to explain all the complex interactions within such a political body is not an easy task. Whereas the Commission is a public administration with a tightly structured working methodology and process, the Parliament is a political body where two dossiers rarely follow the same path. This makes analysing how the Parliament actually works very challenging and it also makes working with the Parliament very much a case-by-case exercise. This chapter will concentrate on presenting the key players, the key stages and the things to look out for when working with the Parliament. Firstly, it is necessary to start with the macro-view of the Parliament.

3.1 *Roles of the Parliament*

The Treaty articles that define the general role of the Parliament are Articles 13-14 and 16-17 TEU, and Articles 223-234 TFEU. Within these articles the three main powers of the Parliament can be found: legislative, budgetary and supervisory.

Besides these Treaty-based formal powers the Parliament also has very important and extensive informal powers.

1. Legislative power

The Parliament is the legislative equal of the Council (with a couple of sensitive exceptions). The Parliament has **Ordinary Legislative Procedure (OLP)** powers over 95% of all legislation, across 84 policy areas. This means that the Parliament has an equal say on the outcome of legislation with the Council (see Chapter 5 on the Ordinary Legislative Procedure for more detail).

Unlike national parliaments, the European Parliament does not have the formal right to initiate legislation which, as we saw in Chapter 1, is reserved to the Commission (with Member States on some occasions). This

---

European Parliament Rules of Procedure

The European Parliament outlines, in detail, all its offices, powers, procedures and much more in its Rules of Procedure.

Everything from Intergroups (Rule 35) to Question Time in Plenary (Rule 137) is explained in the 241 Rules. In addition you will find 8 annexes which range from issues such as a code of conduct for conflicts of interest to a detailed list of committee responsibilities.

Pay attention because the Rules of Procedure can change. It only needs one MEP to propose a change which will then be assessed by the relevant committee, usually the Legal Affairs Committee (Rule 237).

It is extremely useful, even necessary, to know these rules if you work with the Parliament.

You can find them at:
https://www.europarl.europa.eu/about-parliament/en/organisation-and-rules/organisation

issue is a very sensitive one for the Parliament, and one that some would like to see formally changed. The Parliament does have, under the OLP by virtue of Article 225 TFEU, the right to ask the Commission to submit before it a legislative proposal. To do so the Parliament, as outlined in Rule 54 of its internal Rules of Procedure (RoP), must adopt an Own-Initiative Report (see section 3.5) requesting the desired legislative text.

Parliament can also politely request a proposal in a non-binding non-legislative report, as defined in Rule 53. In either case, it is then up to the Commission to consider this request, but it is under no legal obligation to bring forward a proposal. In the 2019 confirmation hearings for Commission President, Ursula von der Leyen committed to consider every single request from Parliament for a legislative proposal. However, this is not a guarantee that an actual legislative initiative will be presented as the Commission must still respect the Treaty provisions on subsidiarity, proportionality and legal basis.

Aside from its substantial powers under the OLP, the Parliament contributes to the legislative process under the **Special Legislative Procedures (SLP)**, notably the **Consultation and Consent procedures**. For example tax issues still remain under Consultation, and the signing-off of international agreements requires the Consent of the Parliament. These two powers should not be taken lightly because they are important powers that are taken very seriously by the Parliament.

This is particularly the case with the Consent procedure, which came to the fore in 2010 when the Parliament withheld its consent on the SWIFT data transfer deal between the EU and the United States. The Consent procedure is a very powerful tool for the Parliament. As a result of the Lisbon Treaty, the Parliament also has the right to approve or reject (but not amend) the EU's trade agreements with third countries, such as CETA (Canada-EU) and TTIP (USA-EU).

2. Budgetary role

The second major power of the Parliament is its budgetary power. The Council and the Parliament together form the EU budgetary authority, whereby the Parliament jointly agrees the annual budget with the Council, monitors the execution of the annual budget, and finally gives discharge to the budget.

The Parliament first gained budgetary powers in 1970, under the Treaty of Luxembourg, and further extended these powers during the following decades. Budgetary powers may thus be regarded as the first real powers the Parliament had and, with the Treaty of Lisbon giving it full equality in budgetary decision-making

The Power of the purse

Since the entry into force of the Treaty of Lisbon, the Parliament shares equal authority with the Council over the EU budget. Its main competences are:

- agreeing the annual budget;
- monitoring the Commission's execution of the annual budget;
- giving discharge to the budget.

with the Council, it continues to be a major power (Articles 310-325 TFEU). In fact, the annual budget negotiations offer the Parliament a heavyweight negotiating opportunity because the Parliament has succeeded in gaining concessions from the Council and/or Commission by linking its priority legislative (and other) issues to the annual budget negotiations.

3. Supervisory role

The third major category of powers of the Parliament is the right of supervision and control functions. The most visible of these is its control of the executive power, namely the Commission. The mechanisms for electing a new College, and removing a College, were dealt with in Chapter 1.3.

In addition, the Parliament has further supervisory powers. These include powers to set up Committees of Inquiry to look into violations or wrong applications of EU law by Member States (e.g. several Committees have investigated unfair tax practices); to request answers to questions from the other institutions, and ultimately directly petition the Court of Justice of the EU; and to exercise control through its budgetary powers by having a Member State, the Commission, other EU institution or EU Agency appear before its Committees to give account, present annual statements, etc. In addition the Committee on Petitions hears up to 1,500 public complaints a year. The Parliament also has considerable powers of supervision in the realm of delegated and implementing legislation (see Chapter 6).

Aside from these formal powers, the Parliament also has significant informal powers, notably ones that supplement its powers to supervise and control. As a political body it is able to effectively exert pressure where it feels its formal mechanisms are not being respected, or where they do not exist. For the three formal powers cited above one must consider that all of them are flanked by a vast array of informal powers to try and achieve its objectives. This can be anything from media coverage, events, reports, high-level networking and political connections.

While the powers described above are presented in three separate categories for the sake of clarity, the Parliament often mixes its powers for maximum effect. There is, therefore, always a possibility of an issue getting tied into other debates and inter-institutional conflicts. It is imperative to never neglect the informal powers of the Parliament because by a simple Own-initiative Report or Question from MEPs (both covered later) an issue can come alive.

> **The Parliament and the media**
>
> The Parliament is the closest of the EU institutions to the European and national media.
> The Parliament, through its MEPs, seeks media coverage of its issues and positions. This is something that should always be taken into consideration when dealing with the Parliament – what are the media opportunities and/or risks?

3.2 Internal structure of the Parliament: Outline

The Parliament is made up of MEPs who are elected to represent over 320 million eligible EU voters – making elections to the Parliament the biggest transnational elections in the world. Elections were last held between 23 and 26 May 2019, and all Member States used variations of proportional representation to elect their MEPs. The majority of MEPs are elected from national party lists, and there are MEPs from more than 140 national parties who are affiliated to one of the seven European Political Groups. The implications of this national list system are extremely important when considering the motivations and drive of an MEP in Brussels, and they will be discussed in more detail later in the chapter.

The allocation of seats is done according to the principle of 'degressive proportionality', whereby the size of population alone, while taken into account, is not the sole criterion for the number of MEPs attributed to a Member State. In this way, the smaller Member States are ensured meaningful (actually over-proportionate) representation in the Parliament. For example, an MEP in Germany represents around 850,000 residents whereas an MEP in Malta represents about 80,000 residents. The number of MEPs per country is highlighted in Table 3.2 below.

Table 3.2: Number of seats in the European Parliament by Member State after Brexit (2020-2024)

Country	*Seats*			Austria	19
Germany	96			Bulgaria	17
France	79			Denmark	14
Italy	76			Slovakia	14
Spain	59			Finland	14
Poland	52			Ireland	13
Romania	33			Croatia	12
Netherlands	29			Lithuania	11
Greece	21			Latvia	8
Belgium	21			Slovenia	8
Portugal	21			Estonia	7
Czech Rep.	21			Cyprus	6
Hungary	21			Luxembourg	6
Sweden	21			Malta	6
				TOTAL	**705**

Source: *https://www.europarl.europa.eu/meps/en/home*

The number of MEPs (total and by Member State) is important for several reasons, all of which will become increasingly apparent as the chapter proceeds. In essence the Parliament is all about the numbers game – the number of MEP votes. It is always vital to follow the number of MEPs from a National Delegation, within a Political Group, supporting an issue, etc. This issue will be raised on a number of occasions.

Every MEP has one (or several) **Accredited Parliamentary Assistants (APAs)** who support their MEP in their tasks. You can find a list of accredited assistants on the Parliament's website at: http://www.europarl.europa.eu/meps/en/assistants. The role of an assistant varies enormously from one MEP to another, with some providing only secretarial support and others offering detailed substantive assistance with drafting and negotiations. You will only ever discover this through your interactions with MEPs and their office. Irrespective of the previous consideration, an assistant is always a vital gatekeeper to the MEP, privy to a wealth of information about substance, process and procedure.

From these broad areas of competence and power, and the number of MEPs sitting in the Parliament, the next stage is to look at the structure of the Parliament itself, as outlined in Figure 3.1.

Figure 3.1: The internal structure of the European Parliament

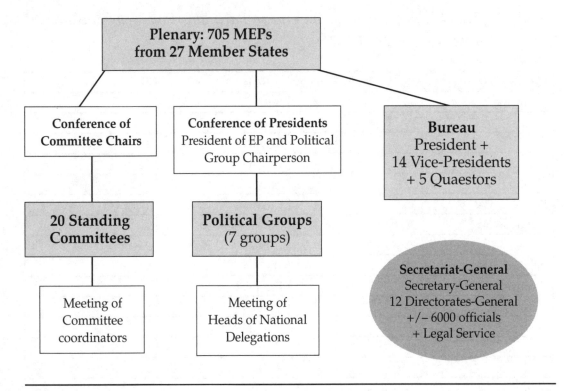

1. The Political Group

MEPs align themselves with one of the seven Political Groups at the European level, or decide to sit as a Non-Attached Member (NI) with no political affiliation.

2. The President

Once MEPs have been elected, and have joined their Political Group of choice, there will be a secret ballot of all MEPs for the election of the President and Vice-Presidents. Since 1979 there has been a gentleman's agreement between the two main Groups in the Parliament, the European People's Party (EPP) and the Socialists & Democrats (S&D), to divide the five-year term of President into two equal mandates. This system is not without criticism, notably from the other parties which are excluded. David Sassoli, from the S&D was elected President on 3 July 2019, and the EPP and S&D intend to again divide the post for the 2019-2024 Parliament, meaning that the EP presidency will go to a representative from the EPP Group in early 2022. The only exception to this stranglehold on the President's position came in 2002-2004 when Pat Cox, from the ALDE Group, was elected for a two and a half year term.

3. The Conference of Presidents

This consists of the President of the Parliament and the Presidents of the Political Groups – and as such represents the highest political body in the organisation of the Parliament. It takes decisions on the organisation of the Parliament's work and matters relating to legislative planning; it manages relations with the other institutions and bodies of the EU and with the national parliaments of Member States, and it has responsibility for matters relating to relations with non-member countries and with non-EU institutions and organisations. It meets twice a month to set the agenda for the Plenary sessions. It always aims for consensus although if a vote is required each Political Group President carries the weight of their Group votes.

> ### *President of the Parliament*
>
> - oversees all of the activities of the Parliament and its constituent bodies;
> - presides over all Plenary sessions, part and full;
> - chairs meetings of the Bureau and Conference of Presidents;
> - represents the Parliament in all external relations;
> - attends meetings of the European Council.
>
> ### *Recent Presidents*
>
> 2017-2019: Antonio Tajani
> 2012-2017: Martin Schulz (two terms)

4. The Bureau

This is the highest administrative body for the Parliament, composed of:

1.   the President;
2.   the 14 Vice-Presidents;
3.   the five Quaestors (in an advisory capacity only; the Quaestors are responsible for administrative and financial matters relating directly and personally to MEPs).

The Bureau meets once a month, usually in Strasbourg, to deal with financial, organisational and administrative matters concerning MEPs, the internal organisation of the Parliament, its secretariat and constituent bodies. In the event of a tied vote, the President has the casting vote in the Bureau.

5. The Conference of Committee Chairs

This consists of the chairs of all of the Parliament's Committees. It coordinates the activities of the parliamentary Committees, trying to establish horizontal working practices and a forum for the discussion of common issues and problems. It makes recommendations to the Conference of Presidents about the work of Committees and the drafting of the agenda of Plenary sessions.

6. The Secretariat-General

The final aspect of the organisation of the Parliament is the Secretariat-General (SG). The head of this body is the Secretary-General who is appointed by the Bureau. The Secretary-General assists the President, the Bureau, the Conference of Presidents and the College of Quaestors in the performance of their duties. The Secretary-General is also

> **Parliament Secretariat-General**
> - Secretary-General;
> - approx. 6,000 EP staff;
> - 12 internal administrative structures covering procedure and policy.

the principal authorising officer for the EP budget, and heads a secretariat of about 6,000 officials. The officials are recruited through competitions and they are assigned to one of the 12 internal administrative structures, such as the Directorate-General (DG) Presidency that is responsible, amongst other things, for the organisation and follow-up from Plenary sittings.

There is one final, and very important, element in how the Parliament works that needs to be mentioned and that is the multicolour **Parliament Calendar** that most people who work with the EU institutions have to hand. This is a major pre-determined constraint on the individual MEPs and the European Parliament as a whole. There are four main elements of the Parliament's Calendar, although they are not quite as clear-cut as they first seem:

Committee weeks (Pink)	These are held in Brussels when the Committees of the Parliament meet to advance their discussions. Committee meetings can also exceptionally be held during Plenary weeks in Strasbourg. In a Committee there will usually be between 22-69 MEPs as full members, with an equal number of substitutes. Substitute members can be as, if not more, active in the life and work of a Committee than full members so this needs to be watched on a Committee by Committee basis.
Political Group weeks (Blue)	These are held in Brussels and allow the Political Groups to prepare their positions, notably for the Plenary that is held the week after. Important Political Group meetings are also held in the Plenary week to discuss last minute positions, issues and voting lists.
Plenary weeks (Red)	There are 12 Plenary sessions held in Strasbourg every year. There the full Parliament holds its debates and votes. There are also six red 'mini-Plenary' sessions held in Brussels every year.
Travel and constituency weeks (Turquoise)	These weeks are when MEPs can travel with their Delegations or return to their constituency.

Having a Parliament Calendar close to hand is essential when trying to set up meetings and work out timetables of action with MEPs. Download the Parliament's calendar from: http://www.europarl. europa.eu/plenary/en/meetings-search.html.

3.3   Internal structure of the Parliament: Political Groups

The individual MEPs sit within the seven Political Groups in the Parliament. The 2019-2024 legislature is presented in Figure 3.2.

Figure 3.2: Political Groups in the European Parliament, by size March 2020

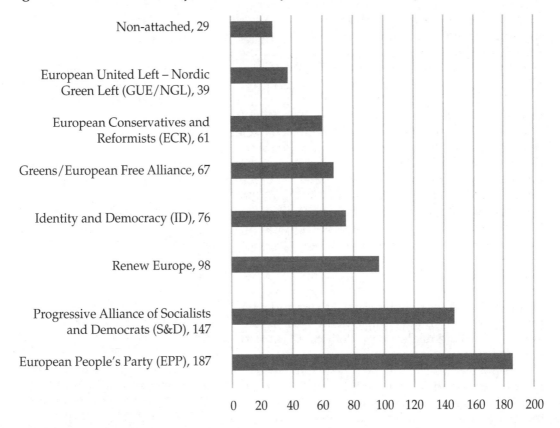

The Political Groups in the Parliament are very powerful and influential bodies as we shall see through the remainder of this chapter. The politics of the Parliament need to be understood in terms of the interaction between these seven Groups and the numbers they represent. To understand the dynamics of Political Groups in the Parliament it is important to always remember that there is no government, or a stable coalition, therefore the political dynamics are different to what we naturally expect in a Parliament with a single-party government or governing coalition. A good way to get a thorough understanding of the differences and similarities between the Political Groups is to visit their websites, read their press releases and manifestos and sign up for their newsletters and alerts.

It is essential to under-
stand the politics be-
tween, and within, the
Groups and their web-
sites offer an important
window into who the
Groups are and what
they are looking to do in
the EU. If you are aiming

EPP Group	www.eppgroup.eu
S&D Group	www.socialistsanddemocrats.eu
Renew Europe Group	reneweuropegroup.eu
ID Group	identityanddemocracy.eu
Greens	www.greens-efa.eu
ECR Group	www.ecrgroup.eu
GUE/NGL	www.guengl.eu

to engage with the Parliament on an issue it is essential to understand the basic Political
Group interplay.

For a Political Group to be formed in the Parliament there need to be at least 25 MEPs
from at least seven Member States, criteria that ensure the trans-nationality of the
Groups. Any MEP who chooses not to belong to a Political Group is termed a Non-Attached Member, of whom there were 29 in March 2020.

Figure 3.2 highlights some fundamental characteristics that define how the Parliament
works in general terms. The first obvious point to make is that no single Political Group
dominates in the Parliament, meaning that solutions in the Parliament have to be cross-
Group compromises: there needs to be a coalition to obtain the majorities needed in Committees and Plenary. This basic fact has to
underpin every effort to work with the Parliament
because there will always be a need to compromise
between the largest Groups. A Plenary is always a
numbers game within, and between, the Groups –
you will always need to follow these numbers because several different coalitions are possible.
From this it follows that it is crucial to try and gain
the support of the main Groups in the Parliament,
and also to avoid neglecting a Political Group, to
have the greatest chances of success.

This point leads to a second key fact. It is essential to understand the internal dynamics of each
Political Group to try and ensure their support. For
this reason it is important to look a little closer at
the composition and functioning of the Political
Groups, which we will do below.

A final point of importance relates to the com-
ings and goings of MEPs in the Parliament, both
within as they change between Political Groups
and Committees, and also outside as a high number of MEPs leave to take up other (usually national) positions. MEPs do not usually have a
stringent mandate in their Brussels work and they
will have less attachment to their European Political Group than to their national party.

Political Group or Political Party?

The Political Groups listed
above are all affiliated to one of
the ten European Political Parties that operate in the EU –
the 'Europarties'.

The Parties are funded and
regulated by the EU and they
operate across the institutions
– notably in the Parliament
through their affiliated Groups
and MEPs.

European Political Parties are
made up of national parties
(from within and outside the
EU) as well as it being possible
to join on an individual basis.
The Parties are very influential
over-arching political structures
that extend beyond the Parliament, with excellent networks
and contacts to influence all aspects of EU business.

Figure 3.3: Organisation of Political Groups in the European Parliament

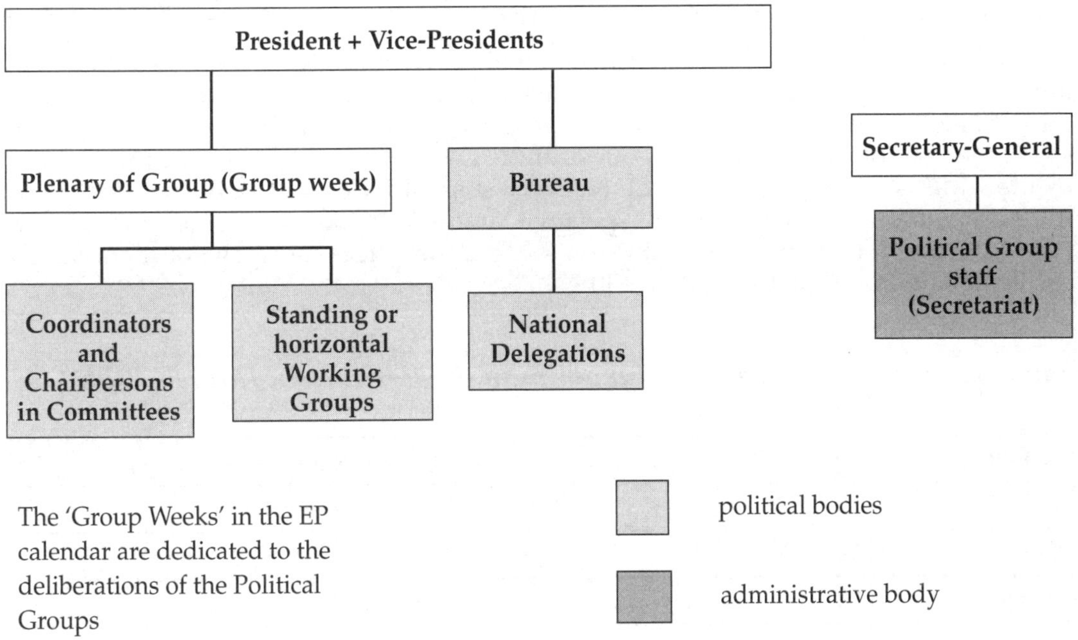

```
┌─────────────────────────────────────────────────────┐                ┌──────────────────────┐
│           President + Vice-Presidents                 │                │  Secretary-General   │
└─────────────────────────────────────────────────────┘                └──────────────────────┘
        │                         │                                               │
┌──────────────────────┐  ┌──────────────────┐                         ┌──────────────────────┐
│ Plenary of Group     │  │     Bureau       │                         │  Political Group      │
│ (Group week)         │  │                  │                         │  staff                │
└──────────────────────┘  └──────────────────┘                         │  (Secretariat)        │
    │            │              │                                       └──────────────────────┘
┌──────────┐ ┌──────────┐  ┌──────────────┐
│Coordinators│ │Standing or│  │  National    │
│and        │ │horizontal │  │  Delegations │
│Chairpersons│ │Working    │  └──────────────┘
│in Committees│ │Groups    │
└──────────┘ └──────────┘
```

The 'Group Weeks' in the EP
calendar are dedicated to the
deliberations of the Political
Groups

☐ political bodies

■ administrative body

Figure 3.3 provides a general view of the organisation within a Political Group in the Parliament. It is not a replica of any Group in particular, but rather it attempts to pull together the main elements of how all Political Groups are structured and work. Common, and important, features are listed below.

1. **The President:** At the head of the Group are the President and Vice-Presidents (VPs) (normally between three and six VPs), usually elected by secret ballot. The President of the Group normally keeps the post for the duration of the legislature.

2. **The Bureau:** The strategic decisions, creation of Working Groups and the approval of financial decisions of the Political Group is all done by the Bureau of the Group, composed of the President, Vice-Presidents, members of the Political Group who are in the Parliament's Bureau, chairpersons of Committees, former Presidents of either the Parliament or the Political Group and one representative of each National Delegation, usually the head of the National Delegation. The main objective of the Bureau is to set the long-term strategy for the Group.

3. **The National Delegations:** Each Political Group is composed of a number of National Delegations, and these will be very important power players within the Political Group. This is because, depending on their size, they can influence the positions of the Group on everything from high-level strategy to detailed voting lists and specific amendments. Knowing the National Delegations within each Group, and understanding their dynamics, is important to working successfully

with the Group as a whole. Each National Delegation can in certain senses represent a separate entity, and National Delegation unity within a Group should never be assumed, as this can change issue by issue.

Of particular interest is whether the national party of the National Delegation is in government in their Member State, in which case they will tend to work closely with their home government positions. It is also important to identify the Delegation spokesperson for your particular issue and the Delegation head. Smaller Delegations of a few MEPs will not have an MEP on every single EP Committee but will still form their opinion on issues covered by specific Committees; likewise, larger Delegations (10+ MEPs) will have multiple MEPs on some Committees, with one of them taking the lead in defining the Delegation's line.

Table 3.3 National Delegation dynamics in the Parliament (March 2020)

Group	No. MEPs	No. Delegations	Largest Delegations
EPP	187	27	29 - Germany (16%)
S&D	147	25	21 - Spain (14%)
Renew	98	22	23 - France (23%)
ID	76	10	29 - Italy (38%)
Greens	67	15	25 - Germany (37%)
ECR	61	14	27 - Poland (44%)
GUE/NGL	39	13	6 - Greece, Spain, France (15%)

What we see in Table 3.3 is that only the EPP have Delegations from all Member States (though the S&D have Delegations from 25 out of 27) and also that, as might be expected, the larger Member States dominate the larger Groups. An interesting number is the percentage of the Groups' MEPs represented by the largest Delegations, where we see that the Renew Europe Group is strongly influenced by its French Delegation, and that the German Delegations in the EPP and Green Groups are relatively dominant. The S&D Group has a strong Spanish Delegation although its German and Italian Delegations are also significant. These considerations help an understanding of the drivers of a Political Group and should always be kept in mind.

At the European level the Political Groups do not have a strong whip sanction system, whereby members can be sanctioned for not following Group lines, such as by not being placed on the next party lists for elections (which is the power of national parties, not the European Groups). But despite the power of National Delegations and the lack of effective whipping, Group voting in the Parliament is in practice seen to be very coherent. This trend is very important and makes working successfully with members of the Group vital. For more on Group voting behaviour and coherence, see www.votewatch.eu (which we come back to in more detail later on).

4. **The Working Group:** The proposals that come before the Political Group Plenary are prepared by a Working Group (WG). In some Groups (Renew Europe, for example) any MEP from the Political Group can sit in a WG, irrespective of its Committee or interests, and in others (S&D, for example) only MEPs from the relevant Committees can attend. The WG meets the week before Plenary, to discuss and decide on amendments and resolutions to be tabled by the Group and on any politically sensitive or controversial dossiers that are coming up in the next Plenary.

The objectives of WG meetings are two-fold:

• To form and agree on Group positions from the various Committees whilst keeping a horizontal overview in mind.

• To find out any sensitive or potentially difficult issues, which would then go to the Group Plenary. This process makes it easier for the Group to be coherent and cohesive when it then comes to full Parliament votes, hence maximising their voting potential.

The main driving forces in these WGs are the rapporteurs and the Committee coordinators who will try to steer their Committee positions through the WG for full Group Plenary support.

5. **The Group meeting:** The main decision-taking body of the Group is the full Group meeting. It takes place at the end of the Political Group week in the Parliament Calendar, and also during Strasbourg weeks to refine voting positions. It is within this body that the positions of the Political Group will be voted and discussed – hence the importance of working with Political Groups and understanding the internal political and voting dynamics. The Groups usually vote by a show of hands and require a simple majority of members present to adopt a Group position. Given the high level of Group voting cohesion in the Parliament (which we come back to later) the vote within the Group is vital for anyone trying to work with a Political Group. The Group's position is usually strictly followed by all of its MEPs in Plenary, except if a 'free vote' is declared beforehand.

6. **The Secretariat:** Each Political Group has its own Secretariat which is led by a Secretary-General. The size of the Secretariat is proportionate to the size of the Group in the Parliament, and all of the staff, or political advisers, can be found on their websites. The Group staff are usually assigned to a Committee (anything from one person covering an entire Committee for a small Group, to three to four advisers per Committee for a larger Group) and they assist their Group MEPs in that Committee by monitoring work, offering research and drafting, liaising with counterparts in other Groups, working on voting lists and keeping important 'work in progress tables'. The Political Group staff are often called into action when an MEP from their Group takes on a rapporteurship as they will assist with the research, discussions and drafting.

7. **The Group coordinator:** The final key person to highlight within the Group architecture is the coordinator. The full members of a Group who sit in a Committee in the Parliament elect from among themselves a coordinator (and vice-coordinator(s) sometimes) for a two and a half year duration, a decision which is confirmed by the Bureau. The coordinator provides political steering and guidance for the

Group on the issues that run through their Committee. They will report back to the Group on developments in their Committee and represent Group positions back in the Committee. A coordinator will also organise the activities of the Group members sitting in their Committee to ensure coherence and consistency and to maximise their efficiency and influence. This will involve nominations of (shadow) rapporteurs, and coordinating any Committee voting. Each Political Group will have one coordinator (and possibly a vice-coordinator) in each Committee (if their numbers allow of course).

3.4 Internal structure of the Parliament: Committees, Delegations and Intergroups

There is one final element of Figure 3.1 on the architecture of the Parliament that needs to be explained: the Committees. The Committees are the specialist engines of the Parliament where the technical and detailed work is done, and where the Political Groups develop their positions on an issue, preparing the work of the Parliament Plenary.

There are 20 Standing Committees in the Parliament, and the list is as follows:

Table 3.4: List of European Parliament Committees

AFCO	Constitutional Affairs	FEMM	Women's Rights and Gender Equality
AFET	Foreign Affairs • DROI Human Rights • SEDE Security and Defence	IMCO	Internal Market and Consumer Protection
AGRI	Agriculture and Rural Development	INTA	International Trade
BUDG	Budgets	ITRE	Industry, Research and Energy
CONT	Budgetary Control	JURI	Legal Affairs
CULT	Culture and Education	LIBE	Civil Liberties, Justice and Internal Affairs
DEVE	Development	PECH	Fisheries
ECON	Economic and Monetary Affairs	PETI	Petitions
EMPL	Employment and Social Affairs	REGI	Regional Development
ENVI	Environment, Public Health and Food Safety	TRAN	Transport and Tourism
Source: https://www.europarl.europa.eu/committees/en/home			

The list of Committees in Table 3.4 is the configuration within the Parliament elected in 2019. The full list of competences can be found in the EP's Rule of Procedure, on the website of each individual Committee, along with other very useful information (see box on the next page).

The Committees vary considerably in how they operate, how they relate to the outside world, how much information they make available on their parliamentary websites and generally in how they conduct their business. These differences make it very difficult to generalise about Committee practice in the Parliament as a whole; each Committee tends to operate in its own separate universe.

> ### Committee websites - A wealth of information
>
> List of members, draft agendas, minutes of previous meetings, calendar of future meetings, work in progress, working documents, reports and opinions of the Committee
>
> In addition, some Committees have: Newsletters, press releases, details of secretariat staff to contact
> *http://www.europarl.europa.eu/committees/en/ home*
>
> Also follow the Committees live: *https://www.europarl.europa.eu/committees/en/meetings/webstreaming*

One thing that they do have in common is the fact that Committees usually meet in Brussels during the two weeks following any Plenary session in Strasbourg, in preparation for the next Plenary. The Committees examine questions referred to them by the Parliament, by debating, preparing reports, opinions and resolutions on legislative and non-legislative dossiers. Committees can also meet, exceptionally, in Strasbourg if the need arises.

Most MEPs serve on one Committee as a full member and on a second as a substitute. It is also possible for an MEP to be a full member of more than one Committee because the number of Committee seats is greater than the number of MEPs.

The formal process is that Committee positions are assigned through a Plenary vote every two and a half years, when seats are granted according to the size of each Political Group. It is then up to the individual Political Groups to decide which MEPs will fill each of the Committee positions they have received. This process varies across Political Groups but is often done through national party delegations. Each MEP will often specialise within their Committee, usually in one specific area of competence of their Committee – which means nearly all MEPs have a specialist area of competence.

Each Committee has its own Secretariat, usually staffed by around six to ten Parliament officials. These staff will offer dedicated support to the MEPs in the Committee for all legislative and non-legislative activities of the Committee. Secretariat staff assist in the drafting of reports, opinions, resolutions and working documents and advise MEPs on questions of substance and procedure. They draw up Committee meeting agendas and voting lists, prepare Committee meetings and assist the chairperson and MEPs in their daily Committee-related duties. Officials of Committees are often allocated to specific dossiers in the Committee, and are hence privy to all information relating to their files.

In addition to Committees, the Parliament also has a plethora of international **Delegations** as listed in Table 3.5.

Table 3.5: Conference of Delegation chairs

Joint parliamentary Committees	14
Parliamentary Cooperation Committees	3
Inter-parliamentary Delegations	25
Parliamentary Assemblies	5
Total	47
Find all Delegations at: ww.europarl.europa.eu/activities/delegations/home.do?language=en	

These Delegations to third countries, regions and organisations often hold a few meetings each year, alternately in the Parliament and in the partner country/region. The Delegations are formed in the same way as a Committee with a chairperson, vice-chairs and a Secretariat. The Delegations have different tasks depending on their partner country or region, so this can be anything from the supervision of the implementation of an accession agreement to an all-encompassing political dialogue.

The Delegations are a very good example of the informal powers of the Parliament, especially in the area of external relations, where the Parliament is able to extend its influence. Delegations are vitally important for anyone working with the partner region/country because they offer another avenue and forum for discussion – and usually wide-ranging discussion. So while they do not take formal decisions, or formally set agendas, they can bring issues to light and make important statements. It is another way to get your point across to your audience and it can be very useful when your interests correspond to Delegation interests.

There are also **Intergroups** (Rule 35, RoP), which are unofficial groupings of MEPs set up to hold informal exchanges, usually with industry and civil society, on specific cross-cutting issues. They are not formal Parliament mechanisms, and as such they exist to offer an informal forum for exchange and information. A distinction needs to be made between the Intergroups that are recognised by the Parliament, and the plethora of informal gatherings and meetings of MEPs that exist. In 2020 there were 27 recognised Intergroups in the Parliament, as decided in December 2019 for the parliamentary term. They usually meet during Plenary weeks in Strasbourg and are open to the public. They are listed below.

Recognised Intergroups for 2019–2024 Parliamentary term

Anti-corruption; Anti-racism and diversity; Artificial Intelligence and Digital; Biodiversity, hunting, countryside; Cancer; Children's rights; Christians in the Middle East; Climate change, biodiversity and sustainable development; Competitive European Industry: long-term and sustainable investment; Demographic challenges, family-work balance and youth transition; Disability; European cultural heritage, Ways of Saint-James and other European cultural routes; Fighting against poverty; Freedom of religion and religious tolerance; Green New deal; LGTBI; Rural, Mountainous and remote areas (RUMRA) and smart villages; SEARICA; Sky and Space; SME; Social economy; Trade Unions; Traditional minorities, national communities and languages; Urban; Welfare and conservation of animals; Western Sahara; Wine, spirit and foodstuffs.

For full details of each of the Intergroups, including their chairpersons and full lists of members go to:https://www.europarl.europa.eu/about-parliament/en/organisation-and-rules/organisation/intergroups.

Both the recognised Intergroups and the unofficial meetings of MEPs are important informal vectors of influence in the Parliament and need to be taken seriously. They are cross-Group gatherings of MEPs interested in the same subject dealing directly with stakeholders, thus offering an extremely privileged platform to those stakeholders involved.

3.5 *How the Parliament works: From the European Commission into a Committee*

Having now outlined the main institutional actors and bodies in the Parliament it is possible to enter into the detail of how the Parliament takes decisions. Decision-making in the Parliament follows a pre-determined path that will be mapped out in the coming pages.

The work of the Parliament that this chapter will base its analysis on is that of **legislative proposals from the Commission** as this is usually the most important. Hence the flow that follows is based on the usual process of dealing with a legislative file.

It is, however, entirely possible that the Parliament drafts a report not based on a Commission proposal. The main mechanism for this is the **Own-Initiative Report**, which can be drafted as a legislative request or as a non-legislative report.

Legislative requests (Rule 47) have to follow a strict format and include the information that the Commission needs to draft legislation: what is the legal basis and what are the financial implications of the proposal. In essence, legislative requests mean that the Parliament does part of the 'homework' of the Commission by showing how it should intervene.

Non-legislative Own-Initiative reports (Rule 53) are more flexible in terms of drafting structure, and are typically used to:

– make an appeal to the Commission to consider legislation in a specific area, instead of an explicit request;

– respond to a Commission consultation or communication, to transmit Parliament's view on a forthcoming initiative;

– establish and solidify Parliamentary consensus around a given topic, to strengthen Parliament's negotiating hand once a proposal is presented and enforce internal cohesion;

– allow MEPs to vent their individual political preferences ('Christmas tree' reports);

– take a position on non-legislative issues, e.g. those reviewing EU Competition Policy or the European Central Bank's Annual Report.

Each Parliament Committee can draft up to six Own-Initiative reports at the same time. However, particularly at times of low legislative activity in the Commission (e.g. around the beginning and end of the mandate), rapporteurs often 'frontload' their work on Own-Initiative reports by starting their drafting informally, before one of the six slots has freed up. Another important feature of Own-Initiative reports is that rapporteurs frequently amend their own draft report, often to circumvent translation limits.

These Own-Initiative Reports follow the same path through the Parliament, but will be subject to differing levels of interest and engagement by MEPs and Political Groups and will also receive different levels of amendments and voting attention.

1. The first stage of the process starts when the Parliament officially receives a proposal from the Commission in its Plenary session, as outlined in Figure 3.4.

Figure 3.4: Proposal: From European Commission to a European Parliament Committee

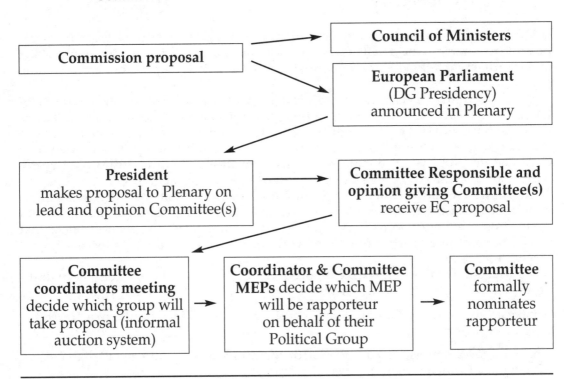

2. Once the Parliament has received the proposal it must announce it in the next Plenary session, and the official process can start.

3. DG Presidency will make a suggestion of attribution of the proposal to the relevant Committee(s) through a formal decision of the President and the Conference of Presidents.

4. The normal procedure would be that the President then makes the formal proposal to the Plenary, usually in the minutes to the part-session and not actually during the sitting itself.

5. In 99% of cases this is the end of a straightforward process, but there can be cases of conflict. In these cases the Conference of Presidents can request the Conference of Committee Chairs to come up with a recommendation, which it will then endorse.

> The legislative terms of the Parliament are split into annual session, part-sessions and sittings: Annual Session – Second Tuesday in March. Part-session – Monthly meetings of the full Parliament. Sitting – The daily meetings of the Parliament.

As it frequently happens that more than one Committee has an interest in a proposal, the most common nomination is for both a **Committee responsible** (also known as a **lead Committee**) and up to three (but usually no more) **opinion-giving Committees**.

The Committee responsible will set the timetable, through the Committee rapporteur, and is where the thrust of the discussion will take place. The opinion-giving Committees will add their expertise on the areas of the proposal that concern them. Their opinions will take the form of amendments and will be submitted for vote in the Committee responsible according to their timetable. Opinion-giving Committees should never be overlooked as their influence can be significant.

Sometimes two (or more) Committees have an equal interest in an issue, which can lead to an **associated procedure** between the Committee responsible and the opinion-giving Committee(s) – with the difference being that the Committee responsible should accept without a vote the amendments of the opinion-giving Committee (Rule 57). Since 2010, the EP has therefore organised frequent **joint Committee meetings**, with joint votes, between associated Committees, under Rule 58 which states that the Conference of Presidents may allow a joint Committee meeting and joint vote on a single draft report.

Conflicts of competence

Despite the clear definitions of Committee competences in the Annex of the EP's Rules of Procedure, Committees sometimes enter into protracted 'conflicts of competence'.

An example is the 2018 European Commission proposal to stimulate green investments (Taxonomy Regulation) which was contested between the Economic and Monetary Affairs (ECON) and Environment, Public Health and Food Safety (ENVI) Committees.

In the end, the ENVI Committee was deemed 'exclusively competent' on the Articles that relate to defining 'green' (a 'technical' environmental matter), whereas the ECON Committee was given exclusive competence over the definitions including what financial firms the rules would apply to.

6. Once the Committees dealing with an issue have been decided, the proposal will be forwarded to them and, usually, announced in the next Committee meeting. The first decision is whether the Committee intends to react or not. After a first discussion of the issue, the chairperson may propose that the Commission proposal be approved without amendment. Unless at least one tenth of the MEPs in the Committee object, the chairperson can present to Plenary a report approving the proposal.

If the Committee decides to react then it is necessary for it to select a **rapporteur**, from the Committee members or substitutes. The rapporteur is the pivotal figure who will steer the dossier through the Committee and into the Plenary. This decision is taken in the **Committee coordinators meeting** – a closed door meeting that usually takes place every few weeks, depending on the individual Committee practice, between the coordinators of all the Political Groups in the Committee.

The **selection of rapporteurs** has taken on rather mythical status due to the complicated, behind closed doors system that is used in most Committees. Each Political Group receives points based on the number of MEPs it has, and it can use these points to bid for reports in these coordinator meetings in a sort of auction. The majority of these decisions are pre-cooked, or subject to negotiated agreement, amongst the Political Groups and the Committee coordinators, and there is rarely prolonged discussion over which Group will take a report.

The most straightforward bidding, and the one costing the least points, is to propose a recognised specialist in the field of the dossier itself, perhaps an MEP who worked on the dossier previously. It is also therefore common for coordinators to come to agreements on future reports in the Committee. For frequently recurring reports, such as annual reports (e.g. the EU Annual Budget) a rotation system between Groups is set up and announced. The choice of rapporteur is very important because it is a fundamental moment in the life of a dossier in the Parliament – the choice of rapporteur will have a large influence on the development and drafting of a dossier.

The majority of politically sensitive files will go to the larger Groups, or expert MEPs.

The majority of report bids that a coordinator places in the Committee coordinators meeting will not have been explicitly discussed by the Group Plenary – it is only the most politically sensitive ones that will come to the attention of the Group as a whole.

7. Once the bidding has taken place within the coordinators meeting and a Group has been accorded a report, it will nominate its rapporteur (in practice, usually already done in the

Political Groups in Committees

Each Political Group will be represented in a Committee by their apportioned number of MEPs. The key figures will be the Group coordinator, the deputy coordinator (not all Groups have one), any rapporteurs and shadow rapporteurs on specific dossiers.

These MEPs will form the Group positions in Committee under the guidance of the coordinator. They will have preparatory meetings in Committee, and also Group weeks to organise their positions, voting lists, compromise suggestions, etc.

These MEPs will drive their position through Committee, Plenary and their own Group discussions.

process of bidding) and the end of the process is that the rapporteur is announced in Committee. The choice of rapporteur will be made by the coordinator and the Group MEPs sitting in the Committee, with the coordinator being the key person involved in this process.

After the rapporteur has been selected the Group will meet regularly to agree and fine-tune its strategy in Committee. The coordinator and the Group in a Committee will also nominate shadow rapporteurs to follow key dossiers and anything of interest to the Group.

The process illustrated in Figure 3.4, from formal reception of a Commission proposal to the nomination of the rapporteur in Committee, can take anything from two weeks to six months, depending on the dossier and the importance attached to its speedy resolution. In this respect the Groups will take an overview of the Commission Work Programme and select which reports to go for in advance – something that will lead to strategic choices and strategic negotiations between the Groups. This can lead to rotation systems, more than one rapporteur at a time and other agreements within Committees. There is also the issue of reports that no one wants or bids for because these also need to be attributed. The practice differs by Committee, but many Committees have a system whereby the Committee chair takes reports that Groups do not bid for.

Before a Commission proposal arrives in the Parliament it is important to have already identified the likely Committees that will be involved and the key MEPs within them. This is possible by looking at past reports, questions, interventions and other activities of the MEPs in the Committees. In this way when the Parliament starts work you are fully prepared and ready to immediately engage with the right MEPs.

3.6 *How the European Parliament works: Preparation in Committee*

Once a proposal has been attributed to a Committee and a rapporteur chosen by the Political Group responsible for the file, the Committee process can begin. The process in a Committee is outlined in Figure 3.5 on the next page.

The preparation of a dossier in the Committee stage is not necessarily as linear as Figure 3.5 would suggest, but nonetheless it captures the essence, and the essential elements, of the process. Basically the rapporteur is responsible for bringing before the Committee a draft report on the Commission proposal which should include amendments with justifications and an explanatory statement (optional). Between the nomination of a rapporteur and the issuing of a draft report into the Committee there are a number of ways in which a rapporteur can get information and prepare their work, which will be determined on a case-by-case basis.

Following the Parliament online

European Parliament committee meetings are systematically made available online, at: https://multimedia.europarl.europa.eu/en/webstreaming You have the opportunity to follow developments on your dossiers both in Committee(s) and in Plenary – from your own desk, in your own language.

Figure 3.5: Process in European Parliament Committee

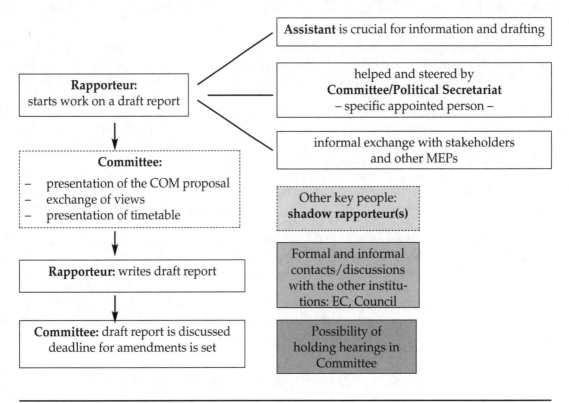

The process in Committee is that the Commission proposal will be outlined in a Committee meeting by the rapporteur with some initial thoughts and ideas. After this, in discussion with the Committee Secretariat, there will be one (or more than one) exchange of views with other Committee members on the proposal at various stages of progress (depending on how sensitive it is). These exchanges take place in the publicly accessible and web-streamed Committee meetings.

This will lead to the rapporteur, after guidance from the Committee Secretariat, issuing a timetable for the report (this can be challenged by the Committee chairperson in exceptional circumstances). The rapporteur will first present a working document and then a **draft report** for discussion, after which a deadline is set for proposed amendments from other members of the Committee (remember that each document needs to be translated into all the working languages of the Parliament). There is also the possibility of holding **hearings** in Committee with experts to further the debate. MEPs are often amenable to the opportunity to offer a hearing in Committee, though the number of hearings which can be held by a Committee is limited.

The Committee votes on the text in one of its Committee week meetings, requiring at least a quarter of members to be present (it can be a majority of component members if this is requested by one sixth of the Committee) before voting by simple majority.

This is usually done by a show of hands unless, exceptionally, one quarter of the members request a roll-call vote (we will come back to voting technicalities later). This means there are no records of who voted how in Committee. The only way to know is to actually be in the room when they vote.

As this chapter has shown, thus far the procedure for any given individual dossier is relatively strict, although flexibility exists over some of the options and the timeline. This makes it difficult to predict the course of any dossier in advance. However, a key moment to look out for is the announcement of deadlines for amendments in Committee to the draft report. From this moment onwards most dossiers move towards a Plenary vote in the same way.

It is possible to follow many of the Committee meetings online. You are also able to follow them in the Parliament itself if you can get an access badge, or get signed in.

The Committee-based discussions, however, represent only the tip of the iceberg when it comes to how a rapporteur drafts a report. There are a myriad of **less formal and less visible processes** at play.

First and foremost, it is important to ascertain the influences surrounding the drafting of an individual report. This will include the influences on, and roles of, the rapporteur, their assistants, Political Group Secretariat staff, Committee Secretariat staff and external experts. The Committee Secretariats often play an important hidden role in this process, shaping the work on a report, and the rapporteur will have a Secretariat official nominated to follow their report.

Political Group staff are also very influential players, even if there are only usually one or two of them per Committee for each Group. So while they might be more pushed for time, they are usually quite senior experts in their field with a detailed understanding of the technical aspects of a file and also the political workings of the Parliament. It is not unusual to see a rapporteur supported by a combination of Committee Secretariat officials, their own assistants and Political Group staff.

Opinion-Giving Committee amendments – What happens?

1. If the opinion-giving Committee amendments are submitted before the Committee responsible deadline they can be taken up by the rapporteur or MEPs in the Committee responsible, and be tabled (i.e. copied) as Committee responsible amendments.
2. If the opinion-giving Committee amendments are tabled close to, or after, the Committee responsible amendment deadline they will need to be inserted into the voting list of the Committee responsible. This can take two forms, either integrated into the voting list article by article alongside Committee responsible amendments, or all put at the end of the voting list. Many of such opinion amendments will not be considered by the lead committee, as they will have already been covered by compromises drafted by the lead committee.

All opinion-giving Committee amendments will potentially be voted on, therefore the opinion-giving Committee needs to be engaged with, and taken seriously.

In addition to this internal support it is also important to establish which external sources of information the rapporteur is relying on. This will be an entirely personal decision of the MEP in question and will, in many cases, be linked to national and personal networks. The Commission is often called on by rapporteurs to provide technical support and facts and figures. Commission officials can also present MEPs with a state of play from the Council discussions and they are always present in Committee meetings to explain and clarify issues that arise about their proposals. The presence of the Commission in Committee is very important for both institutions, as a source of information for the Parliament, and as a source of political intelligence for the Commission.

The other Political Groups in a Committee will usually name a **shadow rapporteur** to follow the work of the rapporteur closely. If it is an important file the other Political Groups will name heavyweight MEPs as shadows, and often you can gauge the importance the Group attaches to a dossier by the shadow they have nominated. The rapporteur can then use these shadows to see how much political support their report will garner amongst other Political Groups – remember that a coalition is always needed. The shadows, for their part, will try to work their Political Group interests into the rapporteur's position.

The coalition-building ability of a rapporteur is one of the most important qualities needed for success. It also goes without saying that a rapporteur has to maintain support for their report within their own Political Group, notably through the coordinator and during Group weeks. In this way the influence of Political Groups on the report will always be very high.

One final element that will come to weigh on the work of the rapporteur in the Committee responsible is the report from the opinion-giving Committee(s). The amendments tabled by the opinion-giving Committee(s) will all potentially be voted on in the Committee responsible and are therefore very important to follow, as outlined in the box on the previous page.

3.7   *How the European Parliament works: Vote in Committee*

Once the rapporteur is ready to table their draft report for vote we enter the second stage of the Parliament workflow, that of a vote in Committee, as outlined in Figure 3.6.

Voting in a Committee is an extremely important stage in the life of a dossier. It is a time when substantive last minute changes are still possible and when voting can remove or approve positions of different actors.

Once the rapporteur has finalised and presented their draft report to the Committee (having consulted their own Committee Group, shadows and external parties to strike the right balance that they hope will succeed) a deadline for amendments will be set (which varies depending on the Committee and the issue under discussion). At this stage any member, or substitute, can table amendments in writing before the deadline and these will be included in the voting list and be voted on in Committee. The key amendments to keep an eye on are those tabled by Group coordinators, or shadows, as they will usually carry more political weight and be subject to negotiations with the rapporteur.

Deadline for amendments	Five working days (one week) from the meeting at which announced (usually when the report is first discussed)
Availability of amendments in all languages	Three days after availability of all amendments
Draft voting list	At the latest four working days before the vote
Final voting list	The evening before the vote (This is the key voting list)

Once the deadline for amendments has been set there is an indicative timetable leading up to the vote, which is as follows:

Figure 3.6: Vote in European Parliament Committee

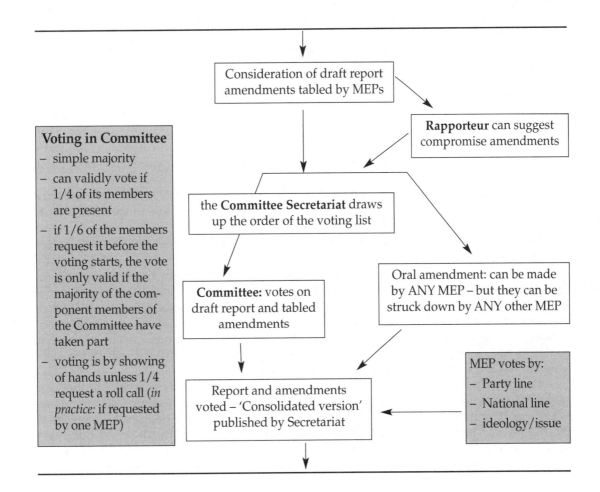

The rapporteur, through the Committee Secretariat, will receive all the proposed amendments and has the possibility of going to the authors and suggesting compromise amendments to make voting easier in Committee. The Committee Secretariat is responsible for drawing up the **final voting list**, which in itself can be done in a strategic way. The order in which amendments are voted on could have an important impact on the final outcome. There are, however, guidelines as to the order of a vote. Compromise amendments are always first, and amendments from the Committee responsible always precede those of an opinion-giving Committee. Once the amendments have been voted there is a vote on the proposal as a whole (as amended).

> ### Voting list – Key document
>
> The voting list is a key document to get hold of – and more importantly to understand.
>
> A preliminary voting list will be drawn up by the Secretariat official and sent to the rapporteur for comments and approval.
>
> After this, a draft voting list will be circulated to Political Group Secretariats.
>
> The final voting list is usually communicated to the Political Groups the evening before the vote.

For the Committee vote there are a few voting technicalities that can be used, and that can be seen on a voting list. For example, there is a separate vote which is a vote on a specific text or paragraph in a report – i.e. if amendments are rejected, the original text shall be deemed adopted unless a separate vote has been requested.

In the Committee meeting that has been designated as the date of the vote, when the issue comes to vote, an individual MEP can ask to make an oral amendment. This request can be rejected if another MEP makes an objection. Nevertheless, it is established practice to use oral amendments to table last-minute compromises, including those agreed only minutes before the vote or during a suspension of voting.

The vote will then proceed along the lines of the voting list and is done by a **simple majority of members** present (as long as one fourth of the members of the Committee are present), usually by a show of hands. The 'simple majority of MEPs present' voting rule is vitally important because not all MEPs will be in Committee and the voting can be very close.

One of the tasks of a coordinator is to make sure all the MEPs from their Political Group are present and voting according to the Group line. The coordinators will have held a preparatory meeting with their MEPs before the Committee meeting to discuss the voting list and also to find out if any MEP cannot make it, therefore perhaps requiring the presence of a substitute to vote. Every Group will have its own voting list to tell its MEPs how to vote on the day – and it is often useful to present voting lists when speaking with MEPs about forthcoming votes.

At the Committee stage the vote is much freer and more fluid than at the Plenary stage. MEPs can vote along a number of different lines, first and foremost according to what was discussed with their coordinator in the preparatory meetings, hence voting a Group line. These core gatherings of Group MEPs are crucial for defining positions and working out compromises. It is also possible that an MEP will vote along National Delegation lines, ideological or issue-based lines or simply for other personal reasons.

It is more likely that you will see an MEP change position, or opinion, in a Committee vote than in a Plenary vote.

Of all the various influences on the vote and preparation of a report in Committee the roles of the Committee Secretariat and Political Group advisers should be firmly highlighted. They will be privy to all developments in substance, procedure and politics, often guiding them due to their experience and influence. They will assist in setting deadlines, drawing up voting lists and (in the case of the Secretariat) finalising the consolidated text after a vote, making them indispensable sources of information.

3.8 How the European Parliament works: From Committee to Plenary vote

After the Committee vote, the final stage of the decision-making procedure within the Parliament is the Plenary vote. This is the final vote to establish the official position of the Parliament as a whole. The Plenary is to the Parliament what the College is to the Commission – the ultimate decision-taking body.

Below we describe the **formal process for completion of the Parliament's 'first reading'**. Non-legislative reports follow this process.

However, in 99% of the legislative procedures in the 2014–2019 Parliament, this process was put on hold to conduct **trilogue negotiations**, which have become the **de facto standard way** of finding an agreement between the Parliament and the Council on legislative proposals.

After the Committee vote, and instead of adopting a formal position in Plenary, the Parliament will use the procedure described in Rule 71 to announce the intention to enter into trilogues in Plenary. Unless a significant number of MEPs ask for a vote, this is deemed to be authorised the next day.

It then conducts trilogue negotiations which are further described in detail in chapter 5.3 of this book, with two possible outcomes:

1. **If an agreement can been found** in trilogue negotiations, the Parliament will reassess the trilogue agreement by referring the procedure back to Committee (Rule 70) and endorse the compromise text through a vote, once legal-linguistic verification of the text is completed. This committee decision will then be approved through a Plenary vote, and form the final agreement.

2. **If no agreement has been found** in trilogues, or the Parliament runs out of time, e.g. before Parliamentary elections, it may choose to complete the first reading anyway.

Figure 3.7: Vote in European Parliament Plenary

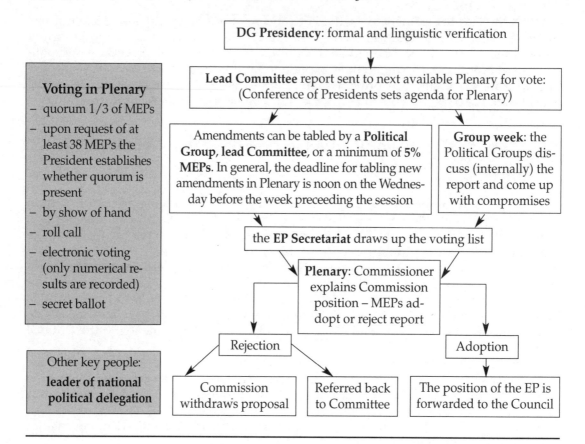

The consolidated version of the report drawn up by the Committee Secretariat is sent to the Parliament's DG Presidency as it prepares the next part-session. Normally the text will be placed on the agenda of the next part-session (unless there is a political or technical reason to hold it back for a future part-session) and this will be made official when the draft agenda is published. From this moment onwards there is the possibility for amendments to be tabled by Political Groups, or a minimum of 38 MEPs, by 12h00 on the Wednesday of the week preceding the part-session. This preceding week is the **Political Group week** and as such is timed for this very reason – to allow the Political Groups to organise themselves for the forthcoming Plenary session. The Political Groups can also meet in Strasbourg on Monday evenings as a preparation meeting, and then again on the Tuesday and Wednesday evenings after the day's proceedings. All of this allows the Group to organise itself and to follow developments closely. As much as the Committee stage of a dossier was all about the rapporteur and the Committee Secretariat, the Plenary stage is all about the Political Groups. They are the drivers of compromise at this point.

The coordinator from the Committee in question will present to its Group Plenary the issues for vote in the next week with recommendations for amendments and compromises, which can then, if supported by the Group, be tabled on their behalf. A key issue for the coordinator, and rapporteur, will be to keep a tight hold over any compromises that were agreed in Committee voting, so as not to unravel any deals already made (for example deals with Council from trilogues or deals made with shadow rapporteurs).

In general coordinators will drive the Group position, although if there is a big politically sensitive dossier the Political Group hierarchy may take over. The Political Group week is thus a very dynamic week in the life of a report, especially a contested or divisive report, as the rapporteur will be trying hard to ensure a political compromise and support, a compromise that honours any deals done in Committee. The result of these negotiations will be **compromise amendments** tabled by the Groups with which there is agreement. The politics at this stage of the Parliament process come to the fore, and a dossier can change radically from the Committee vote. Many of these changes will be done via informal contacts between the rapporteur, coordinators and shadows (and Political Group staff), making it a very difficult week to follow a report on which you are working – which is why previous work and contacts with Political Groups, National Delegations and key Political Group actors is so important.

Voting technicalities

Plenary voting is done by a show of hands unless one of the following is requested/or applies:

Separate vote: vote on a specific text or paragraph in a report, i.e. if amendments are rejected, the original text shall be deemed adopted unless a separate vote has been requested.

Split vote: when an amendment has two or more provisions, or references, that lend themselves to division into two or more parts. This can be used for positioning on very specific (and sensitive) issues.

Electronic vote (EV): The vote is recorded and flashed on the main screen but individual MEP records are not kept.

Roll-call vote (RCV): The vote is recorded and individual MEP voting records are kept (and published). A RCV is obligatory for the final vote on a Parliament resolution under the OLP.

Any of the above may be requested by a Political Group or at least 36 members (5% of MEPs, Rule 179a). These requests are often politically motivated as one Group tries to split, embarrass or cause problems for other Groups.

Once all amendments have been tabled there will be continued discussion to ensure that whatever compromises were reached are delivered in the Plenary vote. A number of amendments tabled at this stage in the process are simply amendments for the gallery, i.e. amendments that do not seek to genuinely contribute to the text or have any real chances of success, but that will play well for political and national constituencies at a later stage.

DG Presidency will draw up the **Plenary voting list** for all reports on the Plenary agenda. Here there are further possibilities with regard to the voting list, such as a request for a split vote, or a roll-call vote, RCV (Rules 185 and 190). A sample voting list is given on the next page, giving a good visual representation of what you need to work with.

Subject	Am No.	Author	RCV etc.	Vote	RCV/EV – remarks
Text as a whole - Block 1 - compromise	63 CP	committee EPP, S&D, RE, Greens, GUE/NGL		+	
Block 2 - amendments by the committee responsible - block vote	1-11 13-25 27-37	committee			
Block 3 - 'all animals'	40-62	ID		-	
Article 3, § 2	63 CP	committee EPP, S&D, RE, Greens	EV	+	435,174,20
	39	Individual Members			
Recital 13	63 CP	committee RE, S&D, Greens, GUE/NGL		+	
	38	Individual Members			
vote: amended proposal			RCV	+	543,56,39
vote: legislative resolution			RCV	+	550,49,41

This example voting list gives an indication of the main things you will see, and need to look for, on a voting list. What is being voted is listed in the first column; in the example we see compromise amendments and individual amendments, with their numbers in the next column. Knowing these numbers at the time of vote can make life much easier for you and your interlocutors. Next is a listing of who drafted and supported the compromise or individual amendment.

In this example there is a mixture of different possibilities: the Committee, Political Groups together and also 5% of individual members (the 'low threshold'). The next column indicates whether a special voting modality has been requested, such as a roll-call vote (RCV) or an electronic vote (EV). The next column indicates whether the amendment was adopted or not and the final column shows the numbers (votes in favour, against, abstentions), if an EV or RCV were used.

The **agenda for the part-session** is finalised on the Thursday afternoon before the sitting, although last minute changes do occur. A typical Strasbourg ordinary part-session, of which there are obligatorily 12 in the year, starts on Monday at 17h00 and finishes on a Thursday afternoon. In addition there are now six additional part-sessions in Brussels which run from Wednesday 15h00 to Thursday 13h00. The order of a typical Strasbourg session is shown on the next page.

Strasbourg is a hive of activity as there is the Plenary sitting itself, meetings of the Political Groups, extraordinary Committee meetings (usually on Monday or Tuesday evenings), media activities and events, visiting dignitaries and politicians and a host of informal talks and negotiations. The timings in Strasbourg are extremely important, and trying to work with a dossier that is subject to a vote there can be very challenging.

Monday	Adoption of final agenda; One-minute speeches Legislative and non-legislative reports – discussion (until 22h00)
Tuesday	<u>Votes on requests for Urgent procedures</u> Legislative and non-legislative reports – major debates: Votes (12h00 -13h00) Legislative and non-legislative reports – major debates Communication by Commission on College decisions of their meeting that day (17h00); Commission question time (17h30 - 19h00) Legislative and non-legislative reports – discussion (21h00 - 24h00)
Wednesday	Major (political) debates <u>Votes (11h00 - 12h00 & 12h30 - 13h00);</u> Major debates with Council Legislative and non-legislative reports – discussion; Council question time Legislative and non-legislative reports – discussion (21h00 - 24h00)
Thursday	Legislative and non-legislative reports – discussion; <u>Votes (11h00 - 13h00)</u> Debates on cases of breaches of human rights, democracy and the rule of law

Watch the Plenary live on http://www.europarl.europa.eu/plenary

Speeches are only transcribed in the original language, but if you need to know what has been said in another language, you can find the recorded audio interpretation of all speeches.

Voting results are available under 'Votes'. For a consolidated text of what has been adopted, you have to wait until these are published under 'Texts adopted', or make one yourself by applying the adopted amendments to the text as tabled for Plenary.

It is important to keep in mind that the Plenary session is streamed live on the internet so all the questions and speeches can trigger wider political and media interest. While the most of what goes on at Plenary is well regimented, and speaking time mostly allocated amongst Political Groups, there is one set of questions that can be interesting to follow, those that take place at the end of any debate when an MEP who manages to 'catch the eye' of the President may make a brief contribution. Introduced in 2008 to stimulate debate and generate publicity and interest in Parliamentary discussions, Plenary debates now always involve a 'catch-the-eye' block (Rule 171.6) where any MEP can raise their hand and request to speak. However, perhaps disappointingly, these interventions also tend to be prepared in advance and not made in response to other MEPs' comments.

To make debates more interactive, the Parliament in 2009 introduced a 'blue-card question' in Rule 171.8 that allows MEPs to respond to another MEP immediately after their speech by asking them a follow-up question. While this has helped debates to become livelier, the blue-card questions often are more statements than questions, meant to show divisions rather than asking for further information on an MEP's position.

Before the final vote takes place, the Commission will state its position on all of the amendments tabled by the Parliament: basically, whether it would accept them or not. This formal procedure is an important right of the Commission, to guarantee that its right of initiative is not infringed by totally remodelled texts. It is also important for the Council because in formal first reading procedures the Commission's opinion on the Parliament's amendments will determine the applicable voting rules in the Council for that amendment (see Chapter 5.2 and 5.4 for more on this). This exercise again underlines the almost omnipresence of the Commission in the decision-making of the other institutions, because to be able to come to this judgement, the Commission needs to be in on all the negotiations. We come back to this in more detail in Chapter 5.3.

The final stage for the report in the Parliament is during one of the three voting sessions in the Strasbourg week. It is worth bearing in mind that during the Plenary week there are a number of press conferences around the topical issues being voted by the Parliament. These are very interesting to follow and also offer opportunities for MEPs to gain media coverage. When the final voting list comes out each Political Group will check to see what voting technicality requests the other Political Groups have tabled, such as split votes or roll-call votes and try to understand the political dynamics behind them. For example, it is often the case that a Political Group will request an electronic vote or a roll-call vote in an attempt to highlight divisions in other Groups on sensitive issues. At this stage it is again important to recall the numbers game and the majorities that are required in the Plenary during the vote as this will have dictated the negotiations within the Parliament in their attempts to find a compromise. The voting requirements are outlined in Figure 3.8.

Figure 3.8: Voting in the Ordinary Legislative Procedure

Absolute majority is needed

1. In Plenary in the second reading:
- to reject the Council position at first reading
- to adopt amendments

Absolute majority in the Plenary	
705	353 votes

Simple majority is needed

1. In Committee votes
2. In Plenary:
- for first reading votes
- in second reading: to approve the Council position at first reading
- in a third reading: to approve the act in accordance with the joint text prepared by the Conciliation Committee

Simple majority
Majority of the members casting their vote

The key numbers in voting are the numbers of MEPs and the majorities needed. If your dossier is to be voted by simple or absolute majority, one factor will be critical: the number of MEPs in the room at the time of the vote. There are now 705 MEPs, and of these there are usually only around 550 in the room for a vote. This can alter the dynamics of a simple majority vote if the absent MEPs are from a Group that supports an issue, but it is even more important when an absolute majority is needed. An absolute majority is notoriously difficult to achieve in the Parliament because of the coalitions that are needed to get 353 MEPs.

When the vote comes there are a number of possibilities:

1. **Show of hands:** this is still the most common way to vote on the majority of issues and is used for reasons of time-efficiency given the large number of votes in any voting session. The President calls the issue and takes a look around the room, deciding on the spot whether the majority required has been attained. With this system there is no record of how individuals voted. If the show of hands is disputed by a Political Group it can request an electronic check, as outlined below.

2. **Electronic votes:** these are used to check disputed and unclear votes. The figures show on the main screen in the Plenary and these aggregated: for, against and abstention figures are recorded. In this case individual voting records for each MEP are not kept (Rule 192.2).

3. **Roll-Call:** this is the only category where a record is kept of how each MEP voted. The final vote on a report is always a roll-call vote (Rule 188), except in sensitive cases (e.g. parliamentary immunity of an MEP). In addition RCV can be used when requested in writing by a Political Group or at least 5% of MEPs the evening before the vote. RCVs can be used to discipline MEPs into following their Group line (as those not respecting the Group line would be exposed); they can also be used to expose divisions and show lack of cohesion in a competing Political Group.

Votewatch.eu

This website is an absolute goldmine of information on the workings of the Parliament. You can find detailed information concerning all voting records, the activity of each MEP such as reports drafted, amended reports, speeches in the Plenary, questions and their attendance records, etc. Votewatch.eu also analyses the voting data to present statistics such as the extent to which an MEP votes according to their European Group line.

Votewatch.eu presents up-to-date complex analysis on how the Political Groups in the EP form coalitions between them, as well as on their internal cohesion. The data is broken down by time intervals and policy areas so that it introduces the reader to the different dynamics of the voting behaviour in the Parliament.

Information on the latest votes is processed and published on the website the same day the votes are cast in the EP Plenary and the general statistics are updated following each part-session.

All of this is possible due to the increased number of roll-call votes in recent years. It allows Votewatch.eu to process the official data of the Parliament and show the voting records and statistics of individual MEPs, Political Groups and National Delegations. This rich set of data is essential for anyone trying to work with (even more so on a vote in) the Parliament as it allows all sorts of possibilities that were not available previously.

See all of this at: www.votewatch.eu

Once the **final vote** on a text has taken place, the Parliament will have either approved the text before it, or will have rejected it. In the first case, for legislative files, the text will be forwarded to the Council so that it can formally engage in its first or second reading. As will be highlighted in Chapter 5.3 on informal trilogues, most legislation is voted by the Parliament after pre-agreement with the Council, leading to a **first reading agreement**, in which case the text is final and only requires endorsement by the Council.

It is also possible that Parliament rejects the text, in which case it can either be returned to the Committee responsible in question for more work (first reading) or be

The final vote?

MEPs can actually change their initial vote, if their voting machine did not work properly at the time of the vote. Sometimes, for this reason, the initial figures (i.e. the number of votes for, against, abstentions) do not match those in the final minutes. However, the initial result (announced by the chair) of the vote cannot be changed, even if, mathematically speaking, after the subsequent individual changes the result would have been reversed.

thrown out altogether (second reading, Conciliation). These voting majorities and requirements will be explained in more detail in Chapter 5.

In the typical Strasbourg session, aside from the key voting time, there are also some final important elements to mention. There is significant time for legislative and non-legislative discussions, which need to be followed carefully. In addition there is also a plethora of opportunities to ask questions, as outlined in the box below.

From 2014 to 2019 the Parliament put more than 45,000 questions to the Commission, all of which the Commission endeavours to answer within six weeks. This is all managed by the SG of the Commission, and once the responses are sent to the EP they are put on the Parliamentary Questions website at: http://www.europarl.europa.eu/plenary/en/parliamentary-questions.html. This very useful site allows you to search questions and answers by MEP, subject, and sitting, therefore giving access to a wealth of questions and answers. These questions should not be neglected because they can

Written and Oral Questions

1. **Oral Questions for answer & debate in Plenary (Rule 136)**
   Questions may be put to the Council or the Commission by a Committee, a Political Group or at least 5% of MEPs, after submission to the President and Conference of Presidents – who decide whether and in what order Questions should be placed on the agenda.
2. **Question time in Plenary (Rule 137)**
   A question may be put to the Council and the Commission by any MEP, after its admissibility has been checked by the President.
3. **Questions for written answer (Rule 138)**
   Any MEP can put Written Questions to any other EU institution, who shall respond within three weeks if it is a priority issue, or within six weeks if not. There is a maximum of 20 questions per MEP, Group or Committee, over a rolling period of three months.

lead to political tensions and ultimately to resolutions by the Parliament; it is one way that an issue can find its way onto the agenda of the Parliament.

3.9 Key stages and key actors – European Parliament

The life of a dossier in the Parliament is significantly less linear than the one it will have followed in the Commission or Council. There are, in essence, three main stages with key aspects and actors that need to be highlighted.

1. The first stage of importance is **when the dossier is assigned to a Committee responsible** and then to a **Political Group**, and ultimately to the key person who shapes the dossier, the **rapporteur**. The choice of rapporteur is important and many stakeholders try to secure the most sympathetic and influential personality for their interests. The drivers in this situation will be the Political Group bidding for the report and then the subsequent choice of rapporteur from among the MEPs on the Committee, an issue that can come down to competing National Delegation interests. The choice of rapporteur is also often down to an MEP's interests, their experience, seniority and reputation. Thus the very early stage of the process can be driven by a Political Group at the level of the Committee, which implies an important role for the Group coordinator. MEPs who have previously worked on a file generally have priority as part of the former EP Negotiating Team. Another key actor at this stage can also be the Committee chairperson who acts as technical rapporteur on some procedural dossiers.

2. **Once the rapporteur has been nominated**, he or she has to draft a response to the Commission proposal by tabling amendments. The other Groups' shadows will be as important as the rapporteur. The rapporteur can hold exchanges of views in Committee and meet with the shadows to discuss the issues at stake, to ensure support. The majority of this work will take place on an informal basis, with the Committee meetings representing a public airing of the state of internal discussions in the Parliament.

An important aspect of this is who the rapporteur chooses to consult and ask for help. Here there are key internal actors such as assistants, Committee Secretariat staff and Political Group staff who will always play important roles and be up-to-date on developments. The MEP will also almost always consult external stakeholders, having probably been flooded by requests for meetings. It is difficult to know in advance who, or how many, external stakeholders an MEP will see and what influence they will have. The basic nucleus for discussions will be between the rapporteur, their Committee coordinator, the assistants, the assigned Committee Secretariat official, the Political Group official and shadow rapporteurs. The exchanges of views in Committee will help you gauge the political temperature and to what extent the rapporteur has the support of their own, and other, Political Groups, but cannot be relied on alone to understand the direction of travel in the compromise meetings.

Once it comes to voting in Committee, the key players are the Political Groups through their shadows and coordinators in the Committees. Group scrutiny of a Committee report varies widely, depending on the discipline of National Delegations, the salience of the issue for national and European politics and the reputations of the coordinator and rapporteur. Having noted that Political Group voting cohesion is very strong in Plenary, it can be less so in Committee as individual votes can count much more, making them a little less predictable.

3. When the dossier passes from the Committee stage to the **Plenary preparation and vote**, the dynamics are almost entirely those of the Political Groups and their attempts to find compromise positions that they can all work with. This takes place during the Political Group week that precedes the Plenary and it can often be a turbulent time for a dossier. Bearing in mind the voting patterns in the Parliament, it is essential to secure the support of the main Political Groups during this stage to have any chance of success when it comes to the final vote itself.

From this analysis the main actors (in chronological order) in the elaboration of a Parliament position are as shown in Table 3.6.

Table 3.6: Key stages and key actors: The European Parliament

Key Stage	Comment	Key people
Reception of proposal by Parliament & Nomination of Committee (Responsible + Opinion-Giving)	Usually an administrative procedure.	DG Presidency Conference of Presidents
Choice of Group to deliver report	The choice of Group and rapporteur is a crucial moment for any dossier because the political leanings of the Group and the personality of the rapporteur will find their way into the report. For both of these choices the Group MEPs in the Committee, led by the coordinator, are key actors as they will decide whether to bid for a report and who to nominate.	
Nomination of rapporteur	Key to this process are the priorities of the Groups in Committees which can be driven by the key Delegations or the coordinator.	
Preparation of draft report	Each rapporteur, in each case, will turn to different sources for information. The most likely and the most influential will be those listed to the right. Drafting can also be linked to Presidency/ Commission priorities. Key here is to understand the dynamics around the rapporteur and shadows from other major Groups.	Rapporteur/Shadow Rapporteur Key issue MEPs MEP Assistants Political Group staff Committee Secretariat Commission/Council External sources/ Network

Key Stage	Comment	Key people
Exchange of views in Committee	The Committee exchange of views will usually offer an insight into both the technical and political developments of a dossier. It is very useful to follow these closely. Key here is to recognise that the exchange will be only a window to the real discussions.	Rapporteur Shadow rapporteur(s) Committee chair Coordinators Key issue MEPs
Deadline for amendments in Committee	It is key to know the deadline for amendments. It is very important in the process.	Rapporteur Coordinators Shadow rapporteur(s) Committee Secretariat
Committee vote	Here individual MEPs can make a much bigger difference than in Plenary. Key to the Committee vote will be the number of MEPs in the room on the day and the positions of the main Groups – even if individual MEPs have more opportunity to vote for themselves.	Rapporteur Shadow rapporteur(s) Coordinators Committee chair Political Group staff Committee Secretariat
Plenary build-up Plenary vote	The Political Groups are the key drivers of both the build up to, and the actual, Plenary vote. The Groups will take their information from the coordinators who will try to keep Committee compromises intact. The Group week that precedes Plenary weeks and the Group meetings in Strasbourg are essential for the formation, or cementing, of compromises.	

OEIL - Legislative Observatory Database

http://www.europarl.europa.eu/oeil/

The Legislative Observatory (OEIL) gives an excellent overview on decision-making files in which the Parliament is involved. Its focus is on the Parliament's role and contributions to legislative files, as well as housing all the documents and noting all the key events relating to a given procedure. The database provides direct links to relevant documents (COM, SEC, EP documents, EP reports, debates and opinions, etc), together with summaries of every stage of the decision-making procedure in which the European Parliament is involved.

The database provides a direct link to IPEX (Interparliamentary EU Information Exchange – www.ipex.eu) where one can find documents and information relating to the scrutiny of National Parliaments as well as on issues related to subsidiary and proportionality.

continues overleaf

OEIL - Legislative Observatory Database – continued

The most straightforward way to search the OEIL database is to use the free text search function. You can search the database and filter using multiple criteria such as: words in title or full-text document, document reference (author, legislative act type, OJ), agent in procedure (rapporteur, EP committee, Political Group, Council, Commission DG) etc. In addition the 'Subject' filter allows one to browse the content of the database by topic (enlargement, the budget, environment, employment, area of freedom security and justice, police, judicial and customs cooperation, consumer protection). This is a very convenient way of following all developments in the legislative process relevant to certain broad subject areas.

The website offers the possibility of subscribing for the Observatory Tracker which allows users to sign up for an automatic notification of new legislative developments.

The European Parliament on Social Media

You can follow the EP on: Facebook, Twitter, Flickr, Linkedin, Youtube, Instagram, Pinterest, Snapchat and Reddit.

In 2020, Twitter remains the key tool for MEP visibility in the policy-making community. However, other social networks such as Facebook and Instagram are more popular to connect with voters and other stakeholders.

4. Other EU Institutions and Bodies

By Erik Akse and Alan Hardacre[1]

The Commission, the Parliament, the Council and the European Council are not the only EU institutions, and they are far from being the only EU bodies. We now look at the most important of these other institutions and bodies inasmuch as they impact on the EU policy cycle, or on the workings of the four core institutions outlined in the previous three chapters.

The box on the right outlines the institutions, bodies, offices and agencies after the Treaty of Lisbon. The first thing to notice is that aside from the four institutions we have described thus far in Chapters 1 to 3, there are in fact three further EU institutions. Two of them fall outside the scope of this book as they are not directly involved in the EU policy cycle, or in mainstream EU lobbying strategies.

The first of these is the European Central Bank (ECB), which is responsible for managing the euro, keeping prices stable, conducting EU economic and monetary policy and supervising the assets of the largest banks in the Eurozone. This powerful financial institution, established in 1998 is based in Frankfurt, Germany.

The second institution outside the scope of this book is the **Court of Auditors (CoA)** because it is likewise not a mainstream EU policy cycle institution. Since its establishment in October 1977 it is tasked with auditing the accounts of the EU institutions – notably to scrutinise if the budget of the EU has been correctly implemented, and if all funds have been spent legally and with sound management.

This leaves the seventh, and final, EU institution – the **Court of Justice of the European Union (CJEU)**, which this chapter will start with.

The principal other EU bodies are listed in the box above. With the exception of the

---

EU Institutions and other Bodies

EU Institutions

- The European Commission
- The European Council
- The Council of Ministers of the EU
- The European Parliament
- The Court of Justice of the EU
- The European Central Bank
- The Court of Auditors

EU Bodies, Offices and Agencies

- European Economic and Social Committee
- Committee of the Regions
- European Investment Bank
- EU Agencies

---

1. *Thanks are due to Nadia Adrien for her work on chapters 4 and 5 in previous editions.*

European Investment Bank (EIB), which was created back in 1958 as a long-term lending institution to support European integration, they all play a role in the EU policy cycle and will be discussed in this chapter.

4.1   *The Court of Justice of the European Union (CJEU)*

The Court of Justice of the European Union ('the Court') constitutes the judicial branch of the European Union. The mission of this EU institution is to 'ensure that in the interpretation and application of the Treaties, the law is observed' (Article 19 TEU). The main elements of the Court are outlined in Table 4.1 below.

Table 4.1: Court of Justice of the EU – Key facts

Name	Court of Justice of the European Union, the Court
Legal basis	Articles 251 – 281 TFEU
Established	1952
Jurisdiction	European Union
President	• Court of Justice: Koen Lenaerts (since 2015) • General Court: Marc van der Woude (since 2019)
Composition	Sits in chambers of: • Court of Justice: 3, 5, 15 or 27 Judges + 11 Advocates-General • General Court: 1, 3, 5 or 15 Judges
Seat	Luxembourg

The Court comprises the **Court of Justice** (supreme body) and the **General Court** (created in 1988). Each has its own responsibilities and ways of working. The former European Union Civil Service Tribunal, a specialised court within the CJEU, ceased to exist in 2016, with the General Court then being doubled in size.

The Court of Justice is currently composed of 27 Judges (one per Member State) and assisted by eleven permanent Advocates-General. The General Court has up to 54 Judges (two per Member State, though not all Member States choose to nominate two Judges).

The Judges and Advocates-General of the Court of Justice and the Judges of the General Court are appointed for a renewable six-year mandate by joint agreement between the governments of the EU Member States, after consultation of a panel which gives an opinion on the suitability of the candidates (Article 255 TFEU).

The role of the Court comes down to guaranteeing that EU law is applied and interpreted correctly by EU Member States and the EU institutions. As part of that mission, the Court reviews the validity of the legal acts adopted by the EU institutions and ensures that the Member States do not fail to act in accordance with the law. It verifies that Member States fulfil their obligations under European law (in terms of legislative instruments and practices) and provides interpretations of Union legislation at the request of the courts and tribunals of the Member States. The Court has the power to settle legal disputes between European institutions, Member States, legal entities and individuals.

The two levels of the Court fulfil very different tasks:

The Court of Justice is tasked with interpreting and enforcing EU law. It is the highest court in the EU, outranking national supreme courts. Its judgements can affect both Member States and individuals, and the Court also acts as a referee between the Member States, institutions and individuals in disputes relating to EU law.

The General Court judges the disputes brought by individuals and Member States against EU institutions.

Although the Treaty of Lisbon has considerably extended its scope, the Court still has almost no jurisdiction in the area of Common Foreign and Security Policy (CFSP) and only limited jurisdiction with respect to the Area of Freedom, Security and Justice (AFSJ) (Articles 275 and 276 TFEU). Since their establishment in 1952, roughly 39,000 judgements and orders have been pronounced by the Courts. Judgements of the Courts are decided by a majority of votes and have binding weight.

While many people working in Brussels will likely never come into direct contact with the Court, it is always useful to understand its powers because they have shaped every EU policy area in some way. The main powers of the Court are outlined in the box below.

Key powers of CJEU

Case Law – The Court creates a system of case law which is often then the established precedent that needs to be followed. You can find the EU case law Digest at https://curia.europa.eu/jcms/jcms/Jo2_7046/en.

Proceedings for failure to fulfil an obligation (also known as infringement proceedings – (Article 258 TFEU). The Court can determine whether a Member State has fulfilled its obligations under Union law. These cases are started by the Commission, which if it deems necessary can involve the Court. This can lead to the Member State having a fine imposed on it.

Actions for Annulment – (Article 263 TFEU). An applicant can seek the annulment of a measure (usually a Regulation, Decision or Directive) adopted by an institution. The Court can declare a measure void.

Actions for Failure to Act – (Article 265 TFEU). The Court can assess the legality of an institution's failure to act. Where a failure to act is found, the institution concerned must end the failure using appropriate measures.

Application for Compensation (non-contractual liability) – (Article 268 TFEU). The Court can hear compensation claims for any damages caused to citizens and undertakings by the institutions in the course of their duties.

Appeals on Points of Law – (Article 256 TFEU). The Court can hear appeals to judgements given by the General Court if it is on a point of law.

References for a Preliminary Ruling – (Article 267 TFEU). National Courts are the frontline of implementation of EU law and on occasion they need to turn to the Court to seek clarification on the interpretation of a point of EU law. Once interpretation is given then all Courts in the EU are bound by it.

In sum, unlike several other institutions and bodies, most of the work of the Court takes place after the actual decision-making process – once legal acts have been formally adopted by the institutions and after these have been implemented by Member States. Nonetheless for certain actors, and sectors, appeal to the Court is a very important avenue for clarification of issues and to pursue the correct implementation of EU legislation, all of which will in turn set important precedents for any future actions by the EU.

4.2 The European Economic and Social Committee

The European Economic and Social Committee (EESC) is one of the two official advisory bodies of the EU (the other being the Committee of the Regions, which we will come on to next). It was set up to give Europe's civil society actors a formal say on EU legislative proposals.

Table 4.2: European Economic and Social Committee – Key facts

Names:	European Economic and Social Committee (EESC, ESC or unofficially 'EcoSoc')
Legal basis:	Articles 300 – 304 TFEU
Type:	EU body
Role:	Formal: Consultative (non-binding opinions) Informal: Involve civil society in EU affairs, promote creation of consultative structures
Members:	329
Groups:	I Employers, II Employees, III Various Interests
Represents:	Social and economic interests
President:	Luca Jahier (since 2018)
Main Seat:	Delors building, Brussels (shared with Committee of Regions)

Founded in 1957 under the Treaty of Rome, the EESC was created with the aim of involving social and economic interest groups in the establishment of a common market, by allowing them to represent their interests in the EU decision-making process. The Committee, among other things, represents the interests of consumers, trade unions, employers and farmers. Serving as a bridge between the Union institutions and its citizens, it encourages participation of civil society in EU decision-making. By informing, and involving economic and social interest groups, it enhances the effectiveness of the EU and strengthens its democratic legitimacy, leading to a more integrated Europe.

Besides its representation, information and integration role, the Committee also plays an advisory role. The Treaty makes the EESC an integral part of the EU decision-making process by obliging the Council, the Commission and the Parliament to consult the EESC before taking decisions on topics that affect economic and social actors. The institutional triangle must consult the EESC when the Treaty so provides, but it may also consult it on a voluntary basis whenever it deems it appropriate. Moreover, the Committee may also issue own-initiative opinions or exploratory opinions at the request of one of the institutions. The box below provides an overview of the areas where consultation of the EESC is compulsory.

European Economic and Social Committee consultation – Policy areas

Agriculture, Rural Development & Fisheries; Climate Change; Cohesion, Regional & Urban Policy; Consumers; Digital Change & Information Society; Economic & Monetary Union; Education & Training; Employment; Energy; Enterprise; Environment; External Relations; Financial Services and Capital Markets; Fundamental & Citizens rights; Industry & Industrial Change; Institutional Affairs & EU Budget; Migration & Asylum; Research & Innovation; Services of General Interest; Single Market; Social Affairs; Sustainable Development; Taxation; and Transport.

The Committee advises the three main decision-taking institutions by issuing **non-binding opinion documents**. The EESC issues between 160 and 190 opinions and information reports a year. About four in five are referrals by the Council, the European Commission and the European Parliament. About one in five are own-initiative opinions and information reports. EESC statistics show that although the opinions are non-binding, the Commission acts on four out of five EESC opinions. Among the success stories where elements of EESC opinions have featured in legislation are the agricultural policy reforms, the Employment recovery plan and the 1989 Charter of Fundamental Social Rights.

The Committee enters into play in the decision-making procedure as early as the pre-legislative phase. It is during this phase, as was described in Chapter 1, that the Commission evaluates policy options, conducts an Impact Assessment (IA) and prepares a legislative proposal. It is usual that the EESC collaborates with the Commission on Impact Assessments.

Once the Commission's proposal is adopted by the College of Commissioners it is forwarded simultaneously to the Parliament, the Council, the national parliaments and, where appropriate, to the EESC and/or the Committee of the Regions. The EESC is then requested to issue a non-binding opinion on the Commission proposal. As soon as the EU institutions start discussing the legislative proposal, the Parliament and the Council are obliged to consult the EESC, which can in turn submit its views on all amendments tabled to the initial Commission proposal. If a legislative proposal is altered during the legislative procedure, the EESC may also adopt a revised opinion on the legislative proposal. This however occurs very infrequently. The views of the EESC are non-binding and can only be taken into account if they are timely and integrated with the Parliament and Council timelines.

The provisions governing the functioning, and the composition, of the EESC are contained in Articles 301 to 304 TFEU and in its Rules of Procedure. The Council is responsible for determining the number of seats allocated to each Member State. These seats will be occupied by representatives of economic and social interest groups who will be appointed to one of the following three Groups:

1. Employers (Group I);

2. Workers (Group II);

3. Diversity Europe – such as professional associations, farmers, consumer groups, environmental organisations, NGOs, etc. (Group III).

The Council formally appoints the members for a renewable five-year term of office, following nominations made by the respective national governments. Once appointed, the members work in a personal capacity in complete political independence. They, moreover, mostly continue to live and work in their own countries and only come to Brussels for meetings. The selection criteria for members are technical expertise and capacity to represent diverse social and economic groups.

Following the departure of the UK, the EESC is made up of 329 members. The allocation per Member State varies by population but smaller Member States are significantly over-represented compared with the larger: thus the three biggest Member States, Germany, France and Italy, with around 47% of the EU population have only a quarter of the seats (24 each).

Table 4.1: Breakdown of seats by Member State: European Economic and Social Committee

Austria	12	France	24	Malta	5
Belgium	12	Germany	24	Netherlands	12
Bulgaria	12	Greece	12	Poland	21
Croatia	9	Hungary	12	Portugal	12
Cyprus	6	Ireland	9	Romania	15
Czechia	12	Italy	24	Slovakia	9
Denmark	9	Latvia	7	Slovenia	7
Estonia	7	Lithuania	9	Spain	21
Finland	9	Luxembourg	6	Sweden	12

Every two and half years the EESC elects, from its midst, a **Bureau** consisting of a President, two Vice-Presidents, the three Group presidents, the section presidents and a number of directly elected members (no more than the number of Member States) (Rule 4 EESC RoP). The Bureau is currently composed of 38 members. The Bureau is mainly

The Sections of the European Economic and Social Committee

ECO	Economic and Monetary Union, Economic and Social Cohesion
INT	Single Market, Production and Consumption
TEN	Transport, Energy, Infrastructure and Information Society
SOC	Employment, Social Affairs and Citizenship
NAT	Agriculture, Rural Development and Environment
REX	External Relations

There is also one so-called Consultative Commission, on Industrial Change (CCMI)

tasked with the general management of the Committee and its work. The full EESC meets in **Plenary Assembly** nine times a year. The Plenary formally adopts, or rejects, the texts and decisions of the Committee prepared by its six '**Sections**'.

When the EESC is asked to produce an opinion or information report by the institutions, the Bureau designates the Section that will be responsible for the work in question. The Section concerned then appoints a rapporteur (+ co-rapporteur) and when necessary a Study Group or Drafting Group which may be set up from among its members to study the question under consideration and collect the views expressed.

To gather the views of civil society, the Sections organise meetings, conferences, hearings, cultural activities, publications, etc. The rapporteur(s) and the Study Group then draw up the draft opinion which they transmit to the responsible Section within the EESC, in order for it to be discussed and voted on. Once the opinion has been voted by this Section it is transferred to the Committee Plenary for formal adoption. In general, texts and decisions of the EESC are adopted by a simple majority of votes cast. As soon as it is adopted, the opinion is forwarded to the Union's decision-making bodies and then published in the Official Journal of the EU. The EESC is also assisted by a Secretariat-General which is accountable to the President.

The EESC is often forgotten by many stakeholders, except those with specific economic and social interests, when it comes to lobbying strategies. As this short description has highlighted, the EESC has a privileged position to give opinions on Commission legislative proposals. Whilst these opinions are non-binding the ideas within them can easily filter into Commission, Council and/or Parliament thinking. Beyond this advisory capacity, members of the EESC also have privileged access to the other institutions and to information, making them extremely useful contacts and partners for any work in Brussels.

4.3 Committee of the Regions

The Committee of the Regions (CoR) is the EU's second advisory body. In many ways the CoR is similar to the EESC. Consisting of representatives of local and regional authorities, the CoR was created in order to provide local and regional interests with a voice at EU level.

Table 4.4: Committee of the Regions – Key facts

Names:	Committee of the Regions (CoR)
Legal basis:	Articles 300, 305 – 307 TFEU
Established:	1994
Type:	EU body
Role:	Formal: Consultative (non-binding opinions)
	Informal: Voice for regional and local interests in Brussels
Members:	329 members and 329 alternates
Principles:	Subsidiarity, Proximity, Partnership
President:	Apostolos Tzitzikostas (since 2020)
Seat:	Delors building, Brussels (shared with EESC)

The CoR was formally established by the Treaty of Maastricht which entered into force in 1993. The rationale behind the creation of this body was two-fold. Firstly, an important percentage of EU legislation is implemented at the sub-national level which makes it important for local and regional representatives to have their say in European policy-making; and secondly, the EU needed a solution to bridge the perceived widening gap between its institutions and its citizens. Involving locally elected officials, who represent a direct link between Brussels and the EU citizens, was intended to help serve this purpose. Besides representing local and regional interests, the Committee also serves as an information source; it channels information from the European institutions to the local authorities (and vice-versa) and as a result seeks to bring Europe closer to the people.

While the Committee is a source of information, and a representative of local and regional administration interests, it is also another policy advisor for the European institutions along with the EESC. Article 300(1) TFEU stipulates that the Commission, the Council and the Parliament must consult the CoR before taking decisions. In exactly the same way as there is a Treaty obligation to consult the EESC, there are obligations to consult the CoR. While its consultation is mandatory, its opinions also have no binding weight. The CoR must be consulted on proposals made in areas that directly affect local and regional interests. The box below provides an overview of the policy areas concerned.

Compulsory consultation of the Committee of the Regions – Policy areas

- Transport
- Employment
- Social policy
- Education, vocational training, youth and sport
- Culture
- Public health
- Trans-European networks
- Economic, social and territorial cohesion
- Environment and climate change
- Energy

The CoR, similarly to the EESC, may also issue **exploratory opinions** and **own-initiative opinions** whenever it judges this appropriate. The latter enables the CoR to put issues on the EU agenda. Moreover, when the EESC is consulted, the CoR may also issue an opinion on the matter if it considers that specific regional interests are likely to be affected.

The functioning and the role of the CoR in the EU decision-making process are very similar to that of the EESC. It however plays two additional roles: firstly, in monitoring the compliance of the EU institutions with the principle of subsidiarity after the formal adoption of EU legislation, and secondly, in monitoring the implementation of EU legislation at national, regional and local level. As a result of the entry into force of the Treaty of Lisbon, the CoR may now initiate infringement proceedings at the Court of Justice if EU legislative acts still do not respect the subsidiarity principle after being formally adopted. The CoR is thus heavily involved throughout the entire legislative process.

The composition and organisation of the CoR are regulated by Articles 305 to 307 TFEU and by its Rules of Procedure. The members of the CoR, who are elected by and/or are politically accountable to an elected regional or local assembly (holders of executive office), are appointed for five years by the Council on a proposal of the respective national governments. These officials may, for example, be local Council members, Regional Parliamentarians or Regional Ministers, City or County Councillors and Mayors.

The CoR is made up of 329 members who each have their alternate. The breakdown of seats by Member State is the same as for the EESC (see Table 4.3).

Again, as for the EESC on which the CoR is to a large extent modelled, the constituent bodies of the CoR are the Plenary Assembly, the Bureau and the Commissions, which are akin to the Sections in the EESC.

The **Bureau**, which is elected by the Plenary Assembly for two and a half years, is, following the departure of the UK, composed of 61 members, comprising the President, the first Vice-President, one Vice-President per Member State (27), 26 other members (the number per Member State reflecting national and political balances) and the chairs of the 6 political groups. The **Plenary Assembly** meets on average five/six times a year. Its role is to formally adopt or reject the texts and decisions of the CoR prepared by its Commissions. These **Commissions** mainly prepare the discussions of the Plenary in terms of content, i.e. they draw up the draft versions of opinions and reports. The CoR may also institute temporary sub-Committees, for particular matters. These sub-Committees are comparable to the Commissions in functioning and role.

The way in which the CoR drafts its opinions is similar to the way in which the EESC works, as described in the preceding section. The Commissions of the CoR are given in Table 4.5

Table 4.5: *Commissions of the Committee of Regions*

CIVEX   –   Commission for Citizenship, Governance, Institutional and External Affairs
COTER   –   Commission for Territorial Cohesion Policy
ECOS   –   Commission for Economic and Social Policy
EDUC   –   Commission for Education, Youth, Culture and Research
ENVE   –   Commission for Environment, Climate Change and Energy
NAT   –   Commission for Natural Resources

One element of the functioning of the CoR differs markedly from that of the EESC in that it is a much more political body. Within the CoR, five of the major Political Groups we saw in Chapter 3 are represented: the European People's Party (EPP), the Party of European Socialists (PES), Renew Europe, the European Alliance Group (EA Group) and the European Conservatives and Reformists Group (ECR Group). Members of the CoR can affiliate with one of these Political Groups, which like the Political Groups in the Parliament, are major actors in the life of the CoR.

4.4   Key stages and key actors – EESC and CoR

As with the core institutions in the preceding three chapters, it is again useful to highlight the key stages and actors within the EESC and CoR. Before doing this, it is important to list their key formal and informal powers. The key powers of the EESC and the CoR are as follows:

1. Giving non-binding opinions, parts of which may find their way into Council, Parliament and Commission texts;

2. Interaction and networks within the EU institutions;

3. Recognised voices of economic, social, and regional interests;

4. Privileged access to Commission, Parliament and Council officials;

5. Privileged access to information.

   These key powers should not be underestimated and any lobbying strategy should ensure that it takes the two consultative bodies into consideration. The key stages and roles of the EESC and CoR are summarised in Table 4.6 below.

Table 4.6: Key stages and actors – The EESC and CoR

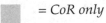 = *CoR only*

Decision-making phase	CoR/EESC role
Pre-legislative phase: European Commission evaluates policy options and prepares legislative proposal	• EESC rapporteur (+ co-rapporteur) and study group organise consultations with civil society organisations. • CoR rapporteur (+ co-rapporteur) organises consultations with local and regional authorities. • CoR rapporteur (+ co-rapporteur) assisted by their commission cooperate with the EC on Impact Assessments. • EESC rapporteur (+ co-rapporteur) assisted by the study group cooperate with the EC on Impact Assessments (EC Cooperation Agreement).
European Commission adopts legislative proposal and must consult both Committees	• CoR rapporteur (+ co-rapporteur) organises consultations with local and regional authorities in order to incorporate their views. • CoR rapporteur in cooperation with the Subsidiarity Steering Group and the Subsidiarity Expert Group analyses compliance with the subsidiarity principle and must ensure that subsidiarity is respected from the point of view of regional and local authorities. The CoR rapporteur also consults with National and Regional Parliaments ('Early Warning Mechanism'). • EESC rapporteur (+ co-rapporteur) assisted by the study group organises consultations with civil society organisations in order to incorporate their views.
EU institutions start discussing legislative proposal. The EP and the Council are obliged to consult the Committees	• EESC rapporteur (+ co-rapporteur) assisted by their study group cooperate with associations representing economic and social interests to incorporate their views on amendments tabled. • CoR rapporteur (co-rapporteur) assisted by the commission cooperates with associations representing local and regional authorities and with the Subsidiarity Monitoring Network to incorporate their views on amendments tabled. • CoR/EESC rapporteurs and their commission/section/study group draft opinion on legislative proposal.

Decision-making phase	CoR/EESC role
In cases where a legislative draft is significantly altered during the legislative process	CoR/EESC rapporteurs assisted by their commission/section/study group may adopt revised opinions on a legislative proposal.
Council and Parliament have adopted EU legislation	The President of the Committee or the commission/section responsible for drawing up an opinion initiates infringement proceedings at the European Court of Justice if adopted EU legislation still does not comply with the subsidiarity principle.
Implementation of EU legislation at national, regional and local level	CoR monitors implementation of EU legislation.

4.5 EU Agencies

The last part of this chapter deals with EU Agencies, one of the most important groups of actors in the EU policy cycle. EU Agencies come in a variety of forms, shapes and sizes and they perform different tasks in different policy areas, but it is essential to understand their role, especially if your policy field involves an EU Agency in some way. This section will detail what EU Agencies are, why they exist, what they do and how they do it.

Table 4.7:   *EU Agencies – Key facts*

Names:	EU Agencies
Legal basis:	Secondary legislation creating each individual Agency
	Own legal personality
	Independent (administratively & financially)
Categories:	Decentralised Agencies (34)
	Agencies under common security and defense (3)
	Executive Agencies (6)
	EURATOM (2)
Staff:	Over 8,000 in decentralised Agencies, ranging from small Agencies with under 50 staff to Agencies with several hundred staff like the European Medicines Agency (EMA) in Amsterdam and the EU Intellectual Property Office (EUIPO) in Alicante.
Annual budget:	4.2 billion euros (2018)
Basic typology:	Regulatory/decentralised
	Executive
Website:	https://europa.eu/european-union/about-eu/agencies_en

EU Agencies are not mentioned in the Treaty (with the exception of the European Defence Agency) and they are not EU institutions. They are EU bodies governed by European law, set up by secondary legislation, operating within the EU policy cycle to fulfil specific tasks. Agencies exist essentially to assist the Commission, and the Member States, in fulfilling various specific tasks. It is for this reason that the majority of Agencies are closely linked to, if not reporting directly to, the Commission.

The first two Agencies appeared in the 1970s, both created to improve effectiveness in specific policy objectives, the European Centre for the Development of Vocational Training (Cedefop) and the European Foundation for the Improvement of Living and Working Conditions (EUROFOUND). The possibility of creating Agencies stemmed from the ability of the Commission to delegate tasks to a separate body, something that was established in the Meroni case of 1958,

> ## *Meroni Case*
> ### *(Case 9-10/56 Meroni v. High Authority)*
>
> - The Commission cannot delegate broader powers than it enjoys itself
> - Only strictly executive powers may be delegated
> - No discretionary powers may be delegated
> - The exercise of delegated powers cannot be exempted from the conditions to which they would have been subject if they had been directly exercised by the Commission
> - The delegated powers remain subject to conditions determined by the Commission and subject to its continuing oversight

now known as the 'Meroni doctrine'. It is from this case that the Commission has proposed, and received Member State support for, the creation of a series of Agencies. It must be noted that the exact interpretation of the Meroni case is still, over 50 years later, highly disputed. The key aspects of the case are highlighted in the box above.

It was not until the 1990s that more Agencies appeared, with 11 further Agencies being created in this decade. This wave of Agency creation was linked to the objective of completing the internal market – notably with attempts to increase technical harmonisation and deliver very specific technical and scientific knowledge in certain sectors. Major Agencies created in the 1990s include the European Union Intellectual Property Office (EUIPO), the European Medicines Agency (EMA), and the European Environment Agency (EEA).

Since then further Agencies have continued to be created with some regularity, some with very specific technical remits (e.g. the European Aviation Safety Agency, EASA) and others with responsibilities in areas of political sensitivity and high salience, such as the European Asylum Support Office (EASO) and European Border and Coast Guard Agency (FRONTEX).

Rationale behind Agencies

- Assist in carrying out Community activities
- Reduce the workload of the European Commission
- Lack of expertise & human resources in the European Commission
- Flexibility: day-to-day management of projects
- Independent expertise and advice
- Increase transparency within policy fields, and across EU decision-making
- Facilitate European-wide cooperation between stakeholders
- Enable more efficient and flexible implementation of EU legislation

From the preceding short historical digest of Agencies, it is important to stress that the numbers have grown for a variety of reasons, all linked to very specific circumstances, needs or objectives. The rationale for the creation of Agencies also helps us understand what Agencies do. In the box on the previous page is a list of some of the main reasons why Agencies have mushroomed since the 1970s.

It is clear from the above rationale behind Agencies, that each Agency is a very specific entity serving specific needs within its policy sector. In this sense no two Agencies are the same, and every Agency is an extremely important actor within its field of competence/speciality.

Table 4.8: List of EU Agencies

Name	Acronym	Location	Created
Decentralised Agencies			
Agency for the Cooperation of Energy Regulators	ACER	Ljubljana, Slovenia	2010
Body of European Regulators for Electronic Communications	BEREC	Riga, Latvia	2009
Community Plant Variety Office	CPVO	Angers, France	1994
European Agency for Safety & Health at Work	EU-OSHA	Bilbao, Spain	1994
European Border and Coast Guard Agency	FRONTEX	Warsaw, Poland	2004
European Union Agency for large-scale IT systems in the area of freedom, security and justice	eu-LISA	Tallinn, Estonia	2011
European Asylum Support Office	EASO	Valletta, Malta	2010
European Aviation Safety Agency	EASA	Cologne, Germany	2002
European Banking Authority	EBA	Paris, France	2011
European Centre for Disease Prevention & Control	ECDC	Solna, Sweden	2004
European Centre for the Development of Vocational Training	Cedefop	Thessaloniki, Greece	1975
European Chemicals Agency	ECHA	Helsinki, Finland	2006
European Environment Agency	EEA	Copenhagen, Denmark	1990
European Fisheries Control Agency	EFCA	Vigo, Spain	2005
European Food Safety Authority	EFSA	Parma, Italy	2002

continued overleaf

continued from the previous page

Name	Acronym	Location	Created
European Foundation for the Improvement of Living and Working Conditions	EUROFOUND	Dublin, Ireland	1975
European GNSS Agency	GSA	Prague, Czech Republic	2004
European Institute for Gender Equality	EIGE	Vilnius, Lithuania	2007
European Insurance and Occupational Pensions Authority	EIOPA	Frankfurt am Main, Germany	2010
European Maritime Safety Agency	EMSA	Lisbon, Portugal	2002
European Medicines Agency	EMA	Amsterdam, Netherlands	1995
European Monitoring Centre for Drugs & Drug Addiction	EMCDDA	Lisbon, Portugal	1993
European Network and Information Security Agency	ENISA	Heraklion, Greece	2004
European Union Agency for Law Enforcement Training	CEPOL	Budapest, Hungary	2005
European Union Agency for Law Enforcement Cooperation	EUROPOL	The Hague, Netherlands	1991
European Public Prosecutor's Office (in preparation)	EPPO	Luxembourg, Luxembourg	2020
European Railway Agency	ERA	Valenciennes and Lille, France	2004
European Securities and Markets Authority	ESMA	Paris, France	2011
European Training Foundation	ETF	Turin, Italy	1994
European Union Agency for Fundamental Rights	FRA	Vienna, Austria	2007
European Union Intellectual Property Office	EUIPO	Alicante, Spain	1994
Single Resolution Board	SRB	Brussels, Belgium	2014
European Union Agency for Criminal Justice Cooperation	EUROJUST	The Hague, Netherlands	2002
Translation Centre for the Bodies of the European Union	CdT	Luxembourg, Luxembourg	1994

continued from the previous page

Name	Acronym	Location	Created
Agencies under common security and defense policy			
European Defence Agency	EDA	Brussels, Belgium	2004
European Union Institute for Security Studies	EUISS	Paris, France	2002
European Union Satellite Centre	SatCen	Madrid, Spain	2002
Executive Agencies			
Education, Audiovisual and Cultural Executive Agency	EACEA	Brussels, Belgium	2006
Executive Agency for Small and Medium-sized enterprises	EASME	Brussels, Belgium	2013
European Research Council Executive Agency	ERC Executive Agency	Brussels, Belgium	2007
Consumers, Health, Agriculture and Food Executive Agency	CHAFEA	Luxembourg, Luxembourg	2005
Research Executive Agency	REA	Brussels, Belgium	2007
Innovation & Networks Executive Agency	INEA	Brussels, Belgium	2006
EURATOM Agencies			
EURATOM Supply Agency	ESA	Luxembourg	1960
Fusion for Energy	F4E	Barcelona, Spain	2007
European Institute of Innovation and Technology	EIT	Budapest, Hungary	2008

Source: data taken from https://europa.eu/european-union/about-eu/agencies_en

Table 4.8 illustrates how Agencies operate in very diverse and specific areas. It also shows how Agencies are geographically spread throughout the EU, with almost all Member States being home to at least one Agency.

A possible major restructuring of the Executive Agencies, including closures but retaining their role, is in planning for 2021 and beyond.

What, then, do the Agencies actually do? This question is not a simple one to answer because Agencies have mushroomed over time within no uniform framework and are based on different reasons and circumstances. As each Agency is created by secondary legislation it can be given very different tasks and powers, so taking a look at the basic act of any Agency in your field is fundamental to know what they do. The main types of Agencies are listed below in Table 4.9.

Table 4.9:   Different Types of EU Agencies

There are two broad types of agency, each with different characteristics and raising different issues: 'Regulatory' Agencies (today more commonly known as decentralised agencies) and Executive Agencies.

Executive Agencies

- Set up under a Council regulation (2002).
- Tasks related to the management of Union programmes.
- Created for limited periods of time.
- Located close to European Commission in Brussels or Luxembourg.

Examples: REA, INEA

Regulatory/decentralised Agencies

- Have their own sectoral basic act.
- Spread around Europe.
- Independent bodies with their own legal personality.
- Most are funded by the EU Budget.

Different types:

- Agencies adopting individual decisions which are legally binding on third parties.

Examples: CVPO, EUIPO, EASA and ECHA

- Agencies providing direct assistance to the Commission and, where necessary, to the Member States, in the form of technical or scientific advice and/or inspection reports.

Examples: EMSA, EFSA, ERA and EMA

- Agencies in charge of operational activities.

Examples: EAR, GSA, CFCA, FRONTEX, EUROJUST, EUROPOL and CEPOL

- Agencies responsible for gathering, analysing and forwarding objective, reliable and easy to understand information/networking.

Examples: CEDEFOP, EUROFOUND, EEA, ETF, EMCCDA, EU-OSHA, ENISA, ECDC, FRA and European Institute for Gender Equality.

- Services to other agencies and institutions.

Examples: CDT

Source: Communication to the European Parliament and the Council: EU Agencies - The Way Forward' (COM (2008)135 final)

Table 4.9 shows the main tasks that Agencies undertake, again highlighting the variety and differences that exist. There is a big distinction between Regulatory Agencies and the others. **Regulatory Agencies**, which are the majority, are actively involved in executive functions by enacting instruments to regulate sectors and some of them have their own decision-making powers. This type of Agency is thus a very powerful and important player in the EU policy cycle in its sector of competence. The Agency will of course be involved in assisting, informing and working with the Commission on all proposals, legislative or Delegated and Implementing Acts, throughout the drafting and decision-making phases. The Agency will also be called on to share its expertise with the Council and Parliament.

An **Executive Agency** on the other hand is created, strictly supervised and dissolved by the Commission – and they are all Brussels or Luxembourg-based. These Agencies are set up for specific time periods to do a fixed job, which is that of managing and implementing a programme.

In an attempt to clarify and standardise the functioning and working methods of the decentralised Agencies which had significantly grown in number and diversity, the Commission adopted the 'Communication to the European Parliament and the Council: EU Agencies – The Way Forward' (COM (2008)135 final) in 2008. This document signified the recognition of the importance of EU Agencies and the need to adopt a common approach to the governance of Regulatory Agencies.

Several years of inter-institutional discussions on ways of improving the efficiency, effectiveness, transparency and accountability of the Agencies, eventually resulted in the endorsement in 2012 of a Common Approach and a Roadmap that translates the approach into concrete implementing initiatives.

The discussions on the role and functioning of EU Agencies continues as is shown in the close attention that the European Parliament dedicates to the topic. In 2018, its research service published a report, 'EU Agencies, Common Approach and Parliamentary Scrutiny', which presented several recommendations to improve management of EU Agencies. The debate about the role and functioning of EU Agencies will surely continue in the coming years and this is an area to keep an eye on.

Agencies are vitally important sector-specific actors in the EU policy cycle and the box below highlights how and why Agencies are important for all stakeholders to understand, and if necessary engage with.

Importance of engaging with EU Agencies

1. An Agency is often the main EU source of technical/scientific expertise on specific subjects: their voice counts.
2. The work of Agencies will directly, or indirectly, influence the work of the Commission and the co-legislators.
3. Agencies will develop their own stakeholder networks – through contacts, events, sub-Committees, open hearings, etc.
4. Agencies are frequently requested to assist the Commission as it drafts legislative texts and Delegated and Implementing Acts, in particular by performing research and stakeholder consultation.

PART II: THE INSTITUTIONS WORKING TOGETHER

5. The Ordinary Legislative Procedure

By Joost Mulder and Alan Hardacre

European decision-making has often been criticised as being too complex and difficult to understand. This is because the processes of decision-making in the EU traditionally involve a multitude of actors and vary according to the policy area concerned and the nature of the act to be adopted. It is also the mixture of formal procedures, informal practices (that have arisen over time) and the evolving inter-institutional relations that are difficult to follow and understand.

But while the EU decision-making procedures may appear complex, this and the next chapter show that in fact they are approachable – and that it is possible to get to grips not only with the formal procedures but also the informal practices. In addition, it should be highlighted that EU decision-making is not necessarily more complex than any national bicameral legislative system.

Before looking in specific detail at the Ordinary Legislative Procedure (OLP), this chapter starts with a general overview of decision-making in the EU.

5.1 EU Decision-Making: The Basics

The first place to start when trying to understand EU decision-making and how it works, is to consider the typology of EU legal norms as outlined in Figure 5.1. This figure shows the basic hierarchy of EU legal norms, and it helps in understanding the decision-making procedures we detail in this and the next chapter.

The **Treaty of Lisbon** is the basic document that lays down which decision-making procedures should be used in different areas of EU activity. Included within the Treaty are specific provisions for where the EU can legislate, and according to which procedure. On the basis of this Treaty provision, which, for example, allows the EU to legislate in the field of the environment, the Commission can come forward with a proposal to start the Ordinary Legislative Procedure, the result of which will be the adoption of a **Regulation**, **Directive** or **Decision**. This level is the most visible level of EU decision-making because it is here that the political objectives of the EU are laid down, and it will be the focus of this chapter.

The level below EU legislation, **Implementing and Delegated Acts**, will be dealt with in the next chapter because it is derived from EU legislation. The Treaty provides for the possibility of EU legislation and in its turn, EU legislation provides the possibility of delegating law-making power to the Commission so it can adopt Implementing and Delegated Acts.

Figure 5.1: Typology of EU legal norms

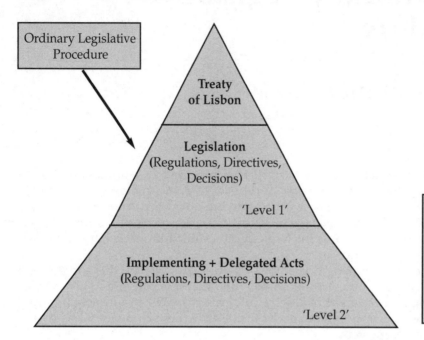

For the adoption of EU legislation, the Treaty of Lisbon provides for two types of procedure.

The first is the **Ordinary Legislative Procedure** (**OLP**, also still referred to under its former name **Codecision**) which 'consists in the joint adoption by the European Parliament and the Council of a Regulation, Directive or Decision on a proposal from the Commission' (Article 289(1) TFEU).

The other is **Special Legislative Procedures** (**SLPs**) which consist in 'the adoption of a regulation, directive or decision by the European Parliament with the participation of the Council, or by the latter with the participation of the European Parliament' (Article 289(2) TFEU).

The policy area under consideration is decisive in determining which one of the two procedures will be followed, and this is always specified in the relevant Treaty article.

With the entry into force of the Treaty of Lisbon in 2009, the Codecision procedure was

Main EU Decision-Making Procedures

1. **Ordinary Legislative Procedure**
   Commission proposal, Council (QMV) and Parliament co-decide in up to three readings. Example: Roaming Charges Regulation

2. **Special Legislative Procedure: Consultation.**
   Commission proposal. Council (unanimity) decides after consulting Parliament (non-binding opinion).
   Example: Competition Law

3. **Special Legislative Procedure: Consent.**
   Role of Commission and Council varies, Parliament has to give its consent.

renamed the Ordinary Legislative Procedure, but the name Codecision continues to be used as common currency – and it will be used inter-changeably with Ordinary Legislative Procedure in this chapter.

The scope of the OLP was significantly extended by the Treaty of Lisbon, making it the rule for passing EU legislation. Considering that this is the most inclusive and arguably the most democratic decision-making procedure in the EU, this was an important development.

Before looking at the OLP in detail, however, we must first take a look at the main forms of **Special Legislative Procedures**, the SLPs.

The SLPs include the Consultation, the Consent and some very specific individualised procedures.

1. The Consultation procedure

In the Consultation procedure, the Council, acting either by unanimity or by qualified majority, adopts acts based on a Commission-initiated proposal after having consulted the Parliament. An important power that the Parliament has under the Consultation procedure is similar to the US-style filibuster principle, because even if the Parliament's opinion is non-binding the Council still has to wait for it to issue one before it can act itself – meaning that the Parliament can delay giving its opinion.

2. The Consent procedure

In the Consent procedure, the Council, acting either by unanimity or by qualified majority, adopts acts based on a Commission-initiated proposal only after obtaining the explicit approval of the Parliament. It is nowadays frequently used in procedures on **judicial co-operation**, e.g. in the context of policy cooperation with third countries, including the UK post-Brexit. This procedure notably applies to **international agreements**, an area in which the Parliament has considerable power. Giving its consent to these agreements is a significant role for the Parliament and can have important consequences.

There are two main differences between the Consent and the Consultation procedure. Firstly, under the Consultation procedure the Parliament can table amendments, which is not possible under the Consent procedure; and secondly, under the Consultation procedure the Council is not bound by the Parliament's position, but it is however obliged to consult the Parliament.

Even though these are the two most important SLPs, a variety of other procedures are used in very specific cases, for example in sensitive areas such as Justice and Home Affairs, EU Budgetary Affairs and for specific aspects of certain policies such as social protection for workers. For these procedures it is necessary to look into the specific Treaty articles for more detail.

This chapter will now focus explicitly on the main legislative decision-making procedure, the OLP. The majority of lobbying work in Brussels is concentrated on the OLP, making it the procedure that external stakeholders work the most with.

Table 5.1:   *Ordinary Legislative Procedure – Key facts*

Names: Ordinary Legislative Procedure (OLP), Codecision

Established: 1992 – Treaty of Maastricht (entry into force 1 November 1993)

Legal basis: Article 294 TFEU

Scope: 85 Treaty articles

Key actors: European Commission (proposal), European Parliament (legislator), Council of EU (legislator)

Process: Up to three readings as follows:
First reading (2014-2019: 89% of legislation adopted at this stage)
Unlimited in time. All amendments possible
Voting: Parliament – Simple Majority, Council – QMV
Second reading (2014–2019: 11% of legislation adopted at this stage – 91% of which are early second-reading agreements)
Limited to 3 and maximum 4 months for each legislator. Amendments limited
Voting: Parliament – Absolute Majority, Council – QMV
Third reading/Conciliation (not used in the 2014–2019 legislature)
Limited to 3 times a maximum of 8 weeks. No amendments possible
Voting: Parliament – Simple Majority, Council – QMV

While previous chapters analysed legislative decision-making from a micro perspective inside the core EU institutions, this chapter will adopt a macro level approach, situating the previously studied internal decision-making systems in a broader context. As a result, the focus will shift from **intra-institutional** dynamics to **inter-institutional** dynamics.

After briefly tracing the origins of Codecision, this chapter will set out the formal steps of the procedure, the informal practices and the evolving inter-institutional dynamics, allowing for the identification of opportunities and challenges when working with OLP.

The functioning of the OLP is laid down in Article 294 TFEU. The main characteristics of this procedure are that the Commission, or a number of Member States or other institutions (in very specific Treaty-based cases), present(s) a legislative proposal that is then subject to negotiation and adoption by the Parliament and the Council (by qualified majority voting, QMV, in the Council).

Thus under OLP, the Parliament and the Council benefit from **equal legislative powers**, consequently a legislative act cannot be adopted as long as the two institutions have not reached a compromise agreement.

5.2   *The rise of Codecision and its transition to the Ordinary Legislative Procedure*

The Codecision procedure has undergone a number of changes since its introduction in 1993. The procedure, and the balance of power between the EU institutions, has developed over time with each Treaty modification. Although it was the Single European

Act, with the adoption of the Cooperation procedure, that paved the way towards 'equal bicameralism', it was the Treaty of Maastricht that formally introduced the Codecision procedure in 1993.

Originally, the Codecision procedure applied to a limited number of 15 legal areas, primarily related to the internal market. The procedure consisted of a minimum of two, and a maximum of three, stages (first reading, second reading, and third reading/Con-

> ### Basic premise of the OLP
>
> The Commission presents a legislative proposal. The Parliament and the Council both have to agree to, and adopt, the same text. This is usually done through inter-institutional negotiations (trilogues) to find a compromise.

ciliation). In 1999, the **Treaty of Amsterdam** extended the scope of the procedure to 39 legal areas, with the main new ones being public health, social exclusion, the environment and transport.

Moreover, it also simplified the Codecision procedure by introducing the possibility of adopting a proposal at first reading, the so-called **first reading agreement**. These agreements are based on negotiations (trilogues, which we introduced in earlier chapters) between the Council, the Parliament and the Commission (acting as a 'broker'). These trilogues will be discussed in more detail later in this chapter because they are the main mechanism for finding agreement in OLP. The development of this early agreement mechanism was seen as a logical next step in the evolution of Codecision since the compulsory second reading had become superfluous in most cases.

First reading deals accounted for 89% of all legislation concluded under the Ordinary Legislative Procedure between 2014 and 2019, up from 85% in 2009–2014 and 72% in 2004–2009. The stages of agreement in 2014–2019 can be seen in Figure 5.2.

The **Treaty of Nice**, which entered into force in 2003, added five more legal areas to the realm of Codecision, the bulk of which were in the area of Justice and Home Affairs. The Treaty did not, however, change the substance of the procedure. With the entry into force of the **Treaty of Lisbon** in 2009, the number of legal bases subject to the OLP almost doubled, reaching 85 articles – the biggest increase since the introduction of the procedure in 1993. Unlike Nice, the Treaty of Lisbon also introdced an important number of amendments to the provisions governing legislative decision-making.

Figure 5.2: When agreements were reached under OLP: 2014-2019

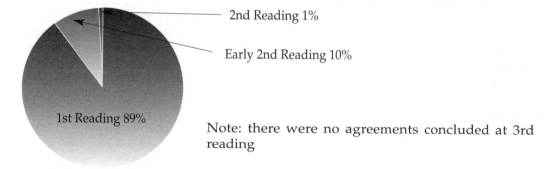

2nd Reading 1%

Early 2nd Reading 10%

1st Reading 89%

Note: there were no agreements concluded at 3rd reading

Table 5.2:   *Policy areas covered and not covered by the Ordinary Legislative Procedure post-Lisbon*

Ordinary Legislative Procedure

- Services of general economic interest
- Intellectual property rights
- Public health (common safety concerns)
- Exclusion of certain activities from right of establishment
- Liberalisation of services in specific sectors
- Implementation of European Research Area space
- Sport/tourism/civil protection/ administrative cooperation
- Economic, financial & technical assistance to third countries

- Humanitarian aid
- Services of general economic interest
- Citizens' initiative
- Statute of Court of Justice (most)
- Statutes of ESCB and European Central Bank
- Modalities for control of Implementing Acts
- European administration
- Financial rules
- EU Staff Regulations
- Fisheries
- Trade Policy (aspects of)

Special Legislative Procedures

- All of CFSP / CSDP
- Parts of agriculture and fisheries ('measures on fixing prices, levies, aid and quantitative limitations and on the fixing and allocation of fishing opportunities')
- Specific R&D programmes
- Detailed rules on electoral rights
- Action to combat discrimination
- Strengthening citizens' rights

- Uniform procedure for EP elections
- System of own resources
- Tax harmonisation, approximation of laws, measures in energy having a fiscal character
- Sensitive areas of social policy
- Family law with cross-border implications
- Operational police cooperation
- European Public Prosecutor's Office

The highlights of the new areas which became subject to OLP after Lisbon were aspects of agriculture, fisheries and EU trade policy. These long-standing preserves of the Council finally became subject to the Codecision procedure, in essence the last major policy areas that had remained outside its grasp.

Table 5.2 also highlights the **main areas still not subject to Codecision**, such as CFSP, some specific elements of agriculture, tax harmonisation and certain areas of social policy – all of which are extremely sensitive domains for the Member States. For example, the elements of fisheries that have remained outside Codecision (Article 43(3) TFEU) require that the Council, on a proposal from the Commission, adopts measures on fixing prices, levies, aid and quantitative limitations and on the fixing and allocation of fishing opportunities.

The progressive increase in the number of legal bases covered by the Codecision procedure was matched by a parallel growth in the number of launched, and adopted, Codecision files (as shown on the next page), making an understanding of its inner workings more important than it was before.

Number of Codecision acts adopted

Maastricht era (1993-1999): 165
Amsterdam and Nice Treaties (1999-2004): 403
6th parliamentary term (2004-2009): 447
7th parliamentary term (2009-2014): 495
8th parliamentary term (2014-2019): 401

Having outlined the rise and spread of Codecision, and before looking in detail at the step-by-step process, it is important to emphasise certain key defining elements:

1. The first reading stage has become the main part of the action for all Codecision files, and in 2014–2019 produced a final agreement in 89% of cases.

2. An understanding of the first reading stage provides the key to understanding the whole procedure, as the later stages cover the same material and use the same formal and informal negotiating processes, just adding constraints as they proceed.

3. For these reasons, the first reading stage, before the Parliament has voted, is the only realistic point of entry for efforts from stakeholders to influence the content of the legislation, as the later stages not usualy reached and in any case are limited by the baselines drawn at first reading.

With these three fundamental points about Codecision in mind, the chapter will now go through the procedure in detail, with a clear focus on the first reading.

5.3 Ordinary Legislative Procedure: First reading

Figure 5.2 highlighted that in the previous legislature 89% of legislation was agreed in first reading, making it essential to understand why, and how, legislation is agreed at the first stage of the process. This section will outline the formal procedure, but more importantly the processes that have been created to facilitate agreement at the earliest possible stage. Figure 5.3 outlines the process of first reading.

Whilst first reading is unlimited in time there are usually political, or technical, reasons to want to conclude the dossier early. In the 2014–2019 legislature the average time required to find agreement at first reading was 18 months.

First reading formally begins when the Commission, through the College, adopts and forwards a legislative proposal to the Council and Parliament. The procedure may also be launched on the initiative of one quarter (i.e. seven), or more, of the Member States (or nine Member States for 'enhanced cooperation' proposals where there is no majority to adopt an existing Commission proposal). This allows a group of like-minded Member States to make a legislative initiative that they wish to pursue.

Before looking at how the legislators deal with a proposal in OLP we also need to consider the other actors who receive the legislative draft and the roles they play. At the same time as the legislators, the draft is sent to national parliaments (see Chapter 1.8) and, where required by the Treaty, to the Economic and Social Committee (EESC) and the Committee of the Regions (CoR) (see Chapters 4.2 and 4.3).

Figure 5.3: First reading of Ordinary Legislative Procedure

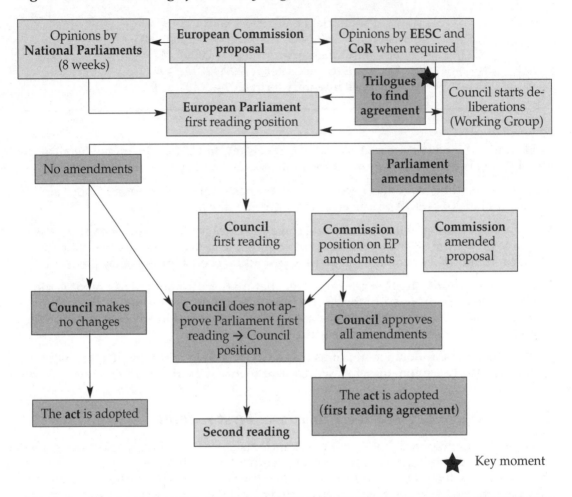

National parliaments have eight weeks to scrutinise Commission legislative proposals to give a reasoned opinion on subsidiarity (Article 12 TEU and Protocol 1). If one-third opposed a draft (one-quarter for Police and Judicial Cooperation in Criminal Matters) (**'yellow card'**), then the draft must be reviewed by the Commission, which must explain any changes, or lack of changes, it decides to make. If a simple majority opposes the draft (**'orange card'**) then it must be reviewed by the Commission. If the Commission decides to maintain the proposal, the Council and Parliament can take account of the position of the national parliaments during their first reading and either of them can stop the Code-cision procedure by a 55% majority in Council or by a simple majority in the Parliament.

A further element of obligatory consultation is that of the Committee of the Regions (CoR) and the European Economic and Social Committee (EESC), as discussed in the previous chapter. Both of these consultative Committees are sent the proposal and are then free to submit their opinion, albeit a non-binding opinion. The opinions of the two consultative bodies are not always followed by stakeholders, as they are non-binding, but elements of their thinking, or their ideas, can be taken up by the legislators.

The subsidiarity check by the national parliaments, and the opinions from the CoR and EESC, do not delay the start of the Codecision procedure. These procedures run in parallel to, and feed into, the start of the internal procedures in the Parliament and Council. That said, a Codecision procedure can obviously not be concluded within these eight weeks (also bearing in mind that the eight weeks scrutiny only actually starts when each national parliament receives the documents in its own language, which can add a few more weeks to the process). It can be worth keeping an eye on developments in the national parliaments, EESC and CoR in the early stages of the process to see if anything important is taking place, even if the obvious focus of the first stage of Codecision is on the co-legislators themselves.

In the formal process of Codecision it is the Parliament that will have to deliver its position first, so the focus of attention is naturally drawn to the Parliament. But this should not mask the fact that the Council also starts work at exactly the same time, in parallel, to find its position for negotiation with the Parliament in the effort to find a first reading agreement. So whilst the Parliament acts first in the formal process, it usually only does so after informal negotiation with the Council, making it essential to consider both legislators at the same time. The Parliament can, of course, and sometimes does, adopt its first reading position without any negotiation with the Council if it wants to make a statement and take a forceful opening position.

> ### National Parliaments
>
> Pay attention to the process of scrutiny and the opinion voiced by National Parliaments. Not because it is likely to lead to objections on the grounds of subsidiarity, but because it will be a good indicator of how the Parliament will pressure its own government and MEPs. Some EU Member States get negotiating mandates from their National Parliaments, and none of them can ignore the opinion of their Parliament(s). These positions will also help you to understand national dynamics, potentially ahead of the Council's orientation debate.
>
> Find out more via IPEX, the platform for EU Interparliamentary Exchange: www.ipex.eu

The internal decision-making system of the Parliament was covered in Chapter 3.5 to 3.8, but we shall reiterate the key elements here. The Parliament has to nominate its responsible and opinion-giving Committee(s) and a rapporteur from the Political Group that 'wins' the dossier. The rapporteur then drafts a report that needs to go through Committee and to Plenary for final adoption. In Codecision, the Parliament has three options in Plenary (all by simple majority voting), it can:

1. Approve the Commission proposal without amendments.

> ### First reading – Negotiating mandates
>
> The early stages of first reading are when each legislator develops its position and identifies its interests. This process is all about preparing a negotiating mandate (formal or informal) for inter-institutional negotiations.
>
> In Codecision procedures, legislation is always the outcome of inter-institutional negotiation. This means it is always necessary to work with both legislators and to understand the actual, and potential, negotiation dynamics.

2. Adopt its own position with amendments to the Commission proposal.

3. Reject the Commission proposal (not foreseen in the Treaty, but in the Parliament's Rules of Procedure, RoP).

It should be clarified that normally a rejection in Plenary would result in the proposal going back to the Committee. The Committee would then try to persuade the Commission to withdraw its proposal, which is the only legally acceptable way to close the file at this stage of the procedure under Treaty rules. This is, however, something that the Commission is reluctant to do, unless it is sure that the EP's negative views are shared by the Council. It does, however, mean that the legislative proposal is, for all intents and purposes, politically dead.

The explicit rejection by the EP is not formally foreseen in the Treaty of Lisbon, but neither is it explicitly prohibited and the Parliament has adapted this into Rule 59 of its Rules of Procedure. Such a rejection happened in July 2018 when the Parliament opposed a controversial Directive on Copyright.

The most common outcome is that the Parliament approves the Commission proposal with amendments. At this stage the Commission may accept some, or all, of the Parliament's amendments and incorporate them into a 'modified' proposal and forward this to the Council (although there have been very few modified proposals up to now).

Internally there is a clear structure for the discussion and adoption of positions on Codecision developments in the Commission, which is spearheaded by the Inter-institutional Relations Group (known by its French acronym GRI). This group prepares all Commission positions on inter-institutional relations for the College, notably therefore on Codecision files, and it is the GRI that will establish coherent Commission positions on all aspects of Codecision files.

These internal deliberations in the Commission are formally aimed at empowering a Commissioner to take a position on behalf of the Commission. The power of this position, which is Treaty-based, is that the Commission can require the Council to act by unanimity at first and second reading when the Commission disagrees with Parliament amendments. The strength of the disciplined internal Commission procedures is the enhanced credibility, and hence political influence, of the Commission in the negotiations, with a view to eventually exercising its power to block a decision by QMV in the Council.

> ### Commission Inter-institutional Relations Group (GRI)
>
> **Who:** Members of all Cabinets in charge of relations with other institutions – meets at least three times a month (Fridays).
> Prepared by Parliament/Council coordinators in each DG (Thursdays).
> **Why:** Main tool of Commission to coordinate its relations with other institutions.
> **What:** All inter-institutional relations, such as OLP and MEP questions.

> ### Council first reading position – Adoption
>
> As a general rule, the Council adopts its position by qualified majority voting. However, when the Council's position differs from the Commission's position, unanimity is required.

When the EP's first reading position is forwarded to the Council, the Council formally has two options. It can either:

1. **Approve all the amendments made by the Parliament** (first reading agreement). To do this, the Council must vote by quali-

Figure 5.4: Processes in OLP First Reading

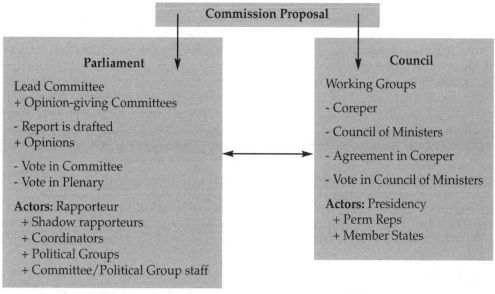

fied majority on the text as a whole (or by unanimity if the Commission did not accept any amendments). Or,

2. **Not approve** the Parliament's first reading position.

In the first case, the act is adopted and the Codecision procedure is finished. In the second case, the Council has to proceed to adopt its own first reading position which may or may not take the Parliament's first reading position into account and which it will return to the latter to launch the second reading.

Just like the European Parliament, the Council does not have the formal (Treaty-based) power to explicitly reject a text, though unlike the EP it has never actually sought or provided for such an outcome. In practice however, the Council has the power to block a text *simply by taking no action* at first reading.

What allows the Council to do this is the absence of time limits at this stage of the procedure. As a result, a dossier becomes pending and will remain so until the Council decides to take action. A withdrawal of the proposal by the Commission would be the only legally acceptable way to close the file at this stage of the procedure. In a majority of cases however, the formal procedures of the first reading will end with an agreed legislative text.

Given that 89% of legislation is now agreed, in an average of 18 months, in the first reading stage, we need to look more closely at what happens within, and between, the institutions (in trilogues) to reach these early agreements.

Figure 5.4 illustrates the *separate* processes that are taking place in parallel within the Parliament and Council at first reading stage, as already identified in the respective chapters on the Parliament and Council. What we will move on to next is understanding how the institutions *work together* towards first reading agreements, and how they interconnect and influence each other.

5.4   First reading agreements – Trilogues

Before looking at these 'interlinkages' it is important to understand the context in which first readings nowadays take place. There is no longer a formal requirement to demonstrate political urgency and trilogue negotiations have become a default feature of the EU decision-making process.

Trilogues, it will be recalled, are trilateral negotiation meetings between the three institutions (Parliament, Council and Commission) towards the end of the first reading, in an attempt to find an inter-institutional compromise agreement and to avoid triggering a second reading. If successful, they lead to an agreed text that is usually first endorsed by the Parliament (in Committee amendments and at Plenary) in a first reading, after which the Council will agree to the Parliament's formal first reading.

If for whatever reason the Parliament must close its first reading without agreement (e.g. at the end of the Parliamentary term), trilogue negotiations can still continue with a slightly amended ratification process: the so-called **early second reading**. In this set-up, the Council will close its first reading with the compromise agreement as its first reading position, to which the Parliament will then agree without amendments in an 'early' second reading.

It is important to understand that in both of these scenarios (first reading agreement and early second reading agreement) there is no time limit for the negotiations, as in both cases the formal first reading has not been completed when the trilogues take place.

The 2016 Inter-institutional Agreement on Better Law-Making includes commitments on the transparency of 'trilateral negotiations', and together with subsequent changes to the EP's Rules of Procedure can be seen as **acceptance of first reading trilogue agreements as the default form** of EU law-making. All legislative proposals under the Ordinary Legislative Procedure will therefore at some point in their institutional lifetime move to trilogue negotiations.

There are, however, political considerations that determine the order of priority given to a specific legislative proposal and its trilogues. Urgency can be determined by external shocks (e.g. financial crisis or a health care or environmental disaster) in combination with institutional factors, especially the end of a Member State Presidency of the Council, elections in a Member State or the end of the legislative term of the EP.

Two of these factors are very important and need to be highlighted.

Firstly, the **end of a legislative term** usually sees a large spike in activity, though this is only once every five years. This is not because of the formal provision that unfinished Parliament business lapses – in reality 80% of negotiations are continued – but because the political composition of the Parliament and its Negotiating Team (rapporteur and shadows) is likely to change, which could change the dynamics of the negotiations.

Secondly, **many Presidencies favour a fast-track approach** to legislation in line with the needs of the dossier, their own political interests and their drive to achieve a 'successful' Presidency – a pressure that is virtually constant given that the Presidency rotates every six months. An incoming Presidency will always announce its priorities in advance, which will, in part, be based on an assessment of what is possible. Each dossier will be evaluated in political and practical terms, which could result in it being fast-tracked by the Presidency. We will come back to this dynamic later in the chapter because it is a source of friction between the institutions, notably because the Parliament can often strategically decide to fast-track, or not, the proposals from the Presidency.

Figure 5.5 highlights the fact that both legislators start work at the same time as they individually try to establish their respective positions, which will eventually form their negotiating mandates. For this reason it is essential to stay abreast of developments in both legislative institutions and to understand what the potential sticking points could be: there will always be negotiating chips created and used as collateral. Once each institution has advanced sufficiently to enter into discussions, trilogues will be planned.

Trilogues take place with the involvement of:

1. **The Council:** it will be represented by the Presidency, usually the official chairing the Working Party and/or the Coreper Chair and representatives from the Council Secretariat (usually from the Directorate dealing with the file, the Legal Service and the Codecision Unit). In exceptional cases the competent Minister from the Presidency Member State might attend a last trilogue to increase political pressure and/or ensure political visibility.

Figure 5.5: The trilogue process

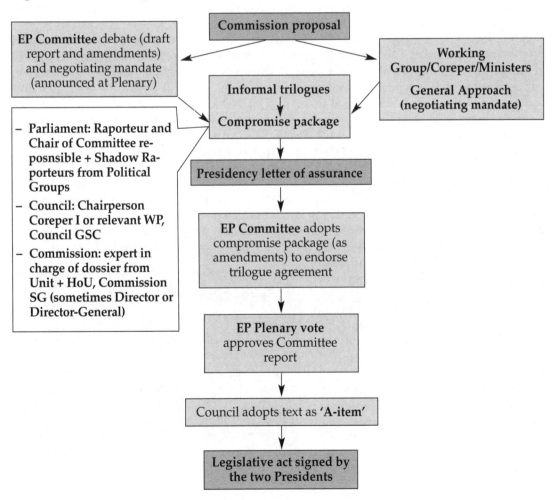

2. **The Parliament**: the EP Negotiating Team will always at least comprise the rapporteur who will lead the team, a shadow rapporteur from each Political Group and the Chair of the Committee responsible (or the Vice-Chair designated by the Chair) who will preside over the team.

3. **The Commission**: it will be represented by the Head of Unit (HoU) in charge of the dossier within the Directorate-General (DG) responsible, as well as by representatives of the Secretariat-General (SG) and the Legal Service. It is also possible that a Director, Director-General or even Commissioner is involved in the Commission delegation, especially as the trilogue process matures and discussions become more political.

These representatives will hold as many trilogue meetings as are required, with the inevitable need to refer back to their institutions to validate proposals and negotiated texts, until they are able, or unable, to find an agreement.

If an agreement is found, the Presidency, via the chairperson of Coreper, will forward **a letter of assurance** that has been approved by Coreper to the chairperson of the relevant Parliament Committee, in which the Council indicates its willingness to accept the text as agreed if it is voted by the Parliament Plenary. This means that the Council promises to adopt as an A point the agreed trilogue text.

The process of trilogues that has just been described is not quite as straightforward as this might suggest. The text that has been agreed in these closed-door meetings still requires the formal approval of the two institutions in their internal decision-making procedures, which can be awkward depending on the stage at which the trilogues find agreement. For example, an agreed text could still need to be subjected to a vote in Parliament Committees and Plenary, as well as in Coreper and Council. This means the compromise text has to be steered through Political Groups, a Committee and Coreper – and with no changes, for it to stay valid. If it is approved then it is forwarded to the Council for approval as an A point, after which the legislative act can be signed by the two institutions and enter into law.

Under the rules as they stand in 2020, a formal Committee decision and Plenary notification is required before negotiations are opened. The procedure is defined in Rule 71 of the Parliament's Rules of Procedure (see box on next page), and requires a majority of Committee members to approve the negotiating mandate in a vote (Rule 71.1). After the Committee vote, there is a notification procedure with an objection opportunity at the next Plenary session. In the highly unlikely event of a successful Plenary objection to the mandate, the report continues into a normal first reading Plenary procedure (amendments and vote).

First reading agreements are the only texts that come from a Committee in the Parliament that are normally not amended by the Political Groups, and that are often adopted in Plenary without modification. It is clear therefore

Following trilogues

A good way to try and keep up with trilogues is to remain in contact with one of the Parliamentary assistants of the MEPs in the Negotiating Team (rapporteur and shadows). Alternatively, you can follow the agendas of Coreper, because you often find points marked 'follow up on trilogue', and although no detail is provided you at least know that the trilogues are happening – and to contact the key actors involved to find out more.

Rule 71 : Negotiations ahead of Parliament's first reading

1. Where a committee has adopted a legislative report pursuant to Rule 51, it may decide, by a majority of its members, to enter into negotiations on the basis of that report.

2. Decisions to enter into negotiations shall be announced at the beginning of the part-session following their adoption in committee. By the end of the day following the announcement in Parliament, Members or a political group or groups reaching at least the medium threshold may request in writing that a committee decision to enter into negotiations be put to the vote. Parliament shall then proceed to that vote during the same part-session.

   If no such request is received by the expiry of the deadline laid down in the first subparagraph, the President shall inform Parliament that this is the case. If a request is made, the President may, immediately prior to the vote, give the floor to one speaker in favour of the committee's decision to enter into negotiations and to one speaker against that decision. Each speaker may make a statement lasting no more than two minutes.

3. If Parliament rejects the committee's decision to enter into negotiations, the draft legislative act and the report of the committee responsible shall be placed on the agenda of the following part-session, and the President shall set a deadline for amendments. Rule 59(4) shall apply.

4. Negotiations may start at any time after the deadline laid down in the first subparagraph of paragraph 2 has expired without a request for a vote in Parliament on the decision to enter into negotiations having been made. If such a request has been made, negotiations may start at any time after the committee decision to enter into negotiations has been approved in Parliament.

that working with the Parliament has to take place *before* it enters into negotiations with the Council, especially as the resulting trilogue agreement could simply be rubber-stamped by the Coordinators meeting, the Committee vote, Political Group week and the Plenary vote.

Having introduced the difficulties that the Parliament faces, it should be underlined that the **Council Presidency also has constraints** – heavy time pressures, difficulties finding agreements in Working Groups and potential problems steering dossiers through Coreper. In addition, the Presidency now only comes around to each Member State once every thirteen-and-a half years, so an incoming Presidency often faces a steep learning curve. It can also be a challenge for a Presidency when it is tasked with negotiating with a coherent delegation from the Parliament that includes long-standing MEPs who were former Ministers, Prime Ministers, etc.

So while the Presidency, representing the Council, is usually able to get an explicit negotiating mandate from Coreper (having been through the Working Group), enjoys internal transparency and is well-placed to know where its limits and lines are, it will also encounter time pressure, internal negotiating problems between Member States and possibly some negotiation imbalances with the Parliament. For example, the interests of the two legislators can be strongly opposed when the drive of a Presidency to conclude a

Presidencies and trilogues

- Presidencies are tempted to try conclude as many dossiers as possible in first reading during their six-month mandate.

- Presidencies need to set priorities – what is feasible in six months (or four months, as Presidencies taking place in the second half of a year can in practice usually only organise negotiations between the end of August and Christmas).

- The Presidency will get in touch with the people it needs to collaborate with (Parliament and Commission) on forthcoming dossiers as soon as possible.

- At the start of the term, the Presidency will meet with the Parliament Committee chairpersons on all OLP files to see how they stand and on which files they are ready to have trilogues.

file at first reading within its Presidency is countered by the desire of the Parliament to take time to consider its position.

Presidencies also have challenges in identifying and driving forward priorities, and agreeing to the substance and mandate they take into negotiations. For the most part these problems can be avoided through the interaction of an incoming Presidency with the Parliament, well before it takes over its role, to discuss what dossiers can be taken forward together.

A final problem that is common to both institutions is that neither the Parliament nor the Council is in fact negotiating with a definitive position, so changes can occur. For example the Parliament negotiators have to steer any agreed text through either/or the Committee, the Political Groups and the Plenary.

It is usually **the Presidency** that **organises the practicalities of trilogues**, such as the venue, the times and the languages to be used – although it must be noted that most trilogues take place in the Parliament (Strasbourg and Brussels). Many trilogues take place in Strasbourg, due to the fact that once a month almost all MEPs are there and usually available (so-called 'Strasbourg weeks'). A good day to organise trilogues in Strasbourg is the Tuesday because it is often the most convenient day of the week for MEPs to find time.

After a trilogue meeting, the Presidency can go back to the Council Working Party or Coreper to report on discussions and, if necessary, get a new negotiating mandate or clarification. These meetings can take place within one week after a trilogue, so a typical trilogue frequency is one meeting every two weeks. Sometimes a Presidency will bring a Minister to trilogues to show the importance that it attaches to a certain dossier, to push negotiations in a specific direction or simply to match the level of seniority presented by the MEPs in the negotiation.

It is also possible that the Presidency could bring along the next Presidency, to ensure a smooth handover. There is a risk that when the next Presidency comes to trilogues it can give the impression that the incumbent Presidency has given up on the file and does not intend or wish to try and finish it (although it can also be a tactic to pressure the Parliament). In addition to the relative ease of getting amended mandates from Coreper, the Presidency, especially from larger Member States, has an additional advantage because it can use its MEPs to get inside information from the Parliament.

A relatively new phenomenon in the world of trilogues is the introduction of **technical trilogues**. At the first **political trilogue**, the institutions agree on the specific paragraphs (line numbers) that are deemed technical, and can be dealt with in special meetings of technical staff – Parliamentary assistants and Political Group staff, the Presidency's national attachés and the Commission desk officers. If there is controversy at the technical trilogue level, individual paragraphs can be sent up in the hierarchy to the political trilogue for further decision-making. In some cases, political agreement is found and announced at the final political trilogue, while technical trilogues can still go on afterwards. It is therefore important to also engage with the participants in technical trilogues and pay attention to what is defined as 'technical' – sometimes it is rather political and/or can have substantial implications.

Although trilogues have been formalised over time, making them more traceable and transparent, there is still a **transparency issue** from a general stakeholder perspective. These informal meetings occur behind closed doors, do not figure on any agenda, do not generate any formal minutes, and only disclose a limited number of documents – so it is difficult to follow them and understand what is happening (before it is too late). Points can be modified, new issues emerge and texts can undergo significant changes, so it is essential to have good contacts within one of the institutions taking part in these meetings: what is agreed in the trilogues has a tendency to be ratified untouched by the respective legislative institutions.

Another way to try and keep up with trilogues is to follow the agendas and minutes of the Parliamentary Committees and Coreper meetings – you will often find points marked 'follow up on trilogue'. Although in the majority of cases very little or no detail is provided, you at least know that the trilogues are happening. The Presidency will typically periodically publish State of Play tables which will show the status of ongoing inter-institutional negotiations. These documents are publicly available in the Council document register.

In Parliament, in oral reports to the Committee meeting and in the minutes of those meetings, you will find relevant information regarding the composition of the Negotiating Team, their mandates, the outcome of discussions, compromise texts and next steps.

The key non-public document used in trilogues is the so called '**four-column document**', an example of which is presented in Table 5.3 on the next page.

Access to trilogue documents

In response to a freedom of information request from a citizen, the European Court of Justice (case T-540/15) ruled in 2018 that Parliament could not restrict public access to four-column documents and cannot only provide partial access. However, the specific case addressed historic documents, and Parliament continues to argue that in the context of 'live' negotiations the 'disclosure of the document would seriously undermine the institution's decision-making process'.

The good news is that there are so many participants in the trilogue room, that it is not that difficult to find someone willing to share a copy of the four-column document and the next trilogue agenda, so you know what issues are going to be discussed.

Table 5.3: Example trilogue four-column document

	Commission	Council	Parliament	Compromise Text
Line – Ref.	*Article 12*	*Article 12*	*Article 12*	*Article 12*
496 – Art. 14b (new)	Text of Commission Proposal	Text of Council position	Text of Parliament position	Text of agreed compromise position [Technical Trilogue]

Source: Own creation generated from variety of four-column documents – this is not a standard format document and each trilogue can use a different variant of something similar to the example presented here

This four-column document forms the basis of discussions and negotiations. With regard to the format, the position of each institution is put into the grid, so that differences and similarities can be highlighted. The obvious prerequisite of the compilation of such a document is that the Parliament and Council have a position in the first place. Once the positions are established, work will begin on column four for a possible compromise text. The final column is also used for other comments and remarks – a kind of commentary or institutional memory for future meetings. It is through this process of trying to complete the compromise text box that the trilogues move towards a final text that can be ratified by both institutions.

A typical trilogue starts by going through the full text to define issues that can be delegated to the technical level, or that can be easily compromised on. As trilogues progress, the list of politically difficult issues becomes shorter and ultimately a degree of horse-trading tends to take place whereby every institution wins some points and loses others.

The dynamics of trilogues within, and between, the Parliament and Council are vital to understand and follow for the simple reason that this is where the majority of compromises come from in Codecision. The success, and institutionalisation, of the trilogue system has brought with it a number of challenges for all the actors involved. It has also increased the risk of the creation of even more informal meetings between the key actors on files. These can be used, for example, to exclude some unwanted actors and to pre-agree certain compromises, making it all the more difficult to keep up with the developments that take place in these meetings.

Whilst this trilogue system is the default for adopting legislation in the first reading stage, it is also a process that continues throughout the further stages of the process should it not prove possible to conclude legislation in the first reading. It is now important to consider what happens to legislation that passes on to the further stages of the Codecision procedure, even though this now happens only in a small minority of cases.

5.5   Ordinary Legislative Procedure: Second reading

The second reading in OLP can lead to one of three possible outcomes:

1. An early second reading agreement in which the Parliament approves the Council first reading position.

2. The Parliament proposing amendments to the Council first reading position, which the Council can either accept (leading to adoption) or not accept (leading to third reading).

3. The Parliament rejecting the Council first reading position, in which case the proposed legislative act lapses.

This section will detail these three possibilities in more detail, starting with the early second reading agreements.

Early Second Reading Agreement

If the Council was not able to agree with all the amendments of the Parliament through the trilogues in first reading, then the Parliament will proceed to its first reading vote and adopt its position. This position will then be forwarded to the Council which will have to proceed to establish its own first reading position with an accompanying statement of reasons which, when accompanied by the Commission's communication is published and transmitted to the Parliament, launching the second reading.

If the Parliament has voted amendments that the Council did not accept in the first reading negotiations, the next chance of agreement in Codecision is an early second reading agreement – but this has to be prepared in the first reading stage. In essence the dynamics of Codecision simply switch from the original attempts of the Council to get its views into the Parliament position, to attempts by the Parliament to get its views into the Council position so that it can lead to a successful early second reading agreement. And it will be the same key actors, again in the trilogues, seeking to further the process. OLP second reading is captured in Figure 5.6 on the next page.

The Parliament and the Council will generally try to avoid having to go to a full second reading because procedurally it changes quite drastically from the first reading. For example, politically sensitive dossiers and major inter-institutional fights will be taken into second reading (along with other issues on which no agreement could be found). As there are no time limits in first reading it is mostly preferable to continue negotiations there rather than pass into second reading, until it becomes evident that there is no possibility of a first reading agreement. This is why further trilogues between the Council and the Parliament frequently take place before the Council adopts its first reading position, in an attempt to find an early second reading agreement.

As this is still in first reading there is no time limit to the continuation of trilogues and discussions to find an agreement that the Parliament can ratify in its second reading. If the Parliament successfully finds a compromise with the Council at the Council's first reading stage by managing, in trilogues, to bridge the difficulties that were not resolved before the Parliament's first reading position was established, the Parliament will send a letter of assurance (from the Chair of the Committee responsible) to the Council to state that it will support the Council position in its second reading.

In this case it will be possible for the Parliament to adopt an early second reading agreement by simply ratifying the Council's position in first reading with no changes at a Plenary session within the three-month (or four-month, see below) deadline (voting by simple majority to accept the Council first reading position). The early stage of the second reading in this case becomes an extension of the first reading. Failing this, there is the more 'classical' full second reading.

Figure 5.6: Second reading of Ordinary Legislative Procedure

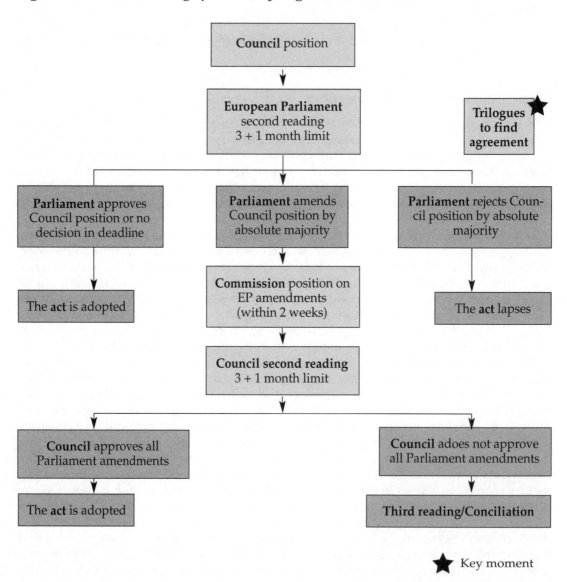

Classical Second Reading

The Parliament has only three months (extendable by one month to a maximum of four, if required) to enact its second reading, which is a very short time limit within which to react. The Treaty provides for the adoption of the Council position should the Parliament fail to deliver an opinion before this deadline, though in practice the Parliament has never missed a deadline.

While the Treaty deadline appears very tight, in reality there is often room for manoeuvre. For example, the second reading only formally starts when the President of the Parliament announces the Council position in a Plenary session, having received the Council position in all its working languages. There is often, therefore, a period of a month (or months) between Council adoption of its position and the formal start of second reading. This period can be used for very informal contacts between the Council Presidency and the rapporteur, with or without the Commission, but not for trilogues as such, to advance the work on finding a compromise.

The Parliament does have the option of extending the second reading by an extra month, on the request of the Committee responsible chairperson, if this is required (Article 294 TFEU, Rule 64 Parliament RoP). Early second reading agreements in the 2014–2019 legislature represented 10% of Codecision agreements (the majority of which were closed in first reading due to the elections), and the full second reading representing a further 1%, and with the average time for a full second reading agreement at 40 months.

In second reading it is only the Committee responsible that continues with a file within the Parliament. Any opinion-giving Committees that were consulted in first reading are no longer included. It is also usually the same rapporteur from first reading who continues with the file unless the reason to close the first reading was that the EP went into elections, and the rapporteur was not re-elected.

Trilogues will then continue as they did in first reading (although the Presidency will usually have changed between readings).

It is theoretically possible at this stage, if the Parliament has real objections to the Council position, that the Parliament rejects the Council position (by absolute majority), in which case the legislative proposal lapses, but this has not happened in the previous Parliamentary mandate (2014–2019).

If there was no early second reading agreement, or an outright rejection of the Council position, the final possibility in second reading is that the Parliament, within the three months (maximum four) allowed, proposes amendments to the Council position (by absolute majority), in which case it is forwarded to the Council for its second reading.

The tabling of amendments in second reading is subject to strict admissibility criteria which severely restrict the room for manoeuvre and the discussions that take place in second reading. **Second reading amendments are only admissible** if:

1. They seek to restore, wholly or partly, a position adopted by Parliament in first reading.

2. They seek to amend a part of the text of the Council's position

Second reading

In second reading the debate becomes inter-institutional and the room for new elements is very limited.

Second reading requires an understanding of the first reading, of the issues that were raised then, and the political sensitivities around them.

which was not included in, or that differs in content from, the proposal submitted in first reading.

3. They seek to take into account a new fact or legal situation which has arisen since the first reading (such as an election for the Parliament).

4. They are a compromise deal between the Council and Parliament.

These amendments are all subject to absolute majority in the Plenary which, as Chapter 3 stressed, is very difficult to attain.

These strict conditions on a second reading amendment, in terms of content and voting rules, have very important consequences for the Codecision procedure, notably because amendments focus on the key differences between the positions of the Council and the Parliament.

While in first reading there are many more amendments due to the less strict admissibility criteria and the fact that a simple majority can carry them through Plenary, it is often true that many amendments are simply 'Christmas tree amendments' – there is something for everybody. In second reading, in contrast, the admissibility criteria restrict what can be tabled and the absolute majority voting rule ensures that only serious amendments with a chance of support will be tabled. While the theory is that new, or different, issues are not introduced at this stage it is not unusual that the Parliament tries to introduce new amendments – though for the most part the rules above are well-adhered to.

The discussions in second reading will therefore focus on the sticking points inherited from first reading, issues that the Parliament will likely have already debated. The fact that the Parliament also has to vote by absolute majority at second reading means there are significantly fewer amendments tabled, and those that are tabled carry heavy political and institutional weight. As a result of these content and voting limitations and the fact that the Council position stands unchanged if the Parliament does nothing in its allotted 3-4 months, the latter has never failed to meet these tight deadlines.

The **Commission** prepares its opinion on the Parliament's second reading position and plays a crucial role by giving an opinion on all Parliament amendments before the Plenary vote – exactly as it did in first reading. Again the importance of this stage is that if the Commission opposes a Parliament amendment, and it is voted by the Parliament, this will oblige the Council to vote by unanimity on this amendment in its second reading. This is again not to be taken lightly as unanimity is an onerous voting requirement in the Council.

The Commission position is reviewed and ultimately agreed by the GRI, and then the College, as was outlined earlier. The Commission will go to the Plenary of the Parliament before the vote on amendments to state which ones it is able to accept in full, or partially, and which not.

This Parliament position, with its voted amendments, is forwarded to the Council for their three (max. four) months second reading. **The Council at this stage only has two choices**:

1. To accept all the amendments tabled by the Parliament, which is something that again will have been pre-agreed in a trilogue meeting before the vote of the Parliament. In this case the act is adopted.

2. If, however, the Council is unable to approve all the Parliament's amendments it will inform the Parliament that it has not accepted its position. Consequently, the President of the Council, in agreement with the President of the Parliament, will convene a meeting of the **Conciliation Committee** within six weeks (which may be extended by two weeks). This is the beginning of the third reading. An important point at this stage is the fact that the Council usually does not indicate to the Parliament which amendments it has not supported in the Parliament's second reading position, as this is not a formal requirement laid down by the Treaty. The Council does this to maximise its negotiating position in the subsequent third reading, although the previous trilogue meetings will have usually made all the points of discord clear.

The second reading stage of Codecision is therefore, as we have seen, very different to the first reading. The procedure is similar, and the use of trilogues (with the same actors) remains, but it is the time limit, amendment admissibility rules and voting changes that constrain discussions to only the most important inter-institutional points of discord.

5.6   Ordinary Legislative Procedure: Third reading/Conciliation

For the sake of completeness, we will describe the third reading (conciliation) phase in detail, even though the number of third readings has steadily gone down, from 5% in 2004–2009 to 2% in 2009–2014. **Since 2014, no third readings have taken place**.

When the Council and the Parliament do not manage to come to an agreement in second reading, the institutions have to go through a third and final reading which can effectively be split into three distinct stages:

1. **Stage 1:** Council second reading can be used to prepare for third reading if it is by this stage obvious that no agreement can be found in second reading.

2. **Stage 2:** The convening of and the actual meetings of the Conciliation Committee and the Conciliation trilogues that prepare their work.

3. **Stage 3:** The approval of any joint text agreed within the Conciliation Committee.

This means, in reality, that third reading is actually three stages of six to eight weeks to find an agreement. This section will detail each of these three stages in turn.

Stage 1: Informally, third reading starts as soon as the Council knows in second reading that it will not be able to find an agreement with the Parliament. This allows extra time to prepare what are usually very difficult negotiations.

Stage 2: The second stage in the third reading process concerns the convening of the Conciliation Committee, which should happen within six, or if necessary eight weeks from the time of the Council's formal decision to reject the Parliaments second reading position. Once the first formal Conciliation Committee meeting takes place the Committee is deemed to have been convened and the formal six to eight weeks of negotiations start. The first six to eight weeks are spent preparing the negotiations that will take place within, and between, the three institutions in the second phase, so here again there are a series of trilogues that bring together small teams of negotiators from the institutions. The delegations are usually as shown in the boxes below.

Parliament delegation – 28

- **Chair** 1 of 3 Vice-Presidents responsible for Conciliation (all in delegation)
- **rapporteur** and **Chair** of the Committee responsible
- 23 other MEPs, mainly from Committee responsible

The composition of the whole delegation must reflect the political balance of the Parliament

Council delegation – 28•

- **Chair**: Minister or Secretary of State from Presidency
- **Coreper I or II**

Commission

- **Commissioner** + support staff

The Commission is there to help 'reconcile' positions

These are the delegations that will take part in the full Conciliation Committee that has to take the final decisions on a text. It is, however, much like first and second readings because it is again within the reduced trilogues that the text will be elaborated. In these conciliation specific trilogues it has been usual to have:

1. The chairperson of Coreper and the chairperson of the Working Party from the Council.

2. The Director-General or Director, and experts from the Commission.

3. The Vice-President of the Parliament heading the Parliament delegation, the Committee chairperson and the rapporteur from the Parliament.

This reduced group will try to agree on a compromise text to be presented to the full Conciliation Committee, as outlined above. They will usually have started their meetings during the second reading stage as identified earlier, meaning that they will be advanced before the six to eight week preparation phase during which the full Conciliation Committee has to be convened. Any agreement that comes from these discussions is usually a delicate package that has been laboriously negotiated. Remember that if a file has arrived in Conciliation it has not proved possible to find agreement at either first or second reading, meaning that positions will be well entrenched.

If an agreement is found within these conciliation trilogue discussions, it will be presented to the two legislator delegations individually, not as a whole Committee. The Council delegation votes by qualified majority and the Parliament delegation by simple majority. It is possible that one, or both, Conciliation delegations will reject the text.

Stage 3: If an agreement on a joint text has been reached in the Conciliation Committee there is an exchange of letters between the co-Chairs of the Conciliation Committee. From here the General Secretariat of the Council, or the Parliament Secretariat, will prepare the draft legislative text to be forwarded to the Presidents of the Parliament and Council.

Figure 5.7: Third reading/Conciliation of Ordinary Legislative Procedure

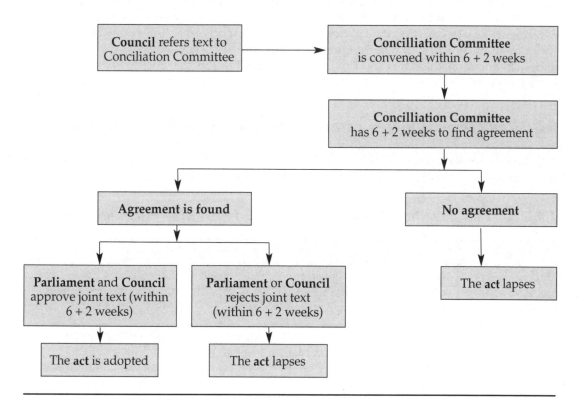

The text will be accompanied by a letter signed by both co-Chairs of the Conciliation Committee. The letter will outline any important statements that were made and that need to be taken into account in the final stage of the third reading, which is the votes on the joint text by the two legislators. This stage of the procedure is limited to six to eight weeks. The Council must adopt the text by qualified majority and the Parliament by simple majority: they are both simple accept or reject votes (i.e. there is no chance to make amendments).

For the Council, this stage has never posed any problems because the delegation of the Council to Conciliation is usually Coreper, and when they have agreed to the joint text in Conciliation they have always approved it afterwards within the Council. For the Parliament the situation is more complicated because the 28-strong delegation to Conciliation is not necessarily representative of the position of the full Plenary. For example a small majority in the Parliament Conciliation Committee vote (simple majority) may not turn out to be a majority in the Plenary.

The Paradox of Transparency

The lack of transparency of the Conciliation Procedure highlights a paradox in the OLP. Council meetings, for legislative files, and Parliament Committee and Plenary meetings are all screened live on the internet. The main arena for compromises and decisions, however, is that of trilogues – which remain totally outside of any public scrutiny.

For the rare dossiers that arrive in Conciliation it is very difficult to follow proceedings as they take place within the restricted trilogues. Of all the parts of the OLP the Conciliation stage has been the least transparent and the most difficult to work with. All of the meetings take place behind closed doors and there are no public information sources on the content or direction of negotiations because there are no minutes or summaries published. In addition, the dates and times of these Conciliation trilogues are difficult to find out in advance so it is not easy to know when the negotiations are happening.

5.7 Key stages and key actors – Ordinary Legislative Procedure

Like previous chapters, this one ends with a table of the main stages and actors in Codecision, along with key comments. The key stages and actors are in Table 5.4.

Table 5.4: Key stages and key actors: Ordinary Legislative Procedure

Key stage	Comment	Key actors
Preparation of legislative proposal	The Commission has the right of initiative and changes to Commission texts require significant majorities within and between the legislators.	Unit within Commission Commissioner Cabinets (see Chapter 1)
Opinions of national parliaments, CoR, EESC	Whilst none of these opinions are binding, the discussions and ideas can easily transfer to the legislators therefore they need to be monitored carefully.	Opinion rapporteurs for both CoR and EESC European Committees of national parliaments (see Chapter 4)
First reading Parliament Committee Council Working Party & Coreper	Whilst Parliament acts first, the Council deliberates at the same time – making it essential to monitor and work with both at once. The formal processes are quite straightforward to follow, although it is easier to access documents and discussions of the Parliament. Each institution needs to be engaged with to build into their position, notably their negotiating mandate for the next stage.	Parliament Committee: Rapporteur Shadow rapporteurs Group coordinators Opinion-giving Committee (see Chapter 3) Council Working Party and Coreper Commission DG, SG and GRI

Key stage	Comment	Key actors
Trilogues Valid for all stages of Codecision hereafter. Trilogues continue until an agreement can, or cannot, be reached	The key forums for inter-institutional negotiations, where the legislators work with their respective mandates to find a compromise text. It is relatively difficult to find information on trilogues, especially ongoing ones. Knowing who sits in them is one way to access information. The key document here is the four- column document that is used to find agreement.	EP: Rapporteur, shadows of Political Groups and Committee Chair (presides the meetings) Council: Working Group chair, Perm Rep or Deputy Perm Rep Commission: officials from DG + SG/Legal Service possible
First reading – Plenary	Any agreement from a trilogue has to be passed by the competent Committee and the Plenary vote (simple majority). Note that pre-agreed trilogue compromises usually get ratified without change.	Rapporteur Shadow rapporteurs Group coordinators Political Groups
First reading – Council	In 89% of cases (2014-2019 data) the Council approves the Parliament position, usually as an A item on the Council agenda. The Council can also vote by **QMV** unless the Commission did not accept EP amendments, in which case the Council votes by **unanimity** on those amendments. If the Council does not agree with the Parliament position then working with the Presidency on the Council position is the objective of all stakeholders, including of course the Parliament.	Presidency Key Member States *If required:* Rapporteur Shadows Key MEPs Commission
Second reading – Parliament Early Second Reading Agreement Classical Second Reading	In 10% of cases (2014–2019 data), the Parliament approves the Council position with no changes. In other cases (1%) it will be necessary to go back to all the key positions from first reading – noting that now there are strict time-limits, amendment admissibility and voting rules, making it more difficult to reach agreement in second reading. The Parliament votes by **absolute majority** of its members.	Parliament Committee: Rapporteur and shadows Coordinators Political Groups

Key stage	Comment	Key actors
Second reading – Council	The Council in second reading only has two possibilities; to agree to the Parliament text with no changes, or to reject the Parliament position. This leaves very little room to work with the Council. The Council votes by **QMV** unless the Commission does not accept EP amendments, in which case the Council votes by **unanimity**.	Presidency Member States Commission
Third Reading Council Second Reading prepares third reading Conciliation Committee and trilogues Votes on joint text by both legislators	Third reading (none in 2014-19 legislature) has three phases as outlined below – but all three are very difficult to engage with, find out about or influence because the battle lines have already been well drawn at the first and second reading stages. 1. Preparation/Negotiation in trilogues 2. Discussion at the Conciliation Committee 3. Ratification in Parliament and Council	EP: Rapporteur and Chair of Committee responsible Vice-Presidents responsible for Conciliation Council: Minister or Secretary of State from Presidency Coreper I and II Commission: Commissioner Support staff

6. Delegated and Implementing Acts

By Alan Hardacre, Michael Kaeding and Sabina Lange

The second category of decision-making that needs to be considered is that of non-legislative acts, which can be either 'Delegated Acts' (Article 290 TFEU) or 'Implementing Acts' (Article 291 TFEU). These two articles of the TFEU introduced major changes to the old system of **Comitology**, creating two new worlds of executive powers for the Commission.

This level of decision-making can be seen with reference to Figure 5.1 (at the start of the previous chapter) where Delegated and Implementing Acts ('D&I Acts') come as 'Level 2' in the typology of EU legal norms.

It is almost impossible to work in, or with, Brussels these days and not come across a reference to D&I Acts or Comitology (see box for clarity on terminology) – it seems to be everywhere. Comitology developed a longstanding reputation as an opaque procedure that was difficult to understand, follow and find out about, let alone work with. This reputation has been changing slowly due to innovations in transparency, the growing involvement of the Parliament and an increasing awareness on behalf of stakeholders that D&I Acts are something that they simply have to engage with. The Treaty of Lisbon, which represented the latest in a long line of adaptations to the Comitology system, was without doubt the most significant reform there has been in terms of legal basis, procedures, institutional balance and

From Comitology to D&I Acts

Comitology is the name given to a system of Committees developed in the 1960s made up of representatives of the Member States, chaired by the Commission. Their job is to assist (and control) the Commission as it drafts implementing measures on technical aspects of EU legislation. Examples include:

- Taking decisions on the detail of the implementation of legislation.
- Taking decisions to implement EU policies, such as how much to spend on what.
- Taking decisions to adapt or update EU legislation in order to take account of technical or scientific developments.

Changing name?

The Treaty of Lisbon created two routes for implementing legislation at the EU level. One of them (Delegated Acts) no longer uses Committees, making the use of the term Comitology partly redundant. This chapter will therefore refer to Delegated and Implementing Acts (D&I Acts), when discussing the post-Lisbon system and to Comitology when recalling the pre-Lisbon system.

openness for interested stakeholders. The last decade or so has thus been marked by the efforts to consolidate this reform. But first, what exactly does Comitology or D&I Acts refer to and why do we hear so much about it?

D&I Acts are all about the **Council** and **Parliament**, the legislators, **delegating tasks to the Commission in secondary legislation** (the process of which was described in the previous chapter). This is the EU equivalent of systems that exist in all EU Member States whereby during the course of agreeing legislation the executive is granted powers to implement or change the legislation – powers which it can subsequently use to propose subordinate legally binding measures. It is therefore indispensable to understand the two systems of D&I Acts.

This chapter will start with a short recap of why the legislators delegate tasks to the Commission. It will then address why and how Comitology has become so important for all stakeholders interested in European Union decision-making. The chapter will then outline the two categories of D&I Acts in turn. These sections will explain in detail what D&I Acts are and how the decision-making procedures work.

The key facts on the D&I Acts can be found below in Table 6.1.

Table 6.1: Delegated and Implementing Acts – Key facts

Names:	Comitology Delegated & Implementing Acts since 2009
Established:	Informally: 1961
Formally:	Single European Act (entry into force 1987) Article 290 TFEU – Delegated Acts – Common Understanding Article 291 TFEU – Implementing Acts – Regulation
Key actors:	European Commission, European Parliament, Council, Comitology Committees, Expert Groups, Agencies
No. Committees:	2018 – 275
No. meetings:	2018 – 718
No. Implementing Acts:	2019 – 1,656
No. Delegated Acts:	2019 – 156
No. Regulatory Procedure with Scrutiny:	2019 – 91
Procedures:	*Delegated Acts (DA)* 1. Commission prepares, drafts and adopts Delegated Act 2. Commission presents adopted, but not yet published act directly to EP & Council 3. EP and Council have a period of time (usually two months) to object (or not) 4. If no objection, act enters into force 5. EP (absolute majority) or Council (QMV) can object to an individual act (on any grounds); the Commission repeals the act

6. EP (absolute majority) or Council (QMV) can revoke (partially or fully) the delegation of powers to the Commission

Procedures:

Implementing Acts (IA)
1. Commission prepares and drafts Implementing Act
2. Commission presents draft act to Comitology Committee
3. Committee (Member State representatives) negotiates the act
4. Committee votes according to one of two procedures:
    – Advisory (Simply majority, non-binding)
    – Examination (QMV, rules for voting in the Council apply)
If Committee approves act by QMV, or has 'no opinion' and no further restrictions apply – Commission adopts the act
If Committee rejects the draft act by QMV, or has 'no opinion' and further restrictions apply – a draft sent to Appeal Committee or the revised draft sent again to the Committee, or act not adopted

Procedures:

Regulatory Procedure with Scrutiny measures (RPS/PRAC)
1. Commission prepares and drafts the measure
2. Commission presents draft act to Comitology Committee
3. Committee (Member State representatives) negotiates the act
4. Committee, following the Regulatory procedure with scrutiny votes:
If Committee approves the measure by QMV the scrutiny by the EP and the Council follows. If they do not oppose the measure, Commission adopts it.
If either the EP or the Council opposes the measure, the Commission must not adopt it. It may present a new draft to the Committee or a new legislative proposal to the legislators.
If Committee does not approve the measure (QMV against it) or has 'no opinion' the Council acts first. If the Council adopts the measure, the Commission may present a new draft to the Council or a new legislative proposal to the legislators.
If the Council envisages to adopt the measure or it does not act, the EP scrutinises the measure.
If the EP opposes the measure, the Commission may resubmit a new draft to the Committee or a new legislative proposal to the legislators.
If the EP does not oppose the measure, Council or Commission may adopt it.

Comitology rose from very obscure beginnings in the agricultural markets in the 1960s to gaining ever-increasing importance and visibility in EU policy-making. It evolved from the delegation of tasks to the Commission such as setting prices and fixing export restitutions in the 1960s. The Commission is now (also) delegated far more sensitive tasks such as supplementing and amending technical annexes of legislation, for example in the Financial Services or Environment policy areas. It is this changing nature of the tasks delegated to the Commission that has required numerous modifications to the decision-making procedures used for the Commission to adopt its Comitology measures, the latest of which was the Treaty of Lisbon and the introduction of D&I Acts.

This introduction of D&I Acts split the ´Comitology world´ into two parts and each has a very different procedure for taking a decision. A **Common Understanding on Delegated Acts** and a **Regulation on Implementing Acts** were negotiated under the Spanish and Belgian Presidencies in 2010 to bring these two new systems fully into force. Parts of the Common Understanding referring to the Commission's preparation of Delegated Acts were later renegotiated and attached to a 2016 **Inter-institutional Agreement on Better Law-Making**. We will see later in the chapter that Delegated Acts are a sharp deviation from the past practice of Comitology, whereas Implementing Acts are the continuation of the 'traditional' Comitology system.

From Table 6.1 we can also notice that D&I Acts involve a significant number of actors, meetings, and ultimately implementing measures. Even with the number of adopted Implementing Acts per year in the last decade dropping, there were still 1,556 Implementing Acts, 156 Delegated Acts and 91 Regulatory Procedure with Scrutiny (RPS, explained below) measures adopted in 2019 – a large number of legal acts with important consequences. It has been, and is increasingly, a crucial decision-making arena of the EU, not only because of this large volume, but more importantly because of the fact that many of these acts have important localised impacts and implications: the devil is often in the detail.

A legislative act, as developed and adopted in Codecision/Ordinary Legislative Procedure (OLP), might frame overall objectives and the broad structure to achieve these, but it is through D&I Acts that the details will be fleshed out – and it is here that many stakeholders will see their interests directly impacted. For example, a chemical company will be impacted by secondary legislation on the quality of the environment, but it will be more impacted by a Delegated Act that bans specific chemical substance from the EU market. It is for this reason that stakeholders need to be able to work with D&I Acts in the same way, and with the same confidence, that they work with the OLP.

Figure 6.1 displays the process of delegating powers to the Commission.

The Lisbon Treaty stipulates that Member States shall adopt all measures of national law necessary to implement legally binding Union acts. But the Council, along with Parliament in cases under OLP, can decide to delegate certain powers to the Commission to either implement or further specify the legislative act. With the Lisbon Treaty this can be done in two different ways: Delegated Acts and Implementing Acts. These two categories represent two different types of tasks and two different procedures for taking decisions once these tasks have been delegated to the Commission:

1. Firstly, supplementing and amending non-essential elements of legislation.

2. Secondly, purely implementing the provisions of the legislation.

Figure 6.1: Delegating executive powers to the Commission

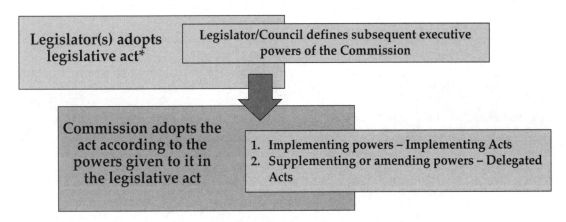

* Note: *Provisions for adoption of Implementing Acts may also be contained in legally binding acts which are not legislative, i.e. those that are not adopted in accordance with a legislative procedure, but are adopted by the Council on a proposal by the Commission.*

These two categories of powers can be delegated to the Commission and form the basis of this chapter's discussions of D&I Acts.

Before looking at why we have such an extensive system of D&I Acts it is important to clarify an often neglected point: D&I Acts need to be engaged with **throughout** the EU policy-making cycle and not just when it comes to the Commission stage of presenting an individual D&I Act. This can be seen more clearly in Figure 6.2 on the next page.

The D&I Acts procedures are decision-making procedures with the objective of applying or specifying particular technical matters of EU legislation that were agreed by the co-legislators. From a sequential perspective, D&I Acts come at the end of the EU policy cycle as seen in Figure 6.2, but practically speaking D&I Acts will already have formed part of the negotiations between the co-legislators and their scope will have been subject to discussions within the Commission when presenting their legislative proposal.

It is therefore crucial to highlight that all D&I Acts will have:

1. **Been framed by the Commission in its legislative proposal** – meaning that at least some aspects of future D&I Acts were likely discussed in Commission Expert Groups, within the Commission Inter-Service Consultation (ISC) and with stakeholders via consultation (formal and informal). The resulting D&I Acts dispositions in the legislative proposal are the ones that the Commission will have found to be the most suitable to undertake the tasks identified and in line with past practice.

Figure 6.2: D&I Acts in the EU policy cycle

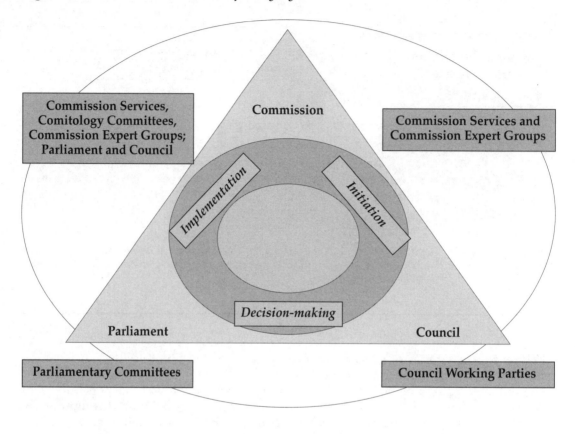

2. **Been subject to negotiation in OLP**. The Treaty of Lisbon limits the Commission's
   executive power and tasks the legislator with specifying the powers delegated to
   it. Legislators therefore take a very keen interest in the tasks delegated to the Commission and their oversight of these tasks. Given different powers given to the three
   institutions when adopting delegated or implementing acts, it is only natural that
   D&I Acts are often subject to OLP negotiations.

Since D&I Acts are present in most legislative acts they are a practically constant subject
of discussion in legislative preparation and decision-making. This means that, firstly, it
is essential to work on D&I Acts throughout the whole policy-making cycle and that,
secondly, working with a legislative file will often involve an appreciation of the D&I
Acts elements within it.

Having outlined the key elements of D&I Acts and the importance they play throughout the EU policy cycle it is now useful to address the question of why Council and Parliament delegate executive powers to the Commission in the first place.

6.1 Why do the legislators delegate executive powers to the Commission?

At the EU level executive powers are delegated to the executive (Commission) by the legislator(s) (Council and Parliament) for a number of important reasons. These come down to the following:

1. Speed and flexibility

Making adjustments to, or implementing, legislation through D&I Acts takes, on average, a few months (or a few days in exceptional cases). This is much faster than the OLP, which had an average for first reading just below 18 months for the 2014– 2019 legislative period. The EU therefore can keep up with events, science and markets by implementing legislation that responds to circumstances effectively and in a timely manner.

2. Efficiency

The D&I system is more flexible than the legislative procedures in terms of time-lines, obligations, etc. Technical expertise is provided by Member State specialists who assist the Commission in the drafting of its acts based on their respective national experiences – an exercise that subsequently facilitates implementation by the national capitals.

3. Technical nature of work

D&I Acts concern technical aspects of legislation. The Commission will draft the acts but will be assisted by Member States and other sources of expertise (Expert Groups, EU Agencies, etc.). The D&I decision-making procedures allow the legislators to concentrate on their core legislative work and move technical work to the level of technical experts, where updates can be adopted more quickly and with greater ease.

4. Oversight and control

D&I Acts are also about Member State control over the Commission while it is exercising the powers delegated to it. In essence, there are a series of different decision-making procedures for the approval of Commission drafted acts, with increasing oversight and control by Member States or by the legislators the more sensitive and political the acts become.

This oversight and control is in particular a counter-balance to the first two points. Speed, flexibility and efficiency are crucial for the EU to get the right information into D&I Acts to be able to respond to policy challenges, markets, events, science, etc. However, there needs to be a political oversight mechanism to ensure this works properly and within the agreed legal boundaries.

The first two reasons were sufficient for Comitology to spread very quickly over the last decades, and across policy areas, such that now there is virtually no area of EU activity that does not have some D&I Acts. This fact is highlighted in Table 6.2 on the next page.

Table 6.2: **Number of Comitology Committees in selected policy**
sectors in 2018

Policy sector	2018
Internal Market, Industry, Entrepreneurship and SMEs (GROW)	44
Environment (ENV)	30
Health and Food Safety (SANTE)	17
Agriculture and Rural Development (AGRI)	11
Mobility and Transport (MOVE)	31
Taxation and Customs Union (TAXUD)	13
Research and Innovation (RTD)	7
Trade (TRADE)	14
Other	108
Total	275
Source: Report of the Commission on the working of Committees COM (2019) 638 final.	

Table 6.2 shows the number of Comitology Committees by policy sector. In some policy areas the Committees are highly specialised while in others, where there is a lower number of Committees, they have a broader mandate.

It is worth bearing in mind a couple of things at this stage. Firstly, a Comitology Committee is established by a legal act, the secondary legislation, so all of the Committees above have a legal basis.

The second thing to be aware of is that a legislative act can refer to an existing Committee if the tasks delegated by the legislation are similar (or the same) as tasks delegated by other pieces of legislation. One Committee can therefore be dealing with several legislative acts at once, a fact that makes the statistics in Table 6.2 a little misleading because the number of Committees is no indicator of the volume of work, or the nature of the actual decisions being taken. The number of meetings and written procedures as well as number of adopted acts varies significantly between policy areas (defined as the policy areas of the Commission's Directorates-General since the data are taken from the Commission's reporting). This is reflected in Table 6.3, which shows the number of Implementing Acts adopted per sector.

Table 6.3 shows Health and Food Safety (SANTE) led by a wide margin in the number of Implementing Acts adopted in 2018, even though it had, as seen in Table 6.2, only 17 Committees in place. Research and Innovation (RTD) came a distant second, though this was achieved with only 7 Committees, and Agriculture and Rural Development, which led the table in the past, came third. In contrast Environment (ENV) and Internal Market, Industry, Entrepreneurship and SMEs (GROW), with 30 and 44 Committees respectively, have far fewer meetings and written procedures and adopt only a small fraction of the Implementing Acts.

Table 6.3: **Number of adopted Implementing Acts by selected policy sector in 2018**

Policy sector	2018
Internal Market, Industry, Entrepreneurship and SMEs (GROW)	53
Environment (ENV)	14
Health and Food Safety (SANTE)	603
Agriculture and Rural Development (AGRI)	145
Mobility and Transport (MOVE)	57
Taxation and Customs Union (TAXUD)	57
Research and Innovation (RTD)	159
Trade (TRADE)	52
Other	316
Total	1,456
Source: Report of the Commission on the working of Committees COM (2019) 638 final.	

6.2 The rise and spread of Comitology

The history of Comitology has been characterised by inter-institutional tensions and by changes in legal basis, procedures and institutional roles. Comitology was not foreseen in the original Treaty of Rome, something that caused the Council a few headaches when it had to start implementing the **Common Agricultural Policy (CAP)** at the beginning of the 1960s. Implementing the CAP required the regular setting of prices, tariffs and quotas, which due to the legal architecture of the Treaty of Rome had to be done by the legislator, the Council. The Commission seized the initiative in 1961 and proposed to the Council that it should delegate these technical executive tasks to the Commission as this was the classical role of an executive. The Council was only too happy to agree to such delegation of tasks, but only on the condition that one representative of each Member State, in a Committee, could check the measures that the Commission was proposing: this was the birth of the Comitology system whereby the Commission was granted the power to adopt technical implementing measures under the control of these Member State Committees.

This was in many senses a natural development because aspects of EU legislation needed to be implemented at the EU level and this practice was already well enshrined in Member States and their executive branches.

The new Committees proved to be very successful fora for cooperation between the Commission and Member States, and they spread quickly through the field of agriculture as the CAP was expanded and deepened. In the 1970s and 1980s, as the Community project spread into new areas and continued to develop, these Committees likewise spread across policy areas.

This growth in the number and functioning of Committees did not, however, take place in any systematic way with, for example, horizontal rules.

Due to this there were many different variations of Comitology Committee procedures. At this time there was also no centralised record of how many Committees there were, what decisions they were taking and how they operated; this effort would not come until much later. There were also no horizontal rules about what types of tasks were delegated to the Commission, and as Comitology covered many policy areas there had been evident moves away from the straightforward technical measures of the 1960s.

From Comitology to D&I Acts

1961	First Committee starts work in field of CAP
1970	Köster case at ECJ validates practice of Comitology
1970s	Expansion of Committee system
1987	Single European Act gives legal basis (Article 145 EEC)
1987	First Comitology Decision
1999	Treaty of Amsterdam gives new legal basis (Article 202 TEC)
1999	Second Comitology Decision
2006	Third Comitology Decision
2009	Treaty of Lisbon Articles 290 and 291 TFEU

It was not until 1987, and the entry into force of the **Single European Act**, that Comitology was given formal legal recognition, through Article 145 EEC. This came some 26 years after the first Committee started working, and some 17 years after the landmark Köster case in which the European Court of Justice legitimised the Comitology system in 1970 in the face of a claim that it was not legal and disturbed the institutional balance. Back in 1987, Article 145 of the Single European Act required secondary legislation to set out, for the first time, some horizontal Comitology procedures. The Council adopted a Decision, later in 1987, which created seven different procedures. The different procedures were rather complicated, and in addition, the Parliament had no role at all in the new system until 1992.

In 1992 the **Treaty of Maastricht** created the **Codecision procedure** which vastly increased the powers of the Parliament in adopting legislation. This development set the stage for a series of inter-institutional clashes over the Parliament's role in Comitology. Simply put, the Parliament wanted a role that was proportionate with its role in Codecision. If the Parliament delegated tasks that were sensitive, it wanted the right to make sure they were being dealt with correctly, otherwise the Parliament could be circumvented by using Comitology.

These tensions were only partially resolved in 1999 with a new **Comitology Decision**, which represents the basis for much of what we see, and understand, in Implementing Acts. It reduced the number of procedures from seven to three; it created Rules of Procedure for Committees; it created an obligation for the Commission to issue an annual Comitology report; and finally it increased the rights of the Parliament. These changes were almost entirely driven by the Parliament and its desire to find out what was happening in Comitology and to get involved. In part the Parliament was waging a symbolic fight with the Council to have equal status as a legislator.

The power granted to the Parliament in 1999 was **the right of scrutiny** (which is described in more detail later in this chapter). This was only a meagre power. A series of inter-institutional tensions and a political crisis over the non-transmission of Comitology documents from the Commission to the Parliament in 2005, as well as the failure of the Constitutional Treaty led to further calls for reform from which a new Comitology Decision arose in 2006.

'Old' Comitology procedures (1999/468/EC as amended by 2006/512/EC)	
Article 3	Advisory procedure
Article 4	Management procedure
Article 5	Regulatory procedure
Article 5a	Regulatory procedure with scrutiny
Article 6	Safeguard procedure

The 2006 revised Comitology Decision added one new procedure, the **Regulatory Procedure with Scrutiny (RPS)**, to grant the Parliament more rights in the Comitology system on measures that were co-decided by it and deemed to be more sensitive (quasi-legislative). At this stage, therefore, under the new Decision there were five different Comitology procedures, all of which engendered the use of a Comitology Committee: Advisory, Management, Regulatory, RPS and the Safeguard procedure. The new RPS granted the Parliament increased powers over a very specific category of implementing measures – those deemed to be the most sensitive and quasi-legislative.

These Comitology procedures were a mechanism to create different levels of control for different types of implementing measures, with more control for those that were more sensitive for the legislators. This brings us to two fundamental questions in Comitology that relate to the procedures and the differing levels of control required by the legislators. Firstly, what are technical and more politically sensitive Implementing Acts and how should they be dealt with; and, secondly, how much should the efficiency of the system be compromised by political oversight and control?

There is in fact no definitive answer to these questions. In the first case, on whether a measure is political or technical, it is always the prerogative of the legislators to decide in the legislative act. While the legislators retain this right, what has become apparent over the years is that there are clearly different categories of tasks being delegated to the Commission – including a grey zone between what is technical and political. It is clear that deciding on the price of an export restitution for barley should not be treated in the same way as modifying an annex of banned substances in the field of the environment.

The second issue is whether the system of deciding implementing measures should lean more towards efficiency in terms of getting measures decided in an appropriate timeframe, or towards legitimacy such that all decisions taken are carefully checked by the legislators to make sure the system is not being abused.

These two questions have framed the debate on Comitology for many years and the system that has been created with Lisbon is the latest attempt to answer them. Let us therefore now consider these two issues in more detail.

The two boxes on the next page highlight the two key questions outlined earlier. Both of these questions have a major influence on the decision-making procedures that have developed for adopting D&I Acts.

Technical or Political?

Comitology in the early days was purely concerned with technical matters. Over time, however, it has taken on more and more quasi-legislative tasks i.e. ones that could have been dealt with by the legislators. The issue of technical or political is at the heart of D&I Acts – essentially at the OLP phase when the legislators have to decide whether to use an Implementing (pure implementation) or a Delegated (amend/modify) Act or to take the decisions in OLP themselves.

Efficiency or Legitimacy?

When matters were purely technical, the legislators required very little control over the Commission. This allowed measures to be taken very quickly. Over time, as more areas came under Comitology, and as the measures became increasingly quasi-legislative, there was a call for more control and legitimacy of the system. This increased control takes time, making the system of D&I Acts less efficient in terms of speed.

Examples of technical and political matters in the boxes below will help complete our understanding of what D&I Acts are.

Example: Technical matter

Policy area:	Common Agricultural Policy
Issue:	A price needs setting.
Technical or political:	The Commission is simply implementing the provisions of the legislative act. This is a very straightforward technical matter (which does not mean it is not important).
Control and oversight:	The Commission act does not need to be subject to a scrutiny by legislator because the Commission is taking a technical decision based on previously defined criteria. The use of a Comitology Committee is sufficient (it is an Implementing Act).
Other examples:	Market authorisations, allocation of grants.

The Commission implements and applies the legislative act respectively.

Example: Political matter

Policy area:	Air Safety.
Issue:	Establish the criteria for a 'Black List' of air companies that cannot fly into, or over, EU airspace. The list of individual air companies is established by implementing the criteria that all airlines have to comply with.
Technical or political:	Because of technical and scientific progress the criteria for the list might need to be updated regularly. It is however a question of policy to have the criteria updated and the legislators' choice to delegate the power to do so to the Commission.
Control and oversight:	This is very sensitive and has important impacts. The legislators require significant oversight and control in return for delegating the power to the Commission (it is a Delegated Act)
Other examples:	Adaptation of annexes, definitions of minimum/maximum requirements.

The Commission supplements or amends non-essential elements of the legislative act.

6.3   *The Treaty of Lisbon and D&I Acts*

As mentioned earlier, with the entry into force of the Treaty of Lisbon on 1 December 2009, the Comitology world was split into two: Delegated Acts and Implementing Acts. The Treaty of Lisbon thus provided the legislators with two legal avenues to use when delegating tasks to the Commission. This change was nothing more than the continuation of developments that had been taking place in the Comitology system for some time. It came as an explicit recognition that there are two fundamentally different types of activities (technical/application vs. political/modification) taking place in Implementing and Delegated Acts and it created two separate systems to deal with them. These two avenues are as described in the two boxes on the next page.

From these short descriptions it becomes clear how the Treaty of Lisbon, and its subsequent implementation under the Spanish and Belgian Presidencies in 2010, split the old Comitology world into two different procedures – notably through the abolition of Committees for Delegated Acts. Both of these avenues will be explored in detail in the following two sections, starting with Implementing Acts.

Implementing Acts (Art. 291 TFEU)

- Traditional Comitology with Committees bringing together Member States' representatives who negotiate Commission drafts and may vote on them.
- The legal base is provided for in legislative and other legally binding acts.
- Rules laid down in new Regulation (Regulation 182/2011).
- Used for measures of general or individual scope.
- A measure of individual scope is always an Implementing Act.
- Implementing Acts cannot add, insert, delete or modify anything.
- An Implementing Act gives effect to the rules laid down in the legislative act.

Delegated Acts (Art. 290 TFEU)

- New system created without Committees. Council and the EP may object to Delegated Acts adopted by the Commission.
- Legal base is provided for in legislative acts only.
- Rules in Treaty of Lisbon with a new Common Understanding.
- A measure of individual scope is never a Delegated Act.
- Delegated Acts are used for measures of general scope that add, insert, delete or modify non-essential elements of the legislative act.

Key moments since the introduction of the D&I Acts

2009	Treaty of Lisbon Articles 290 and 291 TFEU
2012	Schengen border case (C-355/10)
2014	Biocide case (C-427/12)
2016	Interinstitutional Agreement on Better Law Making further consolidates implementation of Articles 290 and 291 TFEU
2019	Agreement on non-binding criteria on delineation

6.4   Implementing Acts

Article 291 TFEU designates Implementing Acts as one of the two categories of acts that can be delegated to the Commission (and in exceptional circumstances to the Council). It is here that we find the 'traditional' Comitology measures and the Committees that were in operation before Lisbon. Article 291 TFEU explicitly required a Regulation to lay out the new decision-making procedures for adoption of Implementing Acts – and this time the Regulation had to be co-decided. The negotiation of this Regulation took 12 months to complete and it entered into force on 1 March 2011 (Regulation 182/2011).

The new Regulation modified the 'old' Comitology procedures, notably by reducing them to only two: the Advisory procedure and a new Examination procedure (which we describe in detail in the next section).

The process for adoption of Implementing Acts is as follows:

I. Establishment of the legal base (i.e. adoption of the so called basic act)

1. The need to have uniform conditions for implementation is established and the power to adopt the implementing acts is delegated to the Commission by the legislators in a legislative procedure or by the Council.

2. The legislators decide what level of control they want to impose on the Commission and choose the corresponding procedure.

3. The legislators refer to an existing Committee or create a new Comitology Committee.

II. Adoption of the Implementing Act

4. The Commission drafts the act.

5. The Comitology Committee negotiates and votes upon the act.

6. The Commission adopts the act (depending on the result of the vote), which gets published in the Official Journal and enters into force.

As the box below shows, the Commission drives the process of Implementing Acts, from drafting the text, calling and chairing meetings, finding compromises and modified texts, trying to ensure a positive vote and then finally adopting the Implementing Act. As stated above, there are now two procedures under which the Commission can operate for Implementing Acts.

The first procedure, the Advisory procedure (Article 4) is shown in Figure 6.3.

Role of Commission for Implementing Acts

1. Drafts the Implementing Act.
2. Organises Comitology Committee meetings.
3. Sets agenda, organises minutes, ensures secretariat, runs Comitology register.
4. Chairs meeting, finds compromises, organises vote.
5. Adopts the final Implementing Act voted upon by Member States in Committee

1. The Advisory procedure

Figure 6.3: The Advisory procedure

Draft Implementing Act of the Commission

The Committee adopts an opinion, if necessary, by simple majority vote

The Commission takes the 'utmost account' of this opinion
Legally it is <u>not obliged</u> to follow this opinion

Figure 6.3 shows the **Advisory procedure** (Article 4), which remains exactly as it was laid out in Council Decision 1999/468/EC as amended by 2006/512/EC – it was not changed by a 2011 **Implementing Acts Regulation**. This procedure is used when the changes being made are not politically sensitive, because it is the least binding on the Commission and also the quickest for taking decisions.

The process is that the Commission presents a draft Implementing Act to the Committee which has to deliver an opinion 'if necessary by taking a vote' (by simple majority) with each Member State having one vote. The Commission then has to take the 'utmost account of the opinion delivered' and inform the Committee of the manner in which its opinion has been taken into account. Legally, the Commission is not obliged to follow the Committee's opinion (although for political reasons the opinion of the Comitology Committee will carry significant weight).

2. The Examination procedure

Next to the unchanged Advisory procedure is the Examination procedure (Article 5), which merged the previous Management and Regulatory procedures.

The Examination procedure has some interesting innovations. Like the Advisory procedure, the Commission presents a draft Implementing Act to the Committee, but for the act to be adopted the Commission has to obtain

Committee voting

Same rules as for voting in the Council apply: at least 55% Members States

At least 65% EU population

Blocking minority must comprise at least 4 Member States

For more information see Chapter 2

Figure 6.4: The Examination procedure

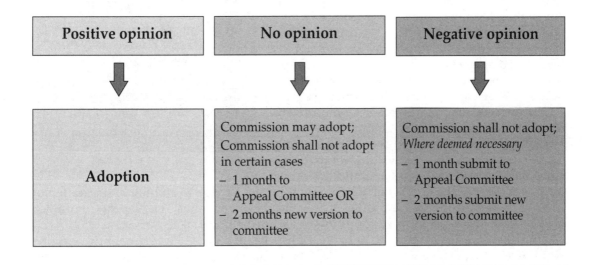

a qualified majority in favour of its draft or, unless stated otherwise, must avoid qualified majority against it.

The procedure allows for two variants in a 'no opinion' situation (see Figure 6. 4). Unless the basic act specifically prohibits it, the Commission may adopt the act in question in the case of 'no opinion'. It is worth noting, however, that in this case the Commission is not obliged to adopt the act, which is an important change from the old Regulatory procedure in which the Commission was obliged to adopt a draft act which did not receive the support of a qualified majority. Now the Commission is able to reconsider and resubmit a new Implementing Act to the Committee, or to send it to the Appeal Committee. In some cases this allows the Commission a greater flexibility where the Member States are divided themselves – making sure that any final decision has the support of the majority of Member States. On the other hand, it still passes the burden of taking a decision onto the Commission in those cases when a decision needs to be taken (e.g. authorisations of a GMO).

If, however, the basic act invokes the provision from Regulation 182/2011 that limits this right, the same rules apply as under the 'negative opinion', i.e. where there is a qualified majority against its draft. A provision in Regulation 182/2011 states that in certain specific policy areas when there is no opinion, such as in taxation, financial services, health and safety and safeguard measures, the Commission shall not adopt. Likewise if there is a simple majority of Member States opposed to the draft Implementing Act the Commission shall not adopt. In this case, the Commission either has to refer the matter to the Appeal Committee (see below), or it has to present a new draft to the Committee.

Likewise, if the Committee votes against the draft measure, by qualified majority, then the Commission shall not adopt it. If the Commission deems it necessary it can forward the rejected draft Implementing Act to the **Appeal Committee** (Article 6). The Appeal Committee has one representative from each Member State (at the appropriate level) and is chaired by the Commission. It has the power to adopt, reject, or vote on changes to the Implementing Act referred to it. This Committee ensures that Member State representatives at a sufficiently high level will make the final decisions on controversial issues, i.e. issues that have been voted against in Committee – which are extremely rare and result in no opinion because Member States are split over the issue.

> ### *Appeal Committee*
>
> Committee of MS representatives 'at the appropriate level' (foremost Coreper level).
>
> Meets to deal with files on which the Comitology Committee issues 'negative' or 'no' opinion.
>
> Can take final decisions on the content of the files.

The introduction of an Appeal Committee reflected the outcome of negotiations between the Parliament and the Council where the Member States wanted to have a political level to look at controversial cases, but a referral to the Council (as it was done in the past) was not an option for the EP due to a notional separation of Member States on one side and Council as legislator on the other. The Appeal Committee is like a high-level Comitology Committee that covers political sensitivities.

This leaves the legislator with only one right when it comes to Implementing Acts: the **right of scrutiny**. This means that for legislative acts adopted under Codecision, either legislator can pass a non-binding Resolution if they feel that the Commission, in the draft Implementing Act, has gone beyond its powers. Despite such resolutions being non-binding, the Parliament tends to use them as 'agenda-setting' instruments, though in a limited number of cases. Member States have the power to vote in the Comitology Committee and in the Appeal Committee and have so far seen little added value in a non-binding right given to the Council.

The Examination procedure is used for (amongst others) Implementing Acts of general scope, programmes with substantial budgetary implications, measures related to the CAP and fisheries, taxation and the Common Commercial Policy (CCP).

Examples of use of Examination procedure: Market authorisations (GMOs for example), setting of limits and classifications.

---

3. The Regulatory Procedure with Scrutiny (RPS)

The Regulatory Procedure with Scrutiny (RPS) dates back to 2006, allowing the legislators more control and oversight over very sensitive modifications of basic acts – where the implementing measures took on a quasi-legislative character.

Between its introduction in 2006 and the entry into force of the Treaty of Lisbon in December 2009, the procedure was written into many legislative acts. Next to the (priority) alignment of the existing acquis throughout 2007 and 2008, any new legislative proposal needed to be tested for potential implementing measures of a 'quasi-legislative' nature.

RPS, as a procedure, has not been inserted in any new legislation since the entry into force of the Treaty of Lisbon. However, the Commission identified over 300 pre-Lisbon basic acts containing provisions for the use of RPS when it prepared the acts for adapta-

Figure 6.5: The Regulatory Procedure with Scrutiny

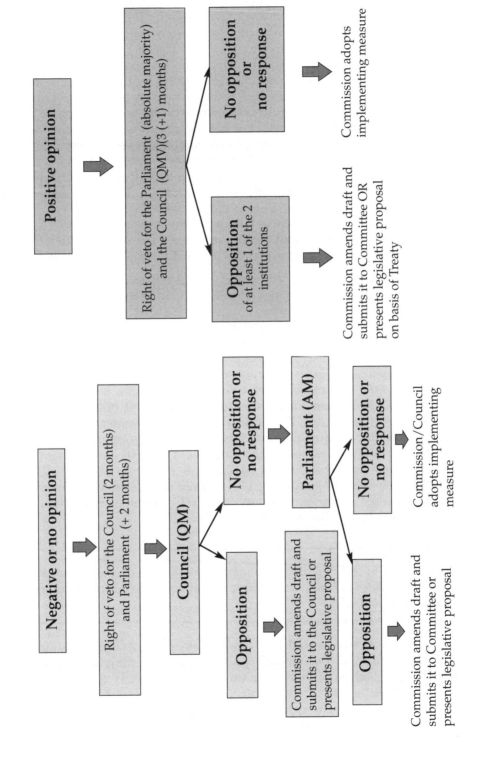

Draft implementing measure of the Commission
The Committee must adopt an opinion by qualified majority

Positive opinion

Right of veto for the Parliament (absolute majority) and the Council (QMV)(3 (+1) months)

No opposition or no response

Commission adopts implementing measure

Opposition of at least 1 of the 2 institutions

Commission amends draft and submits it to Committee OR presents legislative proposal on basis of Treaty

Negative or no opinion

Right of veto for the Council (2 months) and Parliament (+ 2 months)

Council (QM)

No opposition or no response

Parliament (AM)

No opposition or no response

Commission/Council adopts implementing measure

Opposition

Commission amends draft and submits it to the Council or presents legislative proposal

Opposition

Commission amends draft and submits it to Committee or presents legislative proposal

tion to the post-Lisbon situation in the course of 2013. Due to inter-institutional tensions the process of adaptation of the RPS has been slow, with the major breakthrough only at the end of the 8th legislature in 2019. Even so, after the 2019 alignment 106 basic acts referring to RPS are still in place and 98 Implementing measures using the RPS were adopted in 2018.

The RPS is outlined in Figure 6.5 on the previous page.

The RPS was the most constraining procedure for the Commission before the Treaty of Lisbon entered into force because there are two levels of control for it to deal with.

The RPS is a two-tier system of control with firstly a Committee vote and secondly the Parliament and the Council both having a right of veto on the individual measure. So both the Comitology Committee and the legislators have to review the individual measure. The way this works is that if the Committee delivers a qualified majority in favour of the RPS measure then the Parliament and Council each have three months to object to the measure based on three legal grounds. The three legal grounds are if the draft measure:

1.   Exceeds the competences laid out in the basic act;
2.   Is not compatible with the aim or content of the basic act;
3.   Does not respect the principles of subsidiarity and proportionality.

If either legislator objects, using one of these criteria, then the measure is rejected and returned to the Commission to start again in Committee, or to present a legislative proposal on the basis of the Treaty.

In the case of a **qualified majority against** the Commission proposal, or no opinion in the Comitology Committee, the Commission refers the measure first to the Council, which has two months to take a decision on what to do.

The Council can oppose the proposed measure by qualified majority, in which case it goes back to the Commission, which can then submit a revised version to the Council directly (and the Parliament does not get to play a role), or present a legislative proposal on the basis of the Treaty. The Council can also envisage adopting the measure, or not find any opinion by qualified majority within its two months, in which case the Commission submits the measure to the Parliament, which has a further two months to perform the same legal checks outlined above.

If the Parliament objects, using one of these criteria, then the measure is rejected and returned to the Commission to start again in Committee, or to present a legislative proposal on the basis of the Treaty.

Examples of use of RPS: Body scanners in airports, loop-belts in airplanes, detailed implementing rules in Financial Services, lists of authorised substances in the field of public health and food safety.

Besides these two procedures, the Implementing Acts Regulation also foresees two derogations from the Examination procedure for adopting Implementing Acts in **Exceptional Cases** (Article 7) and for adoption of **Immediately Applicable Acts** (Article 8).

Under these variants of the Examination procedure the Commission is empowered to adopt acts for immediate application. In **exceptional cases**, defined in the basic act, which provides for the use of this variant of the examination procedure, the Commission may adopt the Implementing Act even in the case of a negative opinion by the Committee if the Commission needs to do so to avoid significant disruption in agricultural/financial markets. However, in the case of a negative opinion the Commission shall immediately submit the act to the Appeal Committee.

Only a negative vote at this stage means the Commission has to repeal the Implementing Act. The logic behind this is that, for reasons of urgency in the two specific areas, the Commission might need to proceed to immediate application of an act against the will of the Comitology Committee.

In case of **immediately applicable acts** the Commission is empowered, if it has been stated so explicitly in the basic act, to adopt Implementing Acts that have immediate effect, i.e. without first going to the Committee. The Commission must, however, submit the adopted Implementing Act to the Committee within 14 days to get its opinion. The Committee can force the Commission to repeal the act by voting by qualified majority against it. Otherwise, just like in the above case of exceptional cases, it will remain in force.

Many legislative acts provide for the possibility of immediately applicable acts, just in case an emergency requires the Commission to act, but they are seldom employed in practice.

Examples: Health and safety measures (avian flu influenza for example), emergency measures in financial, agricultural markets etc.

Automatic alignment to Implementing Acts took place on 1 March 2011

1. Advisory procedure was maintained (only article number changed)
2. Management and regulatory procedures were replaced by Examination Procedure
3. Regulatory Procedure with Scrutiny is to be adapted to the post-Lisbon situation after screening by the Commission or on a case-by-case basis when individual basic acts are subject to revision

As highlighted in the box above, the Implementing Acts Regulation provided for an automatic alignment process whereby all existing Management and Regulatory procedures were converted to the Examination procedure. Therefore these new procedures are common currency in old and new legislative files alike, with one small distinction only: where the Management procedure applied previously, the Commission may not refer matters to Appeal Committee in case of 'no' or 'negative' opinion.

The new system created by Article 291 TFEU, and the Implementing Acts Regulation, was not such a big break with past practice. The key elements are still in place, notably the Comitology Committees and the Member State representatives, although they only operate under two main procedures now. Referral to the Council was replaced by an Appeal Committee but this is the Council in everything but name and the Commission has been granted flexibility over the obligation to adopt acts that a majority of Member States do not support.

6.5   Delegated Acts

Unlike Article 291 TFEU, Article 290 TFEU did not require any implementation and was therefore immediately applicable. This is because Article 290 TFEU explicitly moved away from a horizontal framework, so the legislators are free to set the modalities, such as objectives, scope, duration and the conditions to which the delegation is subject in each and every legislative act. In this sense there was no requirement to have secondary legislation to set a legally binding horizontal framework – the legislators were empowered to decide case-by-case.

While no legislation was needed to implement Article 290 TFEU there was a concern that it could lead to a piecemeal approach and to more difficult, i.e. longer, negotiations of Delegated Act provisions in the Codecision phase. Therefore, the institutions sought to develop a **Common Understanding** on how to apply and work with Delegated Acts.

Delegated Acts are almost identical in definition to the measures adopted by RPS that was outlined in the previous section. They have been created to deal with the quasi-legislative matters where the legislators are granting extra powers to the Commission for the sake of speed and efficiency but where they secure extra control in return. **Delegated Acts**, like RPS, **grant the Commission the power to supplement or amend** non-essential elements of the legislative act.

Whilst Delegated Acts cover the tasks that were dealt with by RPS measures, there are a number of significant procedural changes to the oversight of the Commission that need to be detailed. Figure 6.6 displays the procedure for Delegated Acts.

This process represented a sharp deviation from past practice, and from the Implementing Acts (notably the RPS) outlined in the last section. It becomes immediately apparent that the two-tier control of RPS has been simplified, because the Commission presents its Delegated Act directly to both legislators simultaneously.

As Figure 6.6 highlights, both legislators have a time determined by the basic act (usually two + two months) to object to the act on any grounds, or to revoke the delegation altogether. There is also the possibility that the legislators can give their approval to a Delegated Act so that the Commission can adopt it faster (so-called 'early non-objection').

Whilst this one-tier procedure is simpler, each legislative act can set out different conditions for Delegated Acts on a case-by-case basis due to the lack of a legally binding horizontal framework. The Common Understanding between the institutions on how to use Delegated Acts includes some model articles, but there is sufficient flexibility allowed for negotiations over the precise conditions of each delegation to take place on a case-by-case basis.

Roughly 40% of all adopted legislative acts post-Lisbon have included delegation to the Commission to adopt Delegated Acts in order to amend or to supplement the basic act. On average there is a handful of such delegations in each act and the Commission adopted between 104 and 137 Delegated Acts per year in the years between 2014 and 2018 and 156 Delegated Acts in 2019.

Figure 6.6: Delegated Acts – The procedure

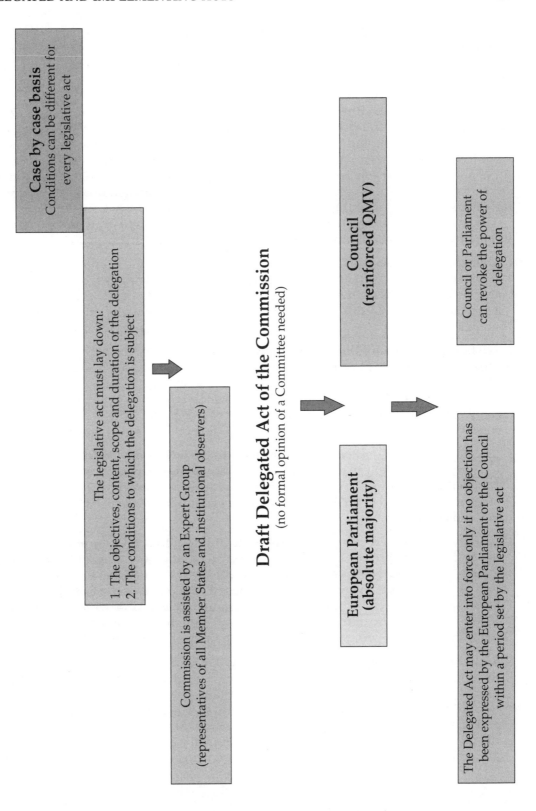

Case by case basis
Conditions can be different for every legislative act

The legislative act must lay down:
1. The objectives, content, scope and duration of the delegation
2. The conditions to which the delegation is subject

Commission is assisted by an Expert Group
(representatives of all Member States and institutional observers)

Draft Delegated Act of the Commission
(no formal opinion of a Committee needed)

Council
(reinforced QMV)

European Parliament
(absolute majority)

Council or Parliament can revoke the power of delegation

The Delegated Act may enter into force only if no objection has been expressed by the European Parliament or the Council within a period set by the legislative act

The **scope, content and objective of delegation** are negotiated for each individual delegation in a basic act. The duration of the delegation of power to the Commission, the principles that bind the Commission when preparing the Delegated Acts and the objection period for the legislator are the same for all delegations in one act and negotiated within the flexibility provided for by the Common Understanding.

When it comes to the **duration of delegation** the Common Understanding suggests this should be for an indeterminable time or for five years, which can be extended for another five years, pending tacit approval by the legislator. When it comes to the period for **objections**, the agreed time is two months, which can be extended by two months by either of the legislators. In both cases – of individually framed delegations and the conditions for their adoption – the modalities chosen are important and need to be addressed early in the preparation of the proposal and throughout the decision-making phase.

The procedure for Delegated Acts since Lisbon is very different from previous practice and there are a number of innovations that were introduced that need to be stressed:

1. **Delegation is optional:** The legislator may decide to ask the Commission to supplement or amend certain non-essential elements of the basic act, but it may also decide to retain this right as legislator. The question of whether delegation is a preferred option (for reasons outlined above) or not is occasionally the subject of negotiations.

2. **No horizontal legally binding framework:** There is no horizontal framework to cover Delegated Acts, so the legislators are free to set the objectives, scope, duration and the conditions to which the delegation is subject in each and every legislative act. The Common Understanding on how to use Delegated Acts includes, most notably, agreed options with regard to duration of delegation, time period for legislators to object as well as principles the Commission follows when preparing the act.

3. **The absence of a Comitology Committee** and the lack of any requirement for the Commission to obtain an opinion by a vote prior to the adoption of a Delegated Act was perhaps the most noticeable change from previous practice. The Committee stage was abolished in favour of much greater control by the legislator (right to object and revocation).

4. **Prominence of expert groups:** In the absence of a Comitology Committee the Member States sought greater involvement in the preparation of Delegated Acts. In the Common Understanding as renegotiated in 2016 it was agreed that the Commission will always consult Expert Groups composed of representatives of all Member States, while the representatives of the legislators attend as observers. The Commission may also use other channels of consultation, but it is required to allow the members of Expert Groups to give their views on the final draft of a Delegated Act.

5. **Right to object on any grounds:** Council and Parliament have the power to object to an individual Delegated Act on any grounds whatsoever. They no longer need to find one of the three legal justifications outlined under the RPS. However, they need to find a majority supporting the objection. The absolute majority in the EP and in particular the reinforced QMV in the Council (a reinforced majority increases the minimum percentage of Member States from at least 55% to 72%) which are required to object to a Delegated Act have proven to present a high requirement. As

Table 6.4: Delegated Acts compared to the Regulatory Procedure with Scrutiny

Regulatory Procedure with Scrutiny (RPS/ PRAC)	Delegated Acts
A framework; Article 5a of the Comitology Decision	No binding framework. Case by case basis
Necessity to obtain an opinion from a Comitology Committee	No compulsory consultation of Committees BUT consultation at expert level including all Member States
EP and Council are not completely on an equal footing	Perfect equal footing between EP and Council
Limited grounds for the right of veto	No limited grounds for the right of objection
	Right of revocation
Source: Based on Council Decision 1999/468/EC as amended by 2006/512/EC and Regulation 182/2011 of the European Parliament and Council	

a result, despite the loosening of the grounds on which the institutions may object, there has not been a rise in the number of objections in both institutions in comparison to the RPS.

6. **Right of revocation:** The final change that needs to be highlighted is that in addition to the right of veto to an individual Delegated Act the legislators are also granted the ultimate control mechanism – the right to revoke the delegation to the Commission altogether. If either legislator becomes so dissatisfied with how the Commission is using its power to issue Delegated Acts it could vote to revoke fully or partially the delegation. While a threat to revoke a delegation might have been used in inter-institutional negotiations to receive concessions, neither the EP nor the Council have revoked the Commission's power to adopt Delegated Acts. In fact, all delegations of powers limited to five years that could be extended following tacit approval by the legislator have been extended.

In sum the procedure for adopting Delegated Acts is fundamentally different to that used to adopt RPS measures.

First, the scope, content and objective of any future Delegated Acts are decided in the legislative decision-making phase and so are the conditions for objection. Further, the process of drafting a Delegated Act involves working with the relevant Expert Groups, and other actors assisting the Commission.

These detailed discussions are vital for the Commission to get the technical expertise of the Member State experts, and to test the political temperature of the Council and the Parliament before presenting a Delegated Act directly to the legislators. The Commission does not want to present Delegated Acts to the legislators without having consulted them in some way before, otherwise it risks an objection to the Delegated Act. In fact, there is much informal contact and also more formalised contact between the Commission and legislator, for example in the form of a presentation of a draft Delegated Act by the Commission in an EP Committee.

Table 6.4 on the previous page makes a direct comparison of the main changes that were ushered in by Article 290 TFEU and the introduction of Delegated Acts.

6.6   *Delegated and Implementing Acts: A summary*

This chapter has shown how Comitology has been fundamentally changed by the Treaty of Lisbon and its subsequent implementation through the co-decided Regulation and an inter-institutional Common Understanding. The name Comitology is now partially redundant because of the creation of two separate regimes: Delegated and Implementing Acts. For both of these categories the procedures are simplified and information is more accessible, making understanding (and working with) this new world of Comitology less difficult than before. The key aspects to retain are that:

1. **Delegated Acts** are an entirely new world created by the Lisbon Treaty, notably with the abolition of Comitology Committees. Instead the Commission now uses Expert Groups, which bring together representatives of all Member States, and with experts from Parliament and Council as observers. The powers of the legislators are now considerable with a discretionary right to delegate to the Commission and, subsequently, the possibility to object to an individual act or to revoke the delegation itself. The high majorities required to object to a Delegated Act (absolute majority in the EP and reinforced majority in the Council) present a challenge to the legislators. Still, the Commission adopted the practice of actively presenting and explaining the draft acts to legislators if it learns of doubts raised by the legislator and in order to avoid difficulties once a Delegated Act is adopted. RPS procedure continues to be in place for implementing measures with a legal base stemming from pre-Lisbon time and requiring the use of RPS.

2. **Implementing Acts** retain the requirement on the Commission to pass through Comitology Committees by submitting draft acts for discussion and vote. There was an automatic alignment that guaranteed an immediate switchover from the old procedures (with the exception of RPS). For Implementing Acts the main changes were that there are only two full procedures: Advisory and Examination. The Commission drafts the acts and chairs the Comitology Committees, while the legislators have only a right of scrutiny. Finally, the Commission may seize an Appeal Committee, chaired by the Commission, but bringing together high-level representatives from the Member States, usually at the level of Coreper.

The importance of choosing the right instrument – Delegated or Implementing Acts – matters considerably in safeguarding the prerogatives of each institution and respecting the Treaty's intentions with regard to the inter-institutional balance. Where the basic legislative act provides for Delegated Acts the legislators have the power to veto. In the case of Implementing Acts the powers of the legislators are more limited.

It is therefore not surprising that several issues arose as the institutions gained experience with implementation of Articles 290 and 291 of the Treaty of Lisbon. The most prominent of the issues has been the so-called question of delineation between the two instruments, but other issues should also be mentioned: the principles the Commission is required to follow when preparing Delegated Acts, transparency surrounding preparation and adoption of Delegated Acts, and joining of several empowerments into one Delegated Act (so called bundling).

The three institutions reached agreement on these issues (and others) in a 2016 **Inter-institutional Agreement on Better Law-Making**. The most important points are:

- Confirmation of the importance of the use of D&I Acts and of the discretion of the legislator when choosing the appropriate instrument. In this way the institutions also reconfirmed the 2014 first decisive judgment of the Court of Justice of the European Union regarding the application of both Articles 290 and 291 TFEU (Case C-427/12 – the so-called 'biocide case'). However, the Court did not provide general guidance on other criteria for choosing between both instruments. It was only in 2019 that the institutions agreed on non-exhaustive, non-binding criteria for delineation between D&I Acts. The criteria present a possible direction over a choice of a Delegated or Implementing Act, but should not be understood as a general guidance.

- The consistent involvement of Member States' experts, appointed by the Member States, in the Expert Groups working with Delegated Acts as well as of observers from the EP and the Council.

- Setting up of the **Register of Delegated Acts**. This inter-institutional Register has been in place since late 2017 and provides documents on preparation of acts as well as documents from and the outcome of the scrutiny process. It offers a one-stop shop to stakeholders for checking the progress of Delegated Acts.

- If the Commission should not join several empowerments from a single act into a single Delegated Act, it needs to be stated so in the basic act.

While the 2016 Inter-institutional Agreement on Better Law-Making helped reach a shared understanding among the institutions on the governance of the worlds of D&I Acts, the delays in adaptation of the pre-Lisbon basic acts to the post-Lisbon situation demonstrate most clearly the difficulties the three institutions continue to have with the implementation of Articles 290 and 291 of the Treaty of Lisbon.

As part of the Commission's 2015 **Better Regulation package** (discussed in Chapter 1) D&I Acts, with some exemptions, are published for feedback. However, there are few specificities. First, there are exemptions for which no obligation of feedback is required, such as in the case of individual authorisations, when agencies conducted consultations, when the margin of manoeuvre is extremely limited, etc. Second, the feedback takes place during 4 weeks and, third, feedback takes place before the Commission's adoption of the act. Feedback gives an opportunity to stakeholders to engage in the preparation of D&I Acts and should be considered and approached similarly to other consultations and feedback.

6.7   Key stages and key actors – Delegated and Implementing Acts

It is possible, in two separate categories, to now present the main stages and actors in preparation, adoption and scrutiny of D&I Acts. It must be remembered that it is vital to work with OLP on the insertion of delegated and implementing provisions into texts, in which case the previous chapter is applicable. Table 6.5 only deals with the actual D&I Acts themselves.

Table 6.5: Key stages and key actors: Delegated and Implementing Acts

Key stage	Comment	Key actors
IMPLEMENTING ACTS		
Drafting of Implementing Act	The Commission will likely require technical assistance in drafting the act, most commonly from the Comitology Committee. In some cases Agencies are mandated to draft Implementing Acts. Public consultation is possible.	Commission Unit/DG Comitology Committee Agency
Commission Inter-Service Consultation (ISC)	A draft Implementing Act has to get approval in ISC.	Lead DG Consulted DGs
Discussion in Committee	The Commission will discuss the Act in Committee to evaluate support, which can lead to major modifications.	Commission Unit/DG Member State representatives Third Parties invited to Committee meeting
Vote in Committee	Adoption is in the vast majority of cases by consensus.	Commission Unit/DG Member State representatives Agency representative
Appeal Committee	Only in case of negative or 'no opinion' vote in the Committee (and for pre-Lisbon legal bases limited to those with Regulatory procedure only).	Member State representatives but at a more political level (Coreper) Commission Unit/DG, Commission Secretariat
Feedback	Unless an exception applies, draft acts are published for feedback after Committee has delivered its opinion.	
Commission adoption	Commission adopts the final Committee text as voted (usually by written procedure or by empowerment).	College Cabinet(s) Director-General
Right of scrutiny	Parliament & Council (under Codecision acts) have the right of scrutiny at any time between referral to Committee and adoption by the Commission.	EP lead Committee Plenary

Key stage	Comment	Key actors
DELEGATED ACTS		
Drafting of Delegated Act	Closely watched by the Member States who all have a representative in an Expert Group involved in the preparation of the draft, broader public consultation possible. In some cases Agencies are mandated to draft acts. Agencies conduct consultation according to rules applicable to them.	Commission Unit/DG Expert Group (with EP and Council Secretariat in an observing capacity) Agency
Commission ISC	A draft Delegated Act has to get approval in ISC.	Lead DG Consulted DGs
Feedback	Unless exception applies, draft acts are published for feedback.	
Commission adoption	Commission adopts the Delegated Act (usually by written procedure or by empowerment) – but the Cabinets have more margin for changes than under Implementing Acts because they are not going against a Committee opinion in this case.	College Cabinet(s)
Parliament objection, Parliament revocation	The Parliament has a period of time (usually two plus two months) to scrutinise the Delegated Act. Objection may be on any ground, but securing absolute majority requires an early start.	Committee responsible Committee responsible chairperson Coordinators Rapporteur from Codecision (standing) Committee member responsible for DA Secretariat Political Groups staff
Preparation and vote on draft Resolution to object to a DA	Delegated Acts are sent to lead and associated Committees for scrutiny. A simple majority in a Committee is needed to pass the draft Resolution onto the Plenary. The Commission engages heavily with the view to maintaining the Delegated Act. EP's rules allow for a Political Group or 5% of MEPs to table a resolution to object to a DA if the Committee hasn't done so by 10 days prior to the last Plenary during which the EP could still object to the DA.	(standing) Committee member responsible for DA Coordinators Committee MEPs Secretariat Political Group advisors

continued overleaf

Key stage	Comment	Key actors
Plenary vote	An absolute majority is needed to carry the draft resolution.	(standing) Committee Member responsible for DA Coordinators Political Groups
Council objection Council revocation	Member States work with the Commission in the Expert Groups and in some cases the same experts who will have assisted the Commission in an Expert Group will be in the Working Group in the Council. However, the formal vote to object to a Delegated Act can only be taken in the Council. In addition, the Council as political body might see issues differently from the expert-level discussions in the Expert Group.	Working Group Key Member States Council Secretariat
Council working party/Coreper discussion	Given that objecting to a Delegated Act is not a question of finding a compromise, the discussions in the Council Working Party are usually brief and Coreper rarely engages in discussions over a Delegated Act. An intention to raise an objection to a Delegated Act goes from the Working Party via Coreper to the Council (normally as I/A item).	Council Working Party Presidency Coreper
Council decision	The Council has to vote by reinforced qualified majority to reject a Delegated Act or to revoke the delegation. The majority is established at the Coreper level.	Presidency Council Key Member States

Index

Page references against a heading with subheadings indicate major coverage of a topic. The following abbreviations are used in the index: EP = European Parliament; D&I Acts = Delegated and Implementing Acts; OLP = Ordinary Legislative Procedure